African American Women Writers' Historical Fiction

African American Women Writers' Historical Fiction

Ana Nunes

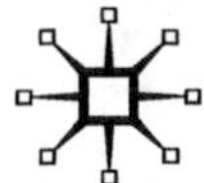

AFRICAN AMERICAN WOMEN WRITERS' HISTORICAL FICTION

First published in 2011 by PALGRAVE MACMILLAN® in the United States—a division of St. Martin's Press LLC, 175 Fifth Avenue, New York, NY 10010.

Where this book is distributed in the UK, Europe and the rest of the world, this is by Palgrave Macmillan, a division of Macmillan Publishers Limited, registered in England, company number 785998, of Houndmills, Basingstoke, Hampshire RG21 6XS.

Palgrave Macmillan is the global academic imprint of the above companies and has companies and representatives throughout the world.

Palgrave® and Macmillan® are registered trademarks in the United States, the United Kingdom, Europe and other countries.

ISBN: 978-0-230-11253-7

Library of Congress Cataloging-in-Publication Data

Nunes, Ana, 1973–
African American women writers' historical fiction / by Ana Nunes.
p. cm.
Includes bibliographical references and index.
ISBN 978-0-230-11253-7
1. American fiction—African American authors—History and criticism. 2. American fiction—Women authors—History and criticism. 3. Historical fiction, American—History and criticism. 4. American fiction—20th century—History and criticism. 5. African Americans in literature. I. Title.

PS153.N5N86 2011
813'.081099287—dc22 2010042331

A catalogue record of the book is available from the British Library.

Design by Scribe Inc.

First edition: May 2011

10 9 8 7 6 5 4 3 2 1

Printed in the United States of America.

With love and deep gratitude to Kieran Burns, who continues to amaze and inspire me. And to Alice Nunes Burns: artist, pirate, fairy, ardent lover of books, and my perfect love.

Contents

Acknowledgments

I am forever grateful to Dr. Ron Callan for direction, encouragement, never-ending patience, and wisdom. My debt is deep to Prof. Elizabeth Ann Beaulieu. I am thankful to the attention that she has given to my work. Her insight, generosity, and encouragement have propelled me forward. I am grateful to Dr. Isabel Caldeira for pioneering African American studies in Europe, her vast store of knowledge, and all the support she has given me throughout the years.

I extended my thanks to Brigitte Shull, my editor at Palgrave Macmillan, for her enthusiasm for the project and for providing answers to so many tiresome questions.

I would like to thank my parents, Conceição and José Luis Nabais Nunes, for their unconditional support. Their lessons in perseverance and commitment made it possible for me to write this book. I am grateful to my brother Pedro Nuno Leal Nabais Nunes and my dearest friend Helena Maria Gil for their unfaltering belief in me.

This book was completed with the kind assistance of the Fundação para a Ciência e Tecnologia.

Introduction

In *African-American History*, Thomas C. Holt states that, although the study of black American history was initiated and developed by African American intellectuals and activists, it was Gunnar Myrdal's *American Dilemma* that "introduced black history to most white Americans."[1] Among the general acceptance with which Myrdal's sociological study of black America was received, there were, as Holt points out, some voices of dissent. Among Myrdal's critics was Ralph Ellison who reviewed *American Dilemma* in 1944, the year of its publication. Ellison's main objection to Myrdal's work was his assertion that "the Negro's entire life and, consequently, also his opinions on the Negro problem are, in the main, to be considered as secondary reactions to more primary pressures from the side of the white dominant majority."[2] Ellison rejects Myrdal's view of African American culture as simply reactive and points to a sense of African American culture with roots in the specific experience of people of African descent in the New World and exposes Myrdal's one-dimensional argument. For Ellison, this is a culture that evolved not merely because of but in spite of the racism that African Americans faced "embod[ing] a *rejection*" of the dominant culture and, thus, holding values and traditions distinct from the hegemonic other. Thus Ellison rebuffs the idea that white culture is a "higher culture," calling attention to the African American contribution to the United States: "In Negro culture there is much of value for America as a whole."[3] However, for Ellison, the "value" of black culture and contribution to American society had yet to be articulated from an African American perspective: "What is needed are Negroes to take it [the value of black culture] and create of it 'the uncreated consciousness of their race.' In doing so they will do far more, they'll help create a more human America."[4] What is implied in Ellison's paraphrase of James Joyce's *Portrait of the Artist*[5] is a call for representations of African American people and experience beyond the prevailing depiction of "Negro culture and personality simply as a product of a 'social pathology.'"[6] What is important to consider here is not the merits or demerits of *American Dilemma*, but the emphasis Ellison puts on the need to challenge the image of the African American as a sociological product of the dynamics established by white hegemony.

His vision of the representation of African American experience and legacy meant that, as Holt puts it, "No longer would black history be simply the history of relations between the races or of black contributions to the nation's life and progress . . . In that history blacks would no longer be relegated to nonspeaking roles, the passive victims of white hostility or beneficiaries of white benevolence. They would be actors with top billing, creating institutions, sustaining communal values, and passing on a legacy of struggle and creativity to their posterity."[7] In 1944 this involved a radical review of the American historical record, one that is evident in Ellison's views. If African American history was to go beyond the analysis of race relations and the contribution of extraordinary people to the country's "progress," the objectification of black people had to be challenged, and they had to be recognized as authoritative narrators of their experience and their place in American society. The extraordinary experience of a minority had to be contextualized to include the "ordinary" lives of the majority of African Americans. This view of historical scholarship would allow African American history and culture to be depicted as valuable in their terms rather than those subservient to the dominant history and culture of whites.

In his review of *American Dilemma*, however, Ellison does not address the sources that document a history and a culture that evolved and developed primarily via word of mouth. This in itself required a fundamental revision of historical research and methodology. But Ellison does address this issue elsewhere, identifying how African American culture is "expressed in a body of folklore, in the musical forms of the spirituals, the blues and jazz; an idiomatic version of American speech (especially in the Southern United States); a cuisine; a body of dance forms and even a dramaturgy."[8] Thus, for Ellison, African American culture is distinctly marked by its orality more than its writing.

In *Living In, Living Out: African American Domestics and the Great Migration*, published in 1994, Elizabeth Clark-Lewis strives to recover the history of African American women who migrated to the North from the rural South to work as domestic servants in the first three decades of the twentieth century. Clark-Lewis collected oral testimonies from her female relatives along with those from 97 other women,[9] all of them former domestics, in order to recreate the unwritten history of her female relatives.[10] Her work constitutes an example of the difficulties faced by historians of a predominantly oral culture. At the close of her book, she stresses the importance of storytelling as a fundamental source for the writing of African American history and appeals to other scholars to listen and record the testimonies that will constitute the cultural heritage of the coming generations: "This is the last time you may find 'the old women gathered.' This is the last song they may ever sing. I challenge you, historians of tomorrow, to scoop up the baton of their rich heritage and carry it along with you as you run."[11] In this way, Clark-Lewis charters the difficulty in recording oral testimonies in a time when communities no longer gather around their elders—the storytellers who wove in their words the fabric of the cultural legacy.

Clark-Lewis had to overcome the lack of written sources from which to draw information about her foremothers' experience while striving to beat the passage of time to record their scattered stories. She makes use of sources often dismissed by traditional approaches to history. In her study she includes the usual references to other historians and political activists, but she also quotes W. E. Du Bois,[12] James Baldwin,[13] and Toni Morrison[14] in order to establish a context for the first-person narratives she collected. In doing so, she establishes a significant relationship between orality, history, and literature and how these sources are interwoven in order to represent African American experience.

Twentieth-century African American literature has been dominated by the notion that the writer should represent and celebrate the uniqueness of African American experience. In this way, contemporary African American writers deal with issues raised by Ellison, issues related to voice and authority over the African American historical record. The characters they create are "actors with top billing, creating institutions, sustaining communal values, and passing on a legacy of struggle and creativity to their posterity."[15] In doing so, they also establish a critical dialogue between orality and literacy and history and literature. This trend toward the definition of a culture that is distinct, though intrinsically related, to the hegemonic other has encouraged black writers, and black female writers in particular, to revise and redefine a history that they view as largely lost or misconstrued.

This study aims at exploring the ways in which African American women writers address the relationship between history and literature, reworking the historical record from the point of view of the silenced female and give origin to an unprecedented narrative of the American experience. For this purpose, I shall focus my analysis on Margaret Walker's *Jubilee* (1966), Gayl Jones's *Corregidora* (1975), Sherley Anne Williams's *Dessa Rose* (1986), Toni Morrison's *Beloved* (1987), and Phyllis Perry's *Stigmata* (1998). In selecting these novels, my primary objective is to consider fictional works that made a unique contribution to the African American historical novel. The main common dominator between these novels is the representation of slavery—the historical center of the African American experience. Writers from Walker to Perry seek different modes of exploring slavery, establish intertextual dialogues with previous works, and root their writing in a tradition that they address and reinvent in order to account for the African American past: "[A]mong the current generation of writers," as Deborah E. McDowell observes, "*women* are at the forefront of reinventing slavery."[16] This exploration does not, however, intend to be an exhaustive overview of African American historical novels published since 1966. The focus will be on the innovative narrative strategies advanced in selected novels, tracing the development of the representation of slavery from Walker's *Jubilee*, published in 1966, to Perry's *Stigmata*, published in 1998. My interest is thus twofold: to examine the narrative and thematic achievements of individual texts and to analyze the main trends and developments of the African American historical fiction written by women in the twentieth century.

These novels rework the nineteenth-century European tradition of the historical novel in order to challenge versions of history established by white hegemonies. Importantly, African American historical fiction combines historical research with imaginary elements in order to recreate the past. Therefore, this body of literature privileges the lives of the socially marginalized, those who remained outside the pages of history. In this context, literature becomes a means to recreate the "historical records" that were destroyed, or never existed; a way of including in the American experience the history of those "who do not speak, . . . who do not have a voice because they/we were so terrified" to make use of Audre Lorde's words.[17]

In Chapter 1, I will focus on some of the texts that have significantly determined the development of twentieth-century African American women's writing. Issues from the accuracy of portraits of black American experience to the establishment of an exceptional literary tradition are, I argue, expressed and defined particularly in the latter part of the nineteenth century. Critical to the establishment of this literary tradition are the works of Harriet Jacobs and Frances E. W. Harper. A central aspect of Harper's work is her call for the establishment of a literary tradition that would assist the "uplifting" of the race, proving intellectual parity with whites, overturning the stereotypical images of blacks, and operating as a didactic medium for both. In this way, Harper prompts the creation of a literary body that would reflect the history of African Americans, one that they had reimagined and written. In this chapter I will also consider how the 1890s represented a seminal decade for the black women's movement and literature. The contribution activists such as Fannie Barrier Williams and Anna Julia Cooper helped consolidate the African American literary tradition by setting the main themes and motifs of the works of contemporary female writers.

Nineteenth-century African American literature, however, presents limitations in its treatment of history. Writers such as Harper in *Minnie's Sacrifice* (1869) and *Iola Leroy, or, Shadows Uplifted* (1892) and Pauline Hopkins in *Contending Forces* (1900) approach the past from a didactic and moral point of view. Confined by the corset of the conventions of the time and too preoccupied with the creation of a black middle-class role model for (and leader of) the masses, they write about exceptional characters, generally educated, and very often light enough to pass for white. In doing so they set aside a black protagonist who could be considered representative.

The silences and the gaps left both by the slave narratives and nineteenth-century historical fiction constitute the open spaces from which the stories of contemporary writers begin to take shape. As Houston A. Baker Jr. observes, only in the last four decades have African American writers traveled "as an extensive and articulate group . . . all the way back to the origins and recorded their insights in distinctive forms designed for a black audience."[18] In fact, Arna Bontemps's *Black Thunder*, a fictional account of Gabriel Prosser's insurrection, published in 1936, is the only significant work to deal with slavery before the publication of Margaret Walker's *Jubilee*.

In the field of black literary studies, *Jubilee* remains "the most famous [novel] nobody knows"[19] to paraphrase the title of an article by Maryemma Graham and Deborah Whaley about Walker. *Jubilee* has often been considered as a groundbreaking novel. For Ashraf H. A. Rushdy, "*Jubilee* marks the transition between the modern and the contemporary history and neo-slave narrative, standing as the final of the modern neo-slave narrative and the harbinger of a new concentrated wave of contemporary neo-slave narratives."[20] For Joyce Pettis, "*Jubilee* is also a vital precursor to complex, nonchronological approaches to Afro-American history . . . *Jubilee* is precedent-setting black historical fiction."[21] However, besides being frequently noted as a benchmarking novel, *Jubilee*, and Walker's work in general, has received little critical attention.[22] Some critics such as Charlotte Goodman attribute this lack of critical attention to "Walker's [imitation of] the conventional linear structure of the traditional slave narrative."[23] Others, such as Barbara Christian, interpret Walker's characters as purely flat figures, "characters, Black and white, who are not subjects so much as they are the means by which we learn about the culture of slaves and slave holders and the historical period."[24]

Jacqueline Miller Carmichael's *Trumpeting a Fiery Sound: History and Folklore in Margaret Walker's Jubilee* is, to date, the only book-length study dedicated to the novel. The first section of this study relates the genesis of the book, adding very little to what can be read in Walker's essay "How I Wrote *Jubilee*." In addition, Carmichael's comparative study of the versions of *Jubilee*, Walker's doctoral thesis and the book format, tends to be quite descriptive. The second section of the book is a comprehensive summary of the criticism on *Jubilee*, but Carmichael does little to revise it. These readings do not seek to address the complexity of Walker's achievement. This is not to say that all criticism on *Jubilee* is flawed. For all its limitations,

Carmichael's study opens the way for more subtle readings of Walker's work. Minrose C. Gwin, for example, addresses Christian's criticism that Walker's characters lack individuality by reiterating that the novel "presents the slavery experience and cross-racial female relationships from the point of view of the black woman."[25] In her reading of *Jubilee*, Elizabeth Ann Beaulieu questions Goodman's one-dimensional view of the text as simple linear narrative and identifies four key episodes, which "illustrate Margaret Walker's break with tradition, a break that is responsible in part for reinvigorating the slave narrative genre."[26] Significantly, Beaulieu also examines *Jubilee* in the context of the contemporary African American historical novel.

One of the primary objectives of this exploration is the contextualization of novels such as Walker's *Jubilee* and Morrison's *Beloved*, which on publication were considered to be benchmarks in African American literature, but tend to be read in isolation rather than as part of a significant trend in black American fiction. This study aims to extricate the selected novels from the literary vacuum in which they are traditionally read and place them within the literary production and ideology that played a central role in the consolidation of the African American literary tradition, which set the main motifs of the works of contemporary female writers. In pursuing this line of investigation, the reading of *Beloved* in the final chapter shall emphasize its innovative narrative strategies and devices in the context of the historical novels that preceded it, removing it from the isolation in which critical acclaim has placed it.

Second, I will examine the origins of African American historical fiction and how this genre has been reworked and reimagined by contemporary authors, tracing the development of the African American historical novel through the last four decades of the twentieth century. My analysis of these novels begins with Walker's *Jubilee*. My work aims to reflect on Walker's achievement in writing historical fiction when African American history remained practically unwritten. Considering the novelist's use of folklore as the framework of her novel, I emphasize the innovative aspects of a novel that have been undervalued on account of its chronological narrative and the common tendency to read its characters as stereotypes. Central to my project's analysis is that Walker's thorough research, concerned with historical accuracy and meticulous representation of the quotidian, free other writers from the constrictions of verisimilitude, creates the possibilities for complex psychological landscapes of the enslaved subject.

Jones's *Corregidora*, which I will examine in Chapter 3, reflects both an acknowledgment of the contribution of *Jubilee* to the African American historical novel and is a departure from Walker's model. In Jones's work, the chronological narrative is abandoned in favor of a mode of narration that mirrors the mental processes by which one remembers, selects, and recreates different aspects of personal history. I emphasize the significance of Jones's first-person narrator and the writer's innovative approach to the use of folk speech. This novel is also influential in its use of the blues patterns of call and response to recreate a notion of history that is circular rather than linear.

In *Dessa Rose*, the focus of Chapter 4, Williams presents yet another way of representing slavery through a number of perspectives. These shifts in the narrative's point of view expose the distortion of African American history and the cultural constructs of race that define and condition the relationships between blacks and whites in the text. Williams exposes preconceived notions of blackness and whiteness, and racializes the latter, an aspect overlooked by the critical texts on *Dessa Rose*. In the final major section of the novel, Williams abandons the variable viewpoint in favor of a first-person narrative, reimaging the African American past by rooting it in the oral tradition that has kept it alive.

My reading of *Beloved* in Chapter 5 considers how Morrison uses magical realism as a means of translating the absences in African American history. I examine how magical realism provides the necessary narrative strategy through which a lost history can be recreated. I conclude the chapter with a reading of Phyllis Perry's first novel, *Stigmata*. I argue that Perry engages with the magical in order to rework the narrative model presented by Morrison. Perry's narrative explores the tension between the Tzvetan Todorov's notion of the fantastic and the supernatural accepted, or magical realism, and her development of a sense of community in the context of the fantastic and magic realism.

1

Contexts

> I would like to do something of lasting service for the race.
>
> —Frances Ellen Watkins Harper

My interest here is to consider a number of texts that significantly determined the development of twentieth-century African American women's writing. Issues from the accuracy of portraits of black American experience to the establishment of an exceptional literary tradition are evident in the work published particularly in the latter part of the nineteenth century. My focus is not simply on the themes addressed but also on the terms of narrative strategies and how literature and politics are closely linked.

The abolition of slavery in 1863 did not bring to an end African Americans' struggle for equal participation in American society. In the postbellum South, as John Hope Franklin and Alfred A. Moss assert, "Depriving blacks of political equality became . . . a holy crusade in which a noble end justified any means. Blacks were run out of communities if they disobeyed orders to desist from voting, and the more resolute and therefore insubordinate blacks were whipped, maimed, and hanged."[1] At length, the compromise of 1877 between Northern and Southern states overthrew Reconstruction and despite the Fourteenth and Fifteenth Constitutional Amendments, as Franklin and Moss go on to say, "Before the dawn of a new century there was a complete recognition in law of what the South had itself accomplished in fact even before the election of 1876."[2] Between 1890 and 1900, the Southern states, led by Mississippi, gradually disfranchised African Americans. Poll taxes, literacy tests, and examinations on the ability to explain a section of the state constitution were some of the measures used to block black people from voting and maintain white rule. Once more, African Americans were silenced, and once more, they had to prove themselves fit for citizenship. The systematic enslavement might be abolished, but the relationships of blacks to whites, blacks to laws, and so on were defined in many cases in terms that reflected the values of slavery.

Social Darwinist ideas, which had a significant influence on American public opinion with the publication of *The Origins of Species* in 1859, were used to suggest that, considering the physiological differences between blacks and whites and the established leadership by the latter, color mattered and whites were the *fittest* to rule by nature. During the eighteenth and nineteenth centuries, African Americans used the written word to defy the logic of the Enlightenment proposed by such philosophers as Immanuel Kant and Jean-Jacques Rousseau, among others, which suggested that a society that did not organize itself around the written word was intellectually inferior. In these contexts, black writers wrote to claim their place in the human race. In the late nineteenth century, black intellectuals turned to the written text as a means of attaining social and political equality. In 1893, at the age of 25, W. E. B. Du Bois wrote in his diary, "These are my plans: to make a name in science, to make a name in literature and thus raise my race . . ."[3] Writing to *The Independent* newspaper in 1898, the poet Paul Laurence Dunbar states, "At this date the Negro has no need to prove his manual efficiency. That was settled fifty years ago, when he was the plantation blacksmith and carpenter and shoemaker. But his intellectual capacity is still in doubt . . . I would not counsel a return to the madness of that first enthusiasm for classical and professional learning; but I would urge that the Negro temper this newer one with a right idea of the just proportion in life of industry, commerce, art, science and letters, of materialism and idealism, of utilitarianism and beauty."[4] This passage implies Dunbar's refutation of Booker T. Washington's accommodationist policy and more specifically the primacy the latter gives to industrial education as the only way to social inclusion. Dunbar's call for and emphasis on the development of African American arts and letters cannot be divorced from the need that both he himself and the writers of his generation felt to deconstruct the representation of African Americans as minstrel figures, as inferior beings, and as ex-slaves.

Once white hegemony was reestablished and secured by law, some writers in the post-Reconstruction South set about trying to repair its image. Works such as Joel Chandler Harris's *Uncle Remus: His Songs and Sayings* (1881) and Nelson Page's *In Ole Virginia* (1887) portray slavery as a benevolent institution and slaves as incapable of attaining self-sufficiency and reliance, living happily and being dependent on and loyal to their charitable masters. In her "Introduction" to *Iola Leroy, or, Shadows Uplifted*, Frances Smith Foster writes, "Afro-Americans and their friends had been urgently calling for novels that would refute these insidious stereotypes. Although autobiographies, biographies, and essays by Afro-Americans directly contradicted those ideas, they did not necessarily reach the same readers on the same level as the fiction of the Plantation School. To fight fire with fire, the call was not just for more facts, but for writers who could shape those facts in ways that would appeal to the aesthetics of the late nineteenth century."[5] One of the first writers to identify the novel as an adequate form to target mass readership and construct positive images of African Americans was Frances Ellen Watkins Harper, whose first novel, *Minnie's Sacrifice*, was serialized in the *Christian Recorder* in 1869. Harper committed herself to the abolitionist movement in 1853, when a law passed in Maryland stated that free blacks entering the state could be sold into slavery. In a letter to William Still, Harper wrote, "Upon that grave [that of a free man captured and sold into slavery] I pledged myself to the anti-slavery cause . . . It may be that God himself has written upon both my heart and my brain a commission to use time, talent and energy in the cause of freedom."[6] In 1854, she gave her first lecture on the "Education and Elevation of the Race" and began a career that spanned over forty years as a lecturer and activist for African Americans' rights. Harper, as Hazel V. Carby points out in *Reconstructing Womanhood: The Emergence of the Afro-American Woman Novelist*, "fought for and won the right to be regarded as a successful public lecturer, a career not generally considered suitable for a woman. But disabilities of gender and race were not automatically overcome. [William] Still recorded that because she was so articulate and engaging as a public speaker, some audiences thought that Harper must be a man, while others thought she couldn't possibly be black and had to be painted."[7] Harper experienced firsthand the interdependency between literacy and identity pervasive in the minds of the public who attended her lecturers. Born of free parents and a well-educated woman who published her first book, *Forest Leaves*, in 1845, when she was only twenty years old, Harper, as Still noted, was well aware of how the color of her skin functioned as a filter through which the audience listened to and interpreted her words. Nevertheless, her work indicates how language and literature could be the means to overcome prejudice by challenging racism through means of representing it. Telling stories in the present and, importantly, developing subtle narrative tactics became a critical matter for the development of race relations in the United States. The novel is politicized in new ways.

Harper's fictional work constitutes a multifaceted project. First, it is as a medium to overturn stereotypical images of African Americans. Second, it articulates the difficulties that the black community experienced during slavery and Reconstruction, and under the Jim Crow laws. Third, it attempts to record and revise history—the novels constitute a search for an African American past from which the reader can draw lessons and directions for the future. Finally, Harper encourages her readers to engage in literary activity as a means of contributing to a change in the status of African Americans at end of the nineteenth century.

An active voice in the women's rights movement, Harper writes of women who are able and willing to take an active part in the life of their community. She revises the figure of the tragic mulatto to create characters that are capable of inspiring and promoting social change. In the conclusion to *Minnie's Sacrifice*, Harper states, "While some of the authors of the present day have been weaving their stories about white men marrying beautiful quadroon girls, who, in doing so were lost to us socially, I conceived of one of that same class to whom I gave a higher, holier destiny; a life of lofty self-sacrifice and beautiful self-consecration, finished at the post of duty, and rounded off with the fiery crown of martyrdom, a circlet which ever changes into a diadem of glory."[8] The central female characters of *Minnie's Sacrifice* and her last novel, *Iola Leroy, or, Shadows Uplifted* (1892), are "beautiful quadroon girls" who discard a white middle-class life, opt to live in a black community, and work for the improvement of living conditions. After guests mistake Minnie for the daughter of the Le Granges, pointing out how she is "the very image of her father"[9] (her master), his angry wife demands that Minnie be sold. Minnie's father chooses not to sell her but to secretly send her to Pennsylvania, where she is adopted by a Quaker family. She grows up ignorant of her past and thinks that she is white. Minnie eventually discovers her origins through her biological mother, who travels with Union soldiers while seeking her long-lost daughter. Minnie's realization that she has "a small portion of colored blood in [her] veins"[10] and her awareness of her "place" in the American society of the time makes her fall ill. When she recovers, however, she decides not to disregard her mother's heritage. Harper carefully prepares her character's decision not to pass as white. The author sets Minnie's childhood with a Quaker family, who supports the abolitionist movement and often gives shelter to runaway slaves. As Minnie's upbringing brings her into contact with slaves, she learns their hardships from their own lips, developing strong antislavery views. The reader is thus not surprised by Minnie's stand: "So, when I found out that I was colored, I made up my mind that I would neither be pitied nor patronized by my former friends; but that I would live out my own individuality and do for my race, as a colored woman, what I never could accomplish as a white woman."[11]

The male protagonist of this novel has a story similar to that of the woman he ends up marrying. Louis also reaches maturity not knowing that his mother was a slave. His mixed ancestry is revealed to him by his black grandmother to prevent him from departing with the Confederate army and, hence, from fighting against his own people. Although he promptly acknowledges his African heritage, this is not an initiation into his foremother's community. Growing up as the heir to a Southern plantation, Louis stood to inherit not just the estate of his father but also the latter's attitude toward his slave workers. Harper does not allow her character to lightly forget his prejudice against black people, and she prepares for him a baptism of fire. Risking death as a deserter, Louis attempts to escape the South and travel north to join the Union army. In his previous trips north, Louis travelled in pursuit of education and pleasure with all the comfort money could buy a member of the hegemonic class, following his white father's steps. This time he walks in his black ancestors' footprints, "guiding himself northward at night by the light of the stars and a little pocket compass."[12] Escaping the South as a runaway slave, Louis learns that to survive he has to trust his life to the very people he despised as his inferiors. The acts of generosity of slaves who help him to reach the Northern army impel Louis to think "with shame of his former position to the race from whom such unswerving position could spring . . . and [begin] to feel that he had never known them."[13] Harper articulates the transformation that Louis undergoes in terms of his feelings toward the land. Once he saw the South as "his mother,"[14] and he would have given his life to protect her. After his descent into darkness as a runaway slave, which anticipates his rebirth as a changed person, he steps onto the "free soil, appreciating that section as he had never done before."[15] Louis's rejection of the Southern land as a maternal figure, the false mother, is equated with the acceptance of his authentic black mother.

As the narrator points out, Louis "had plenty of money, a liberal education, and could have chosen a life of ease"[16] in the North or gone "home and fight mosquitoes."[17] Instead, both he and Minnie go south "to open a school, and devote [their] lives to the upbuilding of the future race."[18] Placing education at the core of their contribution to the Reconstruction project, Harper's characters voice her own views on the significance of formal and practical learning in preparing African Americans' integration into a society organized and ruled by whites. Although Harper transports her characters from a white middle-class milieu and places them at the center of a black village, they never become equal members of that community. "Class differences," as Jacqueline K. Bryant states, "inscribed and implied, reflect the discourse of racial uplifting promoted during the late nineteenth century."[19] These African American leaders are clearly part of the educated middle-class and have a lighter complexion. Thus Harper seeks to promote the establishment of a black middle-class that will lead African Americans into a new era. At the core of this vision is the adoption of white middle-class social values that will facilitate African American integration into mainstream society.

Astute in terms of narrative tactics, Harper's attempt to capture patterns of folk speech constitutes not only a means of characterizing the uneducated ex-slaves but also a means of representing class divisions in the black community. The vernacular establishes the differences between the "us" and "them" pronouns, which punctuate the discourse of both Minnie and Louis. While the Lacroix couple admires and praises the courage and the spirit of endurance of the former bonded men and women, they see themselves apart from them. The community also perceives Minnie and Louis as disassociated from them: "Often would Minnie enter these humble homes and listen patiently to the old story of wrong and suffering. Sympathizing with their lot, she would give them counsel and help when needed. When she was leaving they would look at her wistfully, and say, 'She mighty good; we's low down, but she feels for we.'"[20] Minnie assumes the role of the teacher and mentor of the community. She is a newlywed young woman living in a strange land, but she never goes to others in search of advice and guidance because her social status and formal education gives her a significant leading role in the community. In this construction of her main characters, Harper overlooks valuable forms of empirical knowledge that sustained the black community during slavery. Both Minnie and Louis are role models for would-be leaders of the African American middle classes.

The similarities between *Minnie's Sacrifice* and *Iola Leroy* are manifold. Despite the fact that there are nearly thirty years between the publication of the novels, Harper articulates almost identical subjects through characters that function as mirror images of each other. This suggests that, for Harper, the status of African Americans remained virtually unchanged. Like Minnie, Iola Leroy is also the daughter of a quadroon mother and a white plantation owner. Iola's father had his slave educated in the North, manumitted her, and married her. Iola is raised by her biological parents on their plantation in Mississippi entirely unaware of her lineage. She travels north to finish her education, and though she witnesses strong opposition to slavery, she refuses to go to abolitionist meetings or acquaint herself with antislavery literature.[21] "Iola," as the narrator declares, "being a Southern girl and a slave-holder's daughter, always defended slavery when it was under discussion."[22] The death of her father leaves Iola and all her family in the hands of a white relative who expeditiously nulls both her parents' marriage and her mother's manumission documents, condemning all the family to slavery. Although Harper chooses to make Iola experience a period in bondage to teach her respect for the enslaved people, the novelist spares her brother, Harry. Living in the North taught Harry some lessons and made him sympathetic to the abolitionist cause. Harper chooses not to send Harry into slavery but rather to have him join a black regiment so that he can familiarize himself with the people and culture to whom he is linked by blood. Iola, however, "was destined to drink to its bitter dregs the cup she was so ready to press to the lips of others."[23] At this point, Harper is not necessarily focusing on gender and the fact that women must suffer particular fates. Minnie, though born in slavery, was spared its terror. Minnie's knowledge of slavery came from her childhood with the Quaker family. This family brought her into contact with runaway slaves, and she learned from them the horrific experience of slavery. Iola's time in bondage serves as a period of learning during which stereotypical images about slavery as a benevolent institution have to be necessarily discarded. Harper's strategy here clearly evokes Mary Prince's words: "I have been a slave—I have felt what a slave feels, and I know what a slave knows."[24]

When Iola is finally released from bondage, she is described as "a trembling dove [taken] from the gory vulture's nest."[25] Using the imagery of the dove as a symbol of purity and virginity, the narrator seeks the sympathy of the reader for a helpless woman who was obviously bought and sold as a sexual commodity. However, when the voice of the narrator gives way to that of a fellow slave, he says of Iola that "[d]ey tells me dey's been sellin' her all ober the kentry; but dat she's a reg'lar spitfire; dey can't lead nor dribe her."[26] If the narrator subscribes to the conventions of the sentimental novel and portrays Iola as a powerless woman, the slave recognizes Iola's capacity to endure and resist adversity. Significantly, the powerless yet powerful woman is an ideal of virtue who therefore can be a role model for the community. Iola has learned her lesson: "Although I was born and raised in the midst of slavery, I had not the least idea of its barbarous selfishness till I was forced to pass through it . . . and I hate it, root and branch."[27] Iola's words echo those of Harriet Jacobs: "Only by experience can any one realize how deep, dark, and foul is that pit of abominations."[28] It is only by "hav[ing] felt what a slave feels, and know[ing] what a slave knows" that Iola can have an appreciation of life in bondage and be resolute "to do something of lasting service for the race."[29]

If Jacobs's story ended "with freedom; not in the usual way, with marriage,"[30] Iola has the advantage of being a fictional character and finding both liberty and happy matrimony. She marries not the white man, who could offer her a life among the society she grew up in, but Dr. Frank Latimer, who shares with her a light complexion, a superior education, and a willingness to recognize his black ancestry. Like Louis of *Minnie's Sacrifice,* Frank could have chosen a life of ease if only he had agreed to accept his white Southern grandmother's offer to make him her heir under the condition he would renounce his identity as African American. Frank and Iola follow Minnie's and Louis's steps to the South, where she will teach and he will practice medicine.

Aunt Linda, one of the community elders, foretells Iola's arrival in the community: "I seed it in a vision dat somebody fair war comin' to help us . . . some nice lady to come down yere and larn our gals some sense."[31] Aunt Linda's depiction of Iola resembles that of an angel, an ethereal creature who has come to rescue the afflicted. Iola not only is seen by the community as someone from a separate realm but also sees herself as someone who is on the periphery and who therefore enjoys the privilege of an outsider's standpoint: "I can see breakers ahead which they do not."[32] Iola's double vision, which enables her to see into the future of the community, can be equated with her double position in it. Her position as an outsider working from within is illustrated in the relationship she establishes with Aunt Linda. Iola finds serenity in her house and in her motherly manners, which awakens her memories of the time when she used to "nestle in Mam Liza's arms."[33] Iola sees in Aunt Linda a maternal figure, who she identifies with her black "mummy" but not with her own mother. Although Iola made every effort to be reunited with her family, she does not take any steps toward finding Mam Liza, which shows not only Iola's ambiguous position in the black community but also Liza's place in the Leroy family as a servant. Iola's prejudice is not one based on color of skin but on class and level of education since she establishes a close relationship with her brother's wife and sees her as her equal, though "[n]either [her] hair nor complexion show the least hint of blood admixture."[34] Harper expresses class differences in the black community mainly in terms of education and housing. While Iola has a "cosy home,"[35] she visits "lowly homes and windowless cabins."[36] Although she, like Minnie, is a young newly married woman, "[o]ld age turns to her for comfort, young girls for guidance, and mothers for counsel."[37] Iola's education is valued to the detriment of the other women's experience.

As for Frank, he is a "leader in every reform movement for the benefit of the community."[38] Nevertheless, he does not confine himself to the limits of the community. Both his education and complexion enable him to negotiate "race lines . . . The world is his country, and mankind his countrymen."[39] Harper rewrites the figure of the tragic mulatto to create a character who can simultaneously work in the community for its welfare and be its representative in the white political and economical arena. Thus, in the construction of her characters, Harper points to the establishment integrationist social model and an equitable division of power between blacks and whites.

Harper's novels function as metaphors for the larger African American community. Her stories are deeply rooted in the experience of slavery and the struggle for social equality. *Minnie's Sacrifice* was published four years after the end of the Civil War and, as M. Giulia Fabi observes, "Harper is already at work rewriting history through an epic of slavery and Reconstruction . . . [which] foregrounds the point of view of slaves and the freedmen."[40] Fabi argues that "by consistently using the past tense in ways that expand the small chronological gap between the present narration and the past of the events narrated,"[41] Harper calls on her contemporary black readers to reflect on both the extratextual present and its historical implications. However, Harper's use of fiction as a means of revising history goes beyond the dialogue she successfully establishes with her contemporary readers. She retrieves from oblivion important chapters of African American history and specifically promotes complexity of color and the significance of education.

Shortly after *Minnie's Sacrifice* began to be serialized in the *Christian Recorder*, the Fifteenth Amendment, which sought to remove the individual states' rights to deny the vote to male citizens on the account of race, color, or previous condition of servitude, was sent to the states for ratification. Importantly, in a climate of relative optimism, when, for example, the American Anti-Slavery Society formally dissolved itself and African Americans tried to put down the load of the past and look forward to a place in an apparently transformed society, Harper invites her readers revisit the past. The role of free and enslaved in the American Civil War constitutes a central element in her work. She uses the novel as a means of recording an unwritten history and retrieving it from the obscurity that accompanies the passage of time. In *Iola Leroy*, the fabricated Captain Sybil, voices Harper's concerns: "'I hope,' said Captain Sybil, 'that the time will come when some faithful historian will chronicle all the deeds of daring service these people have performed during this struggle, and give them due credit therefor [*sic*].'"[42]

As a women's rights activist, Harper is particularly eager to record the role of African American women during the conflict, one that she considers significant and also more likely to be forgotten. In *Minnie's Sacrifice*, black women cross the rebel lines to aid suffering soldiers at the risk of being flogged or killed.[43] In *Iola Leroy*, a female slave ingeniously spies for the Union army "by means of hanging her sheets in different ways,"[44] which corresponded to different movements of the rebel forces, while Iola works as a nurse relieving both physical wounds and emotional traumas. After the end of the war, the women continue to have an active role in the community. Aunt Linda, for example, sets up a business making pies and cakes, which she sells to the soldiers and eventually saves enough to, together with her husband, buy a house and land.[45] After the lessons learned during slavery and war, Iola cannot adopt the passive role of a debutante for which she had been educated. In the North, she procures employment and pursues independent living. Iola's endeavor to find a job despite racial prejudice gives Harper opportunity to express overtly her views on Northern racism and black women's position in postbellum America: I have a theory that every woman ought to know how to earn her own living... I am going to join the great rank of bread-winners ... I think that every woman should have some skill or art which would insure her at least a comfortable support. I believe there would be less unhappy marriages if labor were more honored among women.[46] Thus Harper promotes a protofeminism in seeking to record black women's achievements and courage and in suggesting a social function for women as workers outside the home. After being married, Iola and Minnie alike work as teachers and community mentors contributing to the Reconstruction project in a way that is not overshadowed by their husbands and male counterparts. However, it is worth noting that though Harper offers a perspective on the status of women that could also include the condition of white women in America, her interest is fundamentally with the black community.

Harper writes the history of slavery as a usable past on which African Americans can build their future: "'I would have our people,' said Miss Delany, 'more interested in politics. Instead of forgetting the past, I would have them hold in everlasting remembrance our great deliverance ... We have been aliens and outcasts in the land of our birth. But I want my pupils to do all in their power to make this country worthy of their deepest devotion and loftiest patriotism.'"[47] The past, in Harper's work, functions less as a nostalgic era of courageous endurance and deliverance and more as a period from which lessons and directions for the future of the African American community can be drawn. It is with this perspective of the past in mind that Harper calls on the educated youth to write fiction that can give guidance and point out models of conduct. In the conclusion to *Minnie's Sacrifice*, Harper abandons the fictional realm to address her readers in her own voice: "We have genius among us, but how much can it rely upon the colored race for support ... If I could say without being officious and intrusive, I would say to some who are about to graduate this year, do not feel that your education is finished, when the diploma of your institution is in your hands. Look upon the knowledge you have gained only as a stepping stone to a future, which you are determined shall grandly contrast with the past."[48] While politics and formal education are important factors, Harper sees literature not only as a means of proving intellectual parity with whites and overturning the stereotypical images of blacks but also as a didactic medium for both. In *Iola Leroy*, her call for the establishment of a literary tradition that would assist the "uplifting" of the race is threaded into the plot of the novel. Iola's wish "to do something of lasting service for the race" inspires Frank's suggestion to write a novel: "Miss Leroy, out of the race must come its own thinkers and writers. Authors belonging to the white race have written good racial books, for which I am deeply grateful, but it seems to be almost impossible for a white man to put himself completely in our place. No man can feel the iron which enters another man's soul."[49] Frank's words, reverberating with those of Mary Prince and Harriet Jacobs, point to the creation of an exceptional body of literature that reflects African Americans' experiences reimagined and written by them.

When Harper published *Iola Leroy* in 1892, women writers were at the forefront of African American literary activity. In the introduction to Gertrude Mossell's *The Work of Afro-American Women* (1894), Benjamin F. Lee states, "It is worthy of note as well as of congratulation that colored women are making great advancement in literary ventures. In the year 1892 three books were given the world by this class of writers, well worthy of high consideration: Mrs. A. J. Cooper, 'A Voice from the South by a Black Woman of the South;' Mrs. F. E. W. Harper, 'Iola; or, Shadows Uplifted;' and Mrs. W. A. Dove, 'The Life and Sermons of Rev. W. A. Dove.'"[50] To this list, Bishop Lee could have added two other works by women published in the same year, *Southern Horrors: Lynch Law in All Its Phases* by Ida B. Wells-Barnett, and *From the Darkness Cometh the Light or, Struggles for Freedom* by Lucy A. Delaney. A year earlier, Emma Dunham Kelly published her novel *Megda*. In 1893, Victoria Earle's *Aunt Lindy* was issued. Alice Moore Dunbar Nelson's *Violets and Other Tales*, and Wells-Barnett's *A Red Record* appeared 1895. Evidence that the work of these women did not go unnoticed is the emergence of volumes such as Mossell's survey of the achievements of the African American woman, Monroe Major's *Noted Negro Women: Their Triumphs and Activities* (1893), and Lawson Andrew Scruggs's *Women of Distinction: Remarkable in Works and Invincible in Character* (1893).

While black cultural and literary studies, as Carby observes, "have traditionally characterized the turn of the century as the age of Washington and Du Bois, the period was in fact one of intense activity and productivity for Afro-American women."[51] In her address to the World's Congress of Representative Women in 1893, Harper saw herself and her contemporaries "stand[ing] on the threshold of woman's era":[52]

> Today women hold in their hands influence and opportunity ... In the home she is the priestess, in society the queen, in literature she is a power, in legislative halls law-makers have responded to her appeals, and for her sake have humanized and liberalized their laws. The press has felt the impress of her hand. In the pews of the church she constitutes the majority; the pulpit has welcomed her, and in the school she has the blessed privilege of teaching children and youth. To her is apparently coming the added responsibility of political power; and what she now possesses should only be the means of preparing her to use the coming power for the glory of God and the good of mankind.[53]

Harper pronounces a new social order based on principles of Christian democracy and recognition of women's rights, where women could access, influence, and shape all arenas of private and public life.

Fannie Barrier Williams and Anna Julia Cooper, the other two of six African American women to address the World's Congress in the

Columbian Exposition in Chicago, express similar standpoints and aspirations to those of Harper. Williams emphasizes the importance of education in granting access to areas traditionally barred to women: "Today they feel strong enough to ask for but one thing, and that is the same opportunity for the acquisition of all kinds of knowledge that may be accorded to other women. This granted, in the next generation these progressive women will be found successfully occupying every field where the highest intelligence alone is admissible."[54] Along with education, Williams calls attention to three other areas, which are prominent in the black feminist discourse at the end of the century and inform the writing of the time: the conditions of life under the Jim Crow laws, the value of literature as a means of social reform, and the question of black female morality. Discrimination in the work place is the focus of Williams's critique of the Jim Crow laws. Representing a group of women who sought and needed paid employment, she protested against the prejudice experienced by women in all sectors of the economy: "Taught everywhere in ethics and social economy that merit always wins, colored women carefully prepare themselves for all kinds of occupations only to meet with stern refusal, rebuff, and disappointment. One of countless instances will show how the best as well as the meanest of American society are responsible for the special injustice to our women."[55] Williams points to the hopes of her generation (inspired by the prevailing ideas "in ethics and social economy that merit always wins"[56]) and the disappointments owing to the "special injustice" to which black women are subjected. Her concerns, fictionalized in Harper's works and in subsequent novels such as Pauline Hopkins's *Contending Forces,* clearly articulate the link between the black women's movement and the development of a black literature. She also emphasizes the role of literature in black emancipation. American literature, she states, is in need of a "greater variety and . . . deeper soundings which will be written into it out of the hearts of the self-emancipating women."[57] Williams, along with her fellow activists, supports a literary production, which would portray African American experience and concurrently "uplift the race" and educate white America.

Importantly, Williams is attentive to the complexities of the lives of freed slaves. The question of African American female morality was widely debated during this period in fiction and nonfiction, as well as in the nucleus of the National Association of Colored Women. Williams's comments on this subject are characteristic of the 1890s, when, on one hand, the African American middle-classes strove to adopt a sense of morality and decorum promoted by the white hegemony; when, on the other hand, black female activists tried to represent women who had little or no control over most aspects of their lives: "The question of the moral progress of colored women in the United States has force and meaning in this discussion only so far as it tells the story how the once-enslaved women have been struggling for twenty-five years to emancipate themselves from the demoralization of their enslavement."[58] Williams observes that the conduct of female slaves cannot be compared to that of women who lived outside the institution of slavery and more importantly that former slaves were not simply freed from the physical and psychological imprints left by a history of slavery after emancipation. This sense that the African American woman carries with her a terrible legacy from the historical to the psychological emphasizes that the burden of slavery informs the African American novel from its origins till the present day.

Anna Julia Cooper's address to the Columbian Exposition reflects further themes for literature at the end of the century and later works of the twentieth-century. In her speech, Cooper adopts conventions of earlier texts and locates female African American experience within a context revisited by successive generations of writers. She adopts the representative voice of the slave narrative to articulate an experience that is simultaneously personal and collective: "I speak for the colored women of the South, because it is there that the millions of blacks in this country have watered the soil with blood and tears, and it is there too that the colored woman of America has made her characteristic history, and there her destiny is evolving."[59] She identifies the South as the locale of African American history and culture, a region travelled by contemporary female novelists in search of histories and stories. These narratives have their origins in what Cooper calls "the yet unwritten history . . . full of heroic struggle, a struggle against fearful and overwhelming odds."[60] Cooper also identifies the uniqueness of the black female experience, intrinsically separate from that of the middle-class white woman. The latter, in Cooper's words, "could at least plead for her own emancipation; the black woman, doubly enslaved, could but suffer and struggle and be silent."[61] This examination of the particular conditions facing black women and black writers is incisive in that it identifies a double-bind—a social and a personal enslavement. This experience of double-enslavement and required silence is also a recurrent theme of black women's writing from its origins to the present.

Equally prevailing in female African American literature is the self-sacrificial mother figure, the "untrumpeted heroine," identified by Cooper as "the slave-mother, released from self-sacrifice, and many an unbuttered crust was eaten in silent content that she might eke out enough from her poverty to send her young folks off to school."[62] This woman who nearly obliterates herself for the good of her family and especially her children is also, as Cooper tellingly observes, an "entrapped tigress," toiling "to gain a fee simple title to the bodies of [her] daughters . . . [and] to keep hallowed their own [person]."[63] This endeavor to reclaim their bodies and protect those of their daughters is a predominant motif in African American women's literature. Most importantly, Cooper is alert to the tensions evident in the figure of the good mother. More than a simple figure of compliance and passivity, Cooper's mother is also fierce and dangerous. This figure resents the position of black women and acts in complex and subtle ways to change it.

In concluding her speech, Cooper asserts the principles of Christian humanism, which inform and characterize African American literary tradition: "Let woman's claim to be as broad in the concrete as in the abstract. We take our stand on the solidarity of humanity, the oneness of life, and the unnaturalness and injustice of all special favoritisms, whether of sex, race, country, or condition."[64] Here Cooper's concentration on color, on the exceptional lives of black women and men in America gives way to a vision of a world without bias or favoritism—the special conditions facing blacks must concede to the larger interest of humanity.

In this manner, the 1890s represent a seminal decade for the black women's movement and the literature so closely related to it. The publications of this period consolidate the African American literary tradition both by adopting the devices of the slave narrative and by setting what will become the main themes and motifs for the works of twentieth-century female literature. Nevertheless, the thread of continuity between nineteenth-century writers and their modern counterparts has often been disrupted. Nineteenth-century African American female texts have remained outside the literary canon, and therefore the passing on of a literary tradition from one generation to the next has not always been an uncomplicated matter. Some of these texts were dismissed as having little or no literary value; others like Harriet Wilson's *Our Nig; or Sketches from the Life of a Free Black, in a Two-Story White House, North: Showing That Slavery's Shadows Fall Even There* (1859) and Harriet Jacobs's *Incidents in the Life of a Slave Girl: Written by Herself* (1861) were lost and only rediscovered in the 1980s. More recently Henry Louis Gates Jr. discovered the manuscript of Hannah Crafts's *The Bondwoman's Narrative*. This was published in 2002, making a significant contribution to a rich, though poorly studied literary corpus.

Despite the struggle to have their works published and seeing them condemned to literary obscurity, sometimes even during their lifetime, a reading of the works of Harriet Jacobs, Frances Harper, Anna Julia Cooper, and Pauline Hopkins, among others, shows the development of a literary tradition, which establish the major topics, concerns, and aspirations of contemporary literature written by women: the record of African American history as a counter text to that written by the hegemonies; the particular concern with the chronicling of the experience of the black woman, left in the margins of both historical and political discourse due to her race and sex; the importance of the knowledge of the past in directing the future; the challenge presented by patriarchal ideology and institutions; the portrait of African Americans and the creation of characters and situations with a view to overturning stereotypical images of black people; and the presence of a humanist tradition, which informs and shapes the tone of the works by black women writers.

2

Setting the Record Straight

Margaret Walker's *Jubilee*

Contexts

One of the twentieth-century writers who followed in the steps of her African American literary foremothers, taking into account not only the content and direction of her artistic project but also the course of her life, was Margaret Walker: poet, novelist, essayist, political activist, and lecturer. In her introduction to Walker's *How I Wrote Jubilee and Other Essays on Life and Literature*, Maryemma Graham remarks that Walker's concerns as a writer share a common ground to those of Ann Plato, Anna Julia Cooper, and Frances Harper.[1] Like them, Graham states, "Walker pursues her own sense of individual identity while at the same time committing herself to the stream of collective history."[2] Harper, Graham goes on to say, "appears to be Walker's closest literary ancestor in her preoccupation with social issues while at the same time maintaining her reputation as a leading poet of her day."[3]

Margaret Abigail Walker Alexander was born in 1915 in Birmingham, Alabama. At the age of ten, she moved with her family to New Orleans, where she completed her secondary education and began studies at New Orleans University (Dillard University) until, encouraged by Langston Hughes, she left the South and entered Northwestern University in Illinois. In the Deep South, she experienced life under the Jim Crow laws: the rides at the back of the bus and the "segregated churches and segregated hospitals and cemeteries and schools."[4] Segregation left a deep impression on her memory. Later, she wrote about some of the episodes that had a formative effect on her personality: "Once, we climbed the fire escape to see a movie, because there was no Negro entrance, and after that we saw no movies. Another time my mother stood for hours upstairs in a darkened theatre to hear a recital by Rachmaninoff, because there were no seats for colored. My father was chased home one night at the point of a gun by a drunken policeman who resented seeing a fountain pen in a "nigger's" pocket. My grandmother told the story of a woman tarred and feathered in the neighborhood [by a mob] . . . She was horribly burned and scarred."[5] These incidents, lived and told by the people who had a decisive influence in the formation of young Walker's character, remained with her all her life and began to instill in her a desire to understand the roots of racial discrimination and to contest social inequality.

Despite these difficulties, Walker had the advantage of a black middle-class upbringing, which supported and stimulated the writer in the making. Her parents were both university lecturers and placed great emphasis on formal education. From her mother, a music teacher, she inherited a musical ear that would allow her to capture Southern black dialect and also a love for books. It was also her mother who introduced her to the dialect poems of Paul Laurence Dunbar when she was a child. These she reread at several stages of her life, and they helped her to establish the patterns of antebellum plantation speech in her novel *Jubilee.*[6] From her father, a Protestant minister, she learned a strict moral code that would influence her life and her artistic project. Her grandmother introduced her to the oral history of her family and the folk heritage that stemmed from slavery. African American heritage—its history, music, literature, and folk traditions—along with a stern sense of spirituality were the primary forces in Walker's upbringing.

When Walker left the South in 1932 at the age of 17, she was familiar with a wide range of black authors whose works her parents had at home. She had seen Zora Neale Hurston, who Walker considered her literary mentor, at literary events, and she had met Langston Hughes, who remained a friend and "mentor during their thirty-five year friendship."[7] She also carried with her, like other black writers before her, a strong determination to write to change preconceived ideas of African American identity. In the same way as Harper felt compelled to work for the abolitionist cause after the Fugitive Slave Act was passed in Maryland, Walker committed herself to writing as a means of changing the Jim Crow South: "When I went to school, I read the history books that glorify the white race and describe the Negro either as a clown and a fool or a beast capable of very hard work in excessive heat . . . Then I began to daydream . . . Someday, . . . I will understand, and I will be able to do something about it. I will write books that will prove the history texts were distorted. I will write books about colored people who have colored faces, books that will not make me ashamed when I read them."[8] It is interesting to note here how Walker represents her experience in terms of past and future tenses. The history learned on the school benches of the segregated South contributed to this first impulse to set the record of American history straight. In the North, Walker realized that poverty and injustice were not confined to the Southern states or to one side of the racial dividing line. In 1934, the year Walker was a senior student at Northwestern, 17 percent of the white population and 38 percent of the African American population were unable to find employment, and a large number of people were dependent on state relief. However, as John Hope Franklin and Alfred A. Moss observe, "Even in starvation there was discrimination . . . In many of the communities where relief work was offered, blacks were discriminated against, while in early programs of public assistance there was in some places as much as a $6 differential in monthly aid given to white and black families. This was the final proof for African Americans that democracy had escaped."[9] The 1930s were characterized by poverty, mass migration from Southern rural areas to Northern urban centers, and social tensions, which resulted in an intensification of political consciousness. Roosevelt's New Deal sought to revitalize the American economy to prevent a violent social revolution. Among the measures designed to support the rapidly ailing American economy was the establishment of the Works Progress Administration, later renamed the Works Projects Administration (WPA), which, even though it employed mainly manual workers, also supported art projects. The WPA not only gave artists the financial means necessary to subsist but also brought together Southerners and Northerners and, in the North, blacks and whites, giving rise to an unprecedented community of artists. "In cities above the Mason-Dixon where the writers' projects drew no color lines," as Walker writes, "a new school of Black and white writers mushroomed into being overnight."[10] Both black and white writers were influenced by a climate of social unrest, political awareness, and socialist and Marxist thought. This, as Walker states, was a generation of writers driven by a sociopolitical imperative: "The cry of these writers was the cry of social protest: protest against the social ills of the day, including unemployment, slums, crime, juvenile delinquency, prejudice, poverty, and disease. The New Deal struggled to alleviate these social ills, while the writers led the vanguard of literary protest and agitation for a better world."[11] This was no longer the cry for social acceptance or the plea for recognition of their humanity that characterized much of the writing of previous generations of African Americans, who were dependent on white patronage. "These writers," according Walker, "lacked social perspective and suffered from a kind of literary myopia. Poets of the Harlem Renaissance seemed constantly to beg the question of Negro's humanity, perhaps as an answer to the white patron's attitude that Negroes were only children anyway."[12]

Indicative of this new vision was the work of Richard Wright. In his "Blueprint for Negro Writing," published in 1937, a year after Walker joined the WPA in Chicago, Wright criticized the writing of the previous generations for being overly preoccupied with white audiences and their bourgeois values and failing to address the African American masses, their culture, their hardships, and their aspirations. Wright called on African American writers to explore the uniqueness of African American culture within a Marxist framework: "[A] view of society as something becoming rather than as something fixed and admired is the one which points the way for Negro writers to stand shoulder to shoulder with Negro workers in mood and outlook."[13] To produce art that would be meaningful to the African American worker, artists should explore the essence of black culture, which, he argues, is "a folklore moulded out of rigorous and inhuman conditions of life that the Negro achieved his most indigenous and complete expression."[14] Wright saw art interwoven in the social and political fabric and the artist as an agent of social change who "would create values by which his race is to struggle, live and die."[15]

Walker's years in Chicago, her job in the WPA, and her association with the South Side Writers' Group and with Wright laid the foundations for her writing career. During this period, Walker established the bond between political activism and literary creativity that governed all her writing: "I believe my role in the struggle is the role of a writer. Everything I have ever written or hope to write is dedicated to that struggle, to our hope of peace and dignity and freedom in the world, not just as Black people . . . but as free human beings in a world community."[16] It was in her Chicago years, while working on her first book of poems, *For My People*, that folklore became evident in Walker's work as a means of articulating her African American heritage. The use of folk speech and folk beliefs characterizes her poetry and constitutes the creative scaffold of her novel *Jubilee*. The poems of *For My People*, particularly those of the middle section, as Joyce Pettis observes, "reflect the oral and the folk traditions of Southern black culture. Writing in the tradition of James Weldon Johnson, Sterling Brown, and Zora Neale Hurston . . . [Walker] draw[s] characters and speech from the Southern folk tradition."[17]

Walker later saw herself as a writer of the 1930s school of social protest deeply influenced by Wright, "by what he wrote and what he said,"[18] to use her own words. However, both her poetry and prose cannot be contained within the context of the Chicago school of protest. First, Walker's work is rooted in the humanistic tradition of African American literature, which she defines as "a recognition that we are part of nature and the historical process, that we are implicit in the dynamic evolving of mankind to ever higher planes of being, that all life must be richly developed in spirit rather than mere matter, and that one must regard the sacred nature of a brother or sister as one values his own privacy and inner sanctity."[19] Walker placed her concept of humanism in Africa and Asia rather than in the European Renaissance, linking the cultures of the black diaspora in an unbroken tradition: "In literature," as Walker states, "from ancient Africa, the Afro-American humanistic tradition includes search for freedom, truth, beauty, peace, human dignity, and most of all social justice. The most recurrent theme is man's inhumanity to man."[20] This notion of humanism was not fixed but dynamic. It had its foundations in the belief that society was evolving toward a new spiritual and social order that would overthrow racism and create "[a] new respect for the quality of all human life."[21] Walker's humanistic tradition sought inclusiveness as it emphasized human dignity above all else.

Importantly, in her poetry and her fiction, black people lead the way to this new social order. This is a tradition that Walker inherited from generations of African American writers preceding her own. African American literature written before and after the Civil War reflects a preoccupation not only with the suffering and discrimination of the people of African descent but also with the direction of American society as a whole. Writers such as Harriet Jacobs, Frances Harper, and Pauline Hopkins wrote to effect social change, being fully aware of the potential of the "homely tale" that, as the latter writes in her preface to *Contending Forces*, "unassumingly told, cement[s] the bond of brotherhood among all classes and all complexions."[22] In her autobiography, Jacobs's narrator declares that "a man's worth [is measured] by his character, not by his complexion."[23] Discussing the race question in the United States, Harper's character Dr. Latimer proclaims that "instead of narrowing our sympathies to mere racial questions, let us broaden them to humanity's wider issues."[24] These are some examples of how the humanist tradition set the tone and, to some extent, conditioned the content of female African American literature at the end of the nineteenth century. It is this tradition that attracted Walker's interest: "I would not be true to the humanist tradition of Afro-American literature were I pessimistic about the goodness of the future. Change will come and there is hope for a better world. But that world must be founded on a new humanism rather than on the old racism."[25]

The second aspect of Walker's work, which requires a redefinition of her position within the African American literary tradition beyond the boundaries of the 1930s literature of protest, was her urge to piece together the unwritten history of black women. This element of her work set her in the tradition of African American female writers from Phillis Wheatley to Zora Neale Hurston. "For Walker," as Graham states, "to write is to invoke tradition and the past, to celebrate plurality and difference to translate complexity into human understanding, and to construct a model of human society as it is, but more importantly to transform that model as it can be."[26] Walker's extensive research of the historical texts available in the 1940s and 1950s led her to conclude not only that African American history was practically unwritten but that black women's history was still in a state of a tabula rasa. It is important to note that the pioneering study of the slave community by Eugene D. Genovese, *Roll, Jordan, Roll: The World the Slaves Made*, appeared only in 1972, and Angela Davis's *Women, Race and Class* and Deborah Gray White's *Ar'n't I a Woman? Female Slaves in the Plantation South*, both groundbreaking studies of the history of the African American woman, were published in 1981 and 1985, respectively, almost two decades after the publication of *Jubilee*.

The primary and secondary sources available to Walker presented a fragmented and frequently biased African American history. In "How I Wrote *Jubilee*" (1972), she explains that, by trying to frame her grandmother's story in a historical context, she saw herself as "a novelist in the role of a social historian."[27] In her research, Walker was confronted by different accounts of slavery: the Southern-white version, which characterized it as a compassionate and indispensable institution; the Northern-white version, which denounced the evils of slavery but diminished and treated uniformly the experience of the slaves; and finally the African American perspective, which consisted of a small number of chronicles centered on the exceptional lives of a few slaves, most of them male.[28]

Slave narratives were an indispensable source in Walker's attempt to piece together African American history. However, even these personal narratives by the slaves themselves presented limitations. The slaves' "sense of [their own] existence," as Henry Louis Gates Jr. argues, "depended upon memory," and it was that same memory "that gave a shape to being itself,"[29] since any kind of written records had been denied them. However, the memories of those who managed to inscribe them in written text were necessarily limited. For example, in their narratives, ex-slaves indicated, generally speaking, great difficulties in reconstituting the early years of their childhoods, and the recollections of their parents were often vague or nonexistent. Frederick Douglass had no accurate knowledge of his age, did not know who his father was, and was separated from his mother when he was "but an infant."[30] This is a point made general by Barbara Christian: "Slave-owners were aware of the power of memory for they disrupted generational lines of slaves in such a way that many slaves did not *know* even their own parents or children."[31] On the other hand, the slaves' narratives could only be partial, given that their authors' concern was to denounce the institution of slavery to a white audience from a didactic and moral point of view, grounded on an ideology that was also white. Ex-slaves knew that communicating their experiences meant adopting the values of their audience—the white middle classes. In representing their experience in conformity with their audience's sense of good and evil, religiosity, and decorum, they had to leave many things unsaid. "No slave society . . . wrote more—or more thoughtfully—about its own enslavement," as Toni Morrison states; nevertheless, she herself goes on to say that "[i]n shaping the experience to make it palatable to those who were in a position to alleviate it, they were silent about many things, and they forgot many things."[32]

The social determinants that conditioned antebellum African American writing account for, to a large extent, the disappearance of Jacobs's and Harriet Wilson's works for over one hundred years. The main theme of Wilson's work is the discrimination that free blacks were subjected to in the North in the years prior to the Civil War. In the preface to *Our Nig*, Wilson anticipates the criticism of her work from white abolitionists and states that in writing her autobiographical novel, she "purposely omitted"[33] what she considered "would most provoke shame in our good anti-slavery friends."[34] However, her story could not be told without exposing the treatment that her protagonist, Frado, received at the hands of her mistress, and in doing so, Wilson denounces racism in the North and rejects the view that all white Northerners shared abolitionist views. The first black woman to publish a novel in English[35] defied the white Northern values in yet another way. Frado is the result of an interracial marriage between a black man and a white woman, a kind of relationship that was socially unacceptable. Furthermore, the depiction of this marriage as a reasonably successful union,[36] as Gates points out, "did nothing to aid the book's circulation in the North or the South,"[37] condemning it to oblivion until 1983, the date of the publication of its second edition. In writing her story, Wilson, to paraphrase Morrison, did not forget enough and was not silent enough to make her experience, if not "palatable," at least "digestible" to her potential readers.

The silences and the gaps left in nineteenth-century African American narratives are open spaces into which the stories of contemporary African American writers began to enter. Postbellum black women's literature, such as Harper's work, already discussed here, set the tone for subsequent literature by black women. However, writers like Harper and Hopkins, although concerned with retrieving African American history from oblivion, were confined by the corset of the conventions of the time and too preoccupied with the creation of a black middle-class role model for, and leader of, the masses to present a black heroine who could be considered representative. In other words, female novelists of the end of the nineteenth century abandoned the representative voice characteristic of the slave narratives and wrote about exceptional characters who were generally educated and very often light enough to pass for white. Walker wrote at a time when she was free to explore interrelationships of class and race in her treatment of slavery and Reconstruction, and her protagonist differed significantly from Harper's Minnie or Iola: "I was among the first dealing with characters looking up from the bottom rather than down from the top," says Walker.[38]

Walker's interest in history sprang from stories. She grew up listening to the stories about slave life in Georgia told by her maternal grandmother, who lived with the Walkers since Margaret's birth until the author reached adulthood. Throughout these years, Walker became conscious of the significance of the family narrative that her grandmother passed on to her: "As I grew older and realized the importance of the story my grandmother was telling, I prodded her with more questions: 'What happened after the war, Grandma? Where did they go? Where did they live after that place?' I was already conceiving the story of *Jubilee* vaguely, and early in my adolescence, while I was hearing my grandmother tell old slavery-times stories and incidents from her mother's life, I promised my grandmother that when I grew up I would write her mother's story."[39] The story of her great-grandparents populated Walker's imagination from a very early age. She began to work on *Jubilee* when she was a senior student at Northwestern University in 1934, but as she declares, the "genesis [of the novel] coincides with [her] childhood, its development grows out of a welter of raw experiences and careful research."[40] The writer conflated the memory of her grandmother's words with meticulous research carried out over thirty years. She read slave narratives, Civil War novels, newspapers, and pamphlets; traveled to the places where her great-grandparents had lived; and studied legal records and personal documents, such as advertisements for runaway slaves, bills of sale, and letters and diaries, to "authenticate the story [she] had heard from [her] grandmother's lips."[41]

The recognition of the precedence of the oral text over the written word is fundamental to understanding the nature and form of Walker's novel. She saw her artistic project as "the creation of fiction from fact, the development of imagined clothing, of muscle and flesh for the real and living bones of history."[42] Walker's ambition was to recreate the periods of slavery, Civil War, and Reconstruction from a point of view that she understood as historically accurate. Studying the myriad layers of historical narratives, she created a historical context in which to give shape to her grandmother's oral narrative. However, this was not to be a history book. The historical and personal facts were a basis for an imaginative engagement with her past in every sense of the word—gaps could be imagined into existence. In this way, *Jubilee* is a patchwork made up of story, history, and imagination. Walker used written sources to "undergird the oral tradition,"[43] to use her own words. Her artistic task was to write a perspective of African American history that was fundamentally different from a Southern white or Northern white viewpoint or previous black versions but nonetheless a perspective. To validate not only the uniqueness of her grandmother's narrative but also the distinctiveness of African American history and experience, she used black lore as the framework and bedrock of her novel.

"The African impulse to produce and perform music," as Patricia A. Turner states, "survived the horrendous strains of the Middle Passage and became a mainstay of New World African Americans."[44] Walker showed her understanding of the central role that music occupies in black American culture by opening each chapter of her novel with a passage from a song. She also referred to folk speech patterns, storytelling, and sayings; superstitions, religious beliefs and practices, and rituals; food, herbal medicine, and household customs; and quilt making, clothing, and games to represent and express African American history as fully as possible in folk terms. In others words, Walker accounts for those African American traditions and values that were communicated through the ages via word of mouth, revealing a rich culture that survived and developed apart from the printed word.

Walker used folk speech to present an authentic representation of a world both constructed and expressed in folklore terms. She attributed folk speech patterns to her characters to reclaim her ancestors' African American oral tradition. For example, her use of the Georgian slave dialect differed substantially from Harper's application of the vernacular in her novels. Harper made use of dialect in an almost condescending manner to make clear the distance between the uneducated black masses and the educated and well-spoken mulattos. In her interest in black dialect and her attempts to capture it accurately, Walker was closer to Hurston than to any other writer. During the Harlem Renaissance, writers such as Jean Toomer and Hughes turned to folklore to help them define and establish their aesthetics. However, the publication of Toomer's *Cane* in 1923 marked, as Friederike Hajek points out, "both a recognition of the richness of black southern oral heritage and its apparent dissolution. Efforts to preserve and continue folk tradition had little or no success in the decades to follow, as is shown by the case of Zora Neale Hurston, who died poor and forgotten in 1968, at the peak both of Black Power and the Black Aesthetic movements."[45] In this way, it is not surprising that in his "Blueprint for Negro Writing" (1937) Wright called on black writers to root their aesthetics in the indigenous African American oral tradition: "Blues, spirituals, and folk tales recounted from mouth to mouth, the whispered words of a black mother to her black daughter on the ways of men, the confidential wisdom of the black father to his black son."[46] What was surprising, however, was the manner in which Wright failed to acknowledge Hurston's use of folklore. This might have to do with the fact that in her work Hurston recreated the vernacular to give voice to the silenced female. Wright's concept of folklore, as H. Nigel Thomas observed, "embodies the black man's hopes and struggle for freedom as the central focus for the creative black artist. Walker, on the other hand, is in the tradition of Hughes, Bontemps, and Ellison, who use folklore in their fiction to reveal the psychology of black American survival."[47]

The absence of Hurston from Thomas's list was significant. She was a major influence on Walker's work in her use of folklore to articulate the African American female experience. In 1939, as Jacqueline Miller Carmichael observed, "Walker was already interested in Zora Neale Hurston's use of folklore in *Jonah's Gourd Vine*."[48] From the author of *Their Eyes Were Watching God*, Walker saw how to use folk speech patterns to give voice to those historically silenced and to make social comments on African American life and culture. Nonetheless, Walker's use of dialect shows that she went beyond a mimetic response to Hurston's works. Walker, as James E. Spears notes, "is a dialectologist in the strictest sense of the word, and her use of eye dialect for characterization is both accurate and effective. It captures the essence of Black dialect in pronunciation, vocabulary items, and usage of grammar, particularly syntax."[49] This is an important point in that Walker sought levels of accuracy in the representation of the black experience beyond that which had been attempted and achieved. She craved sources, be they historical, personal, and communal, and used them with an attention to detail that was unprecedented. Her use of dialect was yet another example of this.

Community and Language

The first scene of *Jubilee* takes place in 1839 in the slave quarters, giving a clear indication that the slave community is the main focus of the narrative with the presentation of voices speaking in a black dialect:

> "May Lisa, how come you so restless and uneasy? You must be restless in your mind."
>
> "I is. I is. That old screech owl is making me nervous."
>
> "Wellum, 'tain't no use in your gitting so upsot bout that bird hollering. It ain't the sign of no woman nohow. It always means a man."
>
> "It's the sign of death."[50]

In her essay "How I Wrote *Jubilee*," Walker explains that the version of the novel that she presented as her doctoral thesis at the University of Iowa differs greatly from the book form in the sense that in the novel "every dialect word had to be changed for spelling and modernization."[51] Nonetheless, the reader is still exposed to the richness and variety of black dialect in the use of euphemisms and epithets, omissions of auxiliary verbs and prefixes, analogical verb conjugation formation, analogical pluralization, the use of peculiar spelling to translate pronunciation, and other grammatical and syntactical devices.

A close reading of the opening lines reveals the significance of black folk dialect employed by Walker. The verb "to be" is omitted, and the reader (particularly if she or he is unfamiliar with black dialect) has to slow down the reading process to become acquainted with the language. The reading of *Jubilee* becomes a double act of decoding the language to follow the story line while striving to make sense of a life expressed in folk terms. For example, the expression "restless in your mind" is identified by Spears as "belonging peculiarly to Black folk speakers."[52] May Lisa's response includes an example of subject-verb agreement violation, which is characteristic of black dialect: "I is, I is." The usage of double negatives is quite evident: "'tain't no use" and "It ain't no sign of no woman nohow." It is also worth noting the spelling of words such as "gitting," "upsot," and "bout," which are employed to reflect black folk pronunciation and to establish authenticity for the setting.

The structure of the novel illustrates further uses of folklore. Walker not only makes use of folk material in the arrangement of chapters but also employs it to establish a correlation between form and content. Each chapter opens, as was already mentioned, with a quotation from a song, "including spirituals, work songs, popular tunes, and even minstrel songs and favorites [Walker] had heard [her] grandmother say [her] great-grandmother had sung."[53] The passages from songs function as epigraphs that establish the theme or set the tone for each chapter. In a European tradition, these passages printed on the first page of a literary work or at the beginning of a section are, generally speaking, taken from influential works that inspired authors and helped to shape texts and traditions. Choosing extracts from songs sung among black communities as epigraphs, Walker establishes the tradition within which her work is set. Each extract from a hymn or tune is followed by a heading, or title, taken from folk sayings. "Many of the chapter headings," as Walker states, "are exact repetitions of my grandmother's words."[54] The use of folk proverbs and maxims reinforces Walker's purpose in grounding her work in a tradition that is authentically African American and oral and is clearly distinguished from the hegemonic other. Both epigraphs and headings are closely related to the content of the correspondent chapters and, in many cases, lead the reader to anticipate the direction of the narrative. It is clear that folklore not only functions as the scaffold of the novel[55] but also directs and shapes its content.

The first chapter is prefaced by "Swing low, sweet chariot, / Coming for to carry me home . . . ," and the theme of death is reinforced by the chapter heading: "Death is a mystery that only the squinch owl knows." The choice of a spiritual for the first epigraph is significant. On one hand, it embodies a musical tradition with roots in West African chants, which survived the Middle Passage and became one of the first forms of black American expression. The experience of the slave in the New World is engraved in the spiritual song. It also constitutes a form of resistance and endurance that closely reflects the story of the African American characters in *Jubilee*. On the other hand, it represents the profound Christianity that informs the novel. "The spirituals," as Kimberly Rae Connor puts it, "created by enslaved people became a unique means to 'keep on keep on' under the physical and psychological pressures of daily life, testifying to the belief that the supernatural interacted with the natural and the whole world rested in the hands of God."[56] In this way, the spiritual forges the link between oral tradition and religious practice developed throughout the novel. The choice of "Swing Low, Sweet Chariot" is also noteworthy in one other respect. The song celebrates the hope to find liberation in heaven. Another level of meaning is suggested by a footnote in the *Norton Anthology of African American Literature*: the song "signal[s] the plan or the moment—or the general aspiration—to be carried 'home' to freedom by the underground railroad system."[57] Thus the opening epigraph announces both the mother's death and the daughter's desire for freedom in *Jubilee*—it signals Africa, America, life, death, slavery, escape, religion, faith, and transcendence.

The first lines of the narrative are a dialogue between May Lisa and Grandpa Tom during which the title of the chapter is directly addressed: "That old screech owl is making me nervous . . . It's the sign of death." Thus the melody of the well-known "Swing Low, Sweet Chariot" foretells and reflects what will be the slow pace of the chapter: "A hushed quiet hung over the Quarters. There were no children playing ring games before the cabins. The hardened dirty-clay road, more like a narrow path before their doors, was full of people smoking corncob pipes and chewing tobacco in silence."[58] The solemnity of the music and the image of "Sweet Chariot" are reflected in "hushed quiet" and the slow movements of the characters waiting for the inescapable: Sis Hetta's death. Even nature seems to reflect the tune, showing "the quarter moon dripping blood" eight days before Hetta's death,[59] a sign that Granny Ticey interprets as an "evil omen."[60] The novelist constructs meaning by placing one layer of folk material upon another. The reader moves from song, to spiritual, to saying, to symbol, and to omen (evident in folklore) to grasp the significance of the episode. This black community is set within the rigid parameters of the white plantation, so opportunities for expression are specially constructed to reflect the experiences and limitations of the slaves.

In this first chapter, Walker draws the social map of the Dutton plantation: the Big House, headed by Marse John and Mistress Salina, and the slave quarters, where the field hands and the domestic servants wait for Hetta's death. Individuals' identities are tied to the social roles given to them within the plantation structure. Walker plays with stereotypical images of African American identity to deconstruct and revise them. The names of the first two characters introduced illustrate this point. There is an inherent paradox in calling Tom "Grandpa" and describing him as the "stable boy."[61] In turn, May Lisa is characterized as the "Master's upstairs house girl."[62] Both Tom's and Lisa's identities are defined by their slave status. Walker's use of the epithets plays with the way whites imposed fixed identities on black people, robbing them of a sense of individuality.

On the other hand, shattering the cast-iron mask presented to the master, Walker reveals the flesh, the personality, and the humanity of her characters. Accused of being careless and responsible for Hetta's moribund state by a white doctor who came two days too late, Granny Ticey does not respond to the accusations. To the white man, she reveals a "set face"[63] and offers nothing but her silence. He leaves with a mute admission of guilt. Yet the reader has access to an interior monologue that discloses Granny Ticey's feelings: "But she was thinking all she dare not say: How was he expecting me to get all rotten pieces after a dead baby? That's exactly why I sent for him, so's he could get what I couldn't get. If he had come when I sent for him, instead of waiting till now, Hetta might not be dead."[64] Walker works with the slaves' sense of dual identity, the one presented to the hegemonic other and the private self, to document stereotypical images of African Americans and deconstruct them. This is the point when history, and even the ancestor's story, gives way to imagination so that an inner life can be imagined and expressed and the voice of the silenced can be recreated. It is important to reiterate that Walker's imaginative play upon her subjects' lives is drawn from an intense engagement with black culture on a number of levels.

The African American characters in this episode, and throughout the novel, are silenced and silent within the terms set by white discourse. This silence is equated with a sense of powerlessness in relation to Hetta's death, and it permeates almost every aspect of the slaves' lives. Caline fans Hetta in silence, and the repetitious movement reflects both the latter's inescapable death and the former's inescapable life in bondage. Granny Ticey is described as "grim and wordless [as] she watched the night lengthen its shadows outside Sis Hetta's door."[65] Throughout the episode, her lips are "tied" and "tightly set,"[66] suggesting a sense of anger and hopelessness translated in silence—Walker records the impossibility of public expression as she accounts for private responses. Jake, Hetta's husband, remains silent by his wife's deathbed, and again it is by using the narrative mode of the interior monologue or, as in this case, free indirect discourse that the character's thoughts and emotions are revealed to the reader: "Whenever her eyes closed in death, his fate would be sealed. Marster would have no further use for him and he would be sold . . . What would they do with his helpless black child then?"[67] While Walker fills these silences in subtle ways, she insists on a silence beyond her capacity to give voice to the mute. The absence of Hetta's interior monologue leaves such a gap in the narrative, dramatically emphasizing the waste of a human life that dissipates—a mother who leaves behind the children who never got to know her. The inclusion in the narrative of the death of Vyry's mother, Hetta, is Walker's tribute to the silenced black woman whose story is noted but ultimately untold.

Importantly, Walker exposes the brutal way in which men are treated. Jake is dehumanized and stripped of a sense of manhood by a master who "slapped Jake's back and talked down to his slave . . . like he did to one of his good hound dogs"[68] and repeatedly raped his wife in his absence. Jake's feelings can hardly be articulated in words, as the short clauses linked by the copulative conjunction, conferring syncopated and fragmented rhythm to his thoughts, demonstrate: "Jake hated Marster and despised himself and looked at Hetta and got mad and evil. But that was the end of it. He never dared say anything or do anything about it."[69] Jake knew that if he attempted to protect his wife by word or deed, he would put his life at risk. The pressure on the rhythm of the language is but one sign of the repression Jake and his community suffered.

When the omniscient point of view gives way to the interior monologue, the reader perceives that Jake is dehumanized to the extent that he uses the master's language to describe himself: "Guess in a way I'm glad to get away from here. Marster's always said he'll get a fair price for a good stud like me."[70] The way Walker reverses the image of a man turned into a working and breeding brute ("stud") is by evoking his sense of fatherhood while deconstructing the myth that slave fathers were indifferent and slaves did not have a strong of sense of family. Jake's image as a father is gradually constructed. First, the reader sees him holding his anxious child: "Her eyes looked big as saucers in her thin face, and she had her thumb and two fingers in her mouth sucking on all three hard as she could."[71] When the reader has access to Jake's thoughts for the first time, we learn of his main fear: "What would they do with his helpless black child [after Hetta's death]?" However, when we read Jake's interior monologue, he has already laid his baby on a pallet and stepped out of the cabin. His exit from the cabin signals his physical and psychological departure from his family.

His exit does not mean, however, that Walker reverts to the stereotype of the disinterested and unloving slave father, but it exemplifies the lack of control that the slaves had over their families and lives.

This is not to say that the peculiar institution completely disregarded the slave family unit. "[S]lave marriages," as White states, "survived all sorts of problems . . . and the separation of slaves was not universal."[72] However, in Mississippi, "there was much evidence that slave marriages had often been disrupted by sale."[73] In Louisiana, as Franklin and Moss declare, the "law forbade separation of a mother from a child under ten years of age, and some other states discouraged the division of families. These laws, if enforced, would have done much to ameliorate the conditions of slavery; but they were most wholly disregarded."[74] The economic nature of slave trading and slave breeding involved the separation of families and the suppression of the voices of those whose culture and community had opened the novel.

This context is intensified in terms set by motherhood. Each character's perspective of Hetta is influenced by his or her own views. Caline and Granny Ticey think about Hetta in terms of motherhood. Caline never had any children, and Hetta had "all those younguns fast as she could breed them."[75] Granny Ticey remembers her presence at Hetta's difficult deliveries and the frequent childbearing forced on Hetta by her master as she tries to come to terms with the inevitability of her death at the age of 29 after having lost her fifteenth child. With this imagery, conventional connotations of motherhood and its associations with life and nurturing are subverted. Caline is thankful for her barren womb: "Slaves were better off, like herself, when they had no children to be sold away, to die, and keep on having till they kill you."[76] Granny Ticey sees motherhood, at least in relation to Hetta, as an almost destructive force. In her mind she has the almost grotesque image of a woman that pregnancy left "bloated and swollen beyond recognition" and "whose babies came too fast, tearing her flesh in shreds."[77] Sis Hetta's death dramatizes the manner in which female slavery, as White states, "had much to do with work, but much of it was concerned with bearing, nourishing, and rearing children whom slaveholders needed for the continual replenishment of their labor force."[78] Motherhood is for the female a bittersweet experience of giving life and raising and loving children while increasing the value of the master's property. "The white folks," as the former slave Martha Harrison remarks, "was crazy 'bout their nigger babies, 'cause that's where they got their profit."[79]

Such individual cases have to be read in the larger political circumstances of the time. With the closing of the African slave trade to the United States in the beginning of the nineteenth century and despite the violations of the federal legislation of 1808, slavery in America became gradually dependent on the natural increase of the enslaved population. In this peculiar institution very little was left to chance, and the reproduction of the labor force was a topic much discussed by slave owners. In *Ar'n't I a Woman? Female Slaves in the Plantation South,* White states that "[m] ajor periodicals carried articles detailing optimal conditions under which bonded women were known to reproduce, and the merits of a particular 'breeder' were often the topic of parlor or dinner table conversations."[80] White also argues that once reproduction was introduced in the public arena, so was black female sexuality. "People accustomed to speaking and writing about the bondswoman's reproductive abilities," as White observes, "could hardly help associating her with licentious behavior."[81]

The exposure of the black female body stripped and handled in slave auctions and at whipping posts and the lack of clothing appropriate to weather conditions and the prevailing sense of decorum also encouraged the construct of the African woman as an amoral sexual being. The view that black women were naturally promiscuous is elemental to proslavery ideologists in several ways. First, it fits in with the reproduction policies that slave owners adopted. Among them, as Franklin and Moss observe, was "forced cohabitation and pregnancy."[82] Second, the image of the amoral and lustful slave woman is central to the creation of its antithesis: the pure Southern white woman, the very essence of virtue. The virginal and almost ethereal white woman is sustained by the black woman who functions as a safeguard of her honor. Third, the representation of the African American female as a temptress rationalized and legitimatized the abuse of black women by white men. White quotes William Harper, the chancellor of the University of South Carolina, whose speech encapsulates the Southern debate on the immorality of the black woman and the legitimacy of the white man to use her body as he saw fit: "She [the pregnant slave] is not a less useful member of society than before . . . She has not impaired her means of support or materially impaired her character, or lowered her station in society; she has done no great injury to herself, or any other human being. Her offspring is not a burden but an acquisition to her owner; his support is provided for, and he is brought up to usefulness."[83] Against this, the body of the bondswoman—used in agricultural and domestic work, as a means of reproducing the slave labor force, and as means of social control to shield the white woman from the physical compulsions of the white man—is, as Walker exposes in *Jubilee,* a scarred body. "The bearing of children was" as Franklin and Moss declare, "[a] hard time for the slave women. Lack of adequate medical care had a particular negative impact on the health of the slave women during pregnancy, childbirths, and the period immediately after."[84] The resistance offered to the white man's advances was often severely punished with beatings, marking body and mind. The resentful mistress, powerless in relation to her husband, would also make the enslaved woman feel her anger. Many slave women, as Harriet Jacobs's narrative illustrates, had to confront what Minrose C. Gwin calls "the two-faced monster of slavocracy, a lustful master and a jealous mistress."[85]

When John Dutton walks away from Hetta's deathbed, his memories of her are consistent with the image of the black woman as an oversexualized being within easy reach to satisfy all his needs. The figure of a pregnant woman heavy with his children does not emerge in Dutton's recollections. Nor does he consider the children he had with her and who sooner or later he had to sell away to appease his wife. His memories are reduced to Hetta's young body: "Her small young breasts tilted up, and even her slight hips and little buttocks were set high on her body. When she moved lightly and they switched lazily and delicately, they titillated him and his furious excitement grew while watching her walk."[86] Like the other characters, he remembers Hetta on his own terms, and for him she is the temptress whom he has to subdue and possess. Having Hetta's body as the focal point of his reminiscences ties in with his view of the relationship between master and slave: "Miscegenation was no sin to Marse John. It was an accepted part of his world. What he could not understand at first was where Salina had been given such romantic notions, and how her loving parents had kept the facts of life from her."[87] Through the character of John Dutton, Walker depicts the status of both black and white women in the American South. The novelist's representation of the black woman's sexual abuse offers no euphemistic subterfuges, leaving the reader to deal with the raw reality: "Anyway it was his father who taught him it was better for a young man of quality to learn life by breaking in a young nigger wench than it was for him to spoil a pure white virgin girl. And he had wanted Hetta, so his father gave her to him, and he had satisfied his lust with her . . . When she began having babies it was no problem. He gave her Jake for a husband and that was that."[88] The narrator's language is direct and the account is succinct, reflecting a social system where there was no scope for anyone's views but those of the master. The expression that closes the paragraph mirrors a world created and controlled by the white man, which was not to be easily shaken. The reader is forced to contemplate the sense of inescapability that dominated the slave's life. To be born a slave was to have a marked destiny, "and that was that."

In the first chapter of *Jubilee*, as already mentioned, Walker emphasizes the complexity of the social organization of the plantation to introduce the reader to the peculiar institution while exposing a close-knit community that comes together in an hour of grief: the men silently sit outside the cabins in an act of solidarity; the women make themselves busy tending to Hetta; and Brother Zeke, the plantation preacher, comes to pray by the moribund woman's side. This sense of community is further developed when the narrator describes the women's network formed around Hetta's child, Vyry. The little girl's resemblance to the master's legitimate daughter puts her in a particularly vulnerable position, and the women gather around her to protect her the best they can. Mammy Sukey holds her in her arms and tries to sooth Vyry in her restless sleep while Aunt Sally worries about what life will unfold to her: "In her mind she thought, 'They could pass for twins—same sandy hair, same gray-blue eyes, same milky white skin.'"[89] Vyry's white skin against the darkness of the night of her mother's death reinforces the tensions about to be unleashed by Hetta's death. In *Minnie's Sacrifice*, the physical similarity between the slave girl and her Big House sister caused her separation from her mother. Notwithstanding, Minnie is given to a compassionate Quaker couple who raise her as their own daughter. In Walker's narrative, based on her family's story and told in a realistic rather than a romantic manner, there is no room for fairy-tale white benefactors who rescue little slave girls. Thus Vyry's fate drastically differs from Minnie's. Her white skin, blonde hair, and blue eyes, instead of granting Vyry a life of privilege, as Charlotte Goodman remarks, "cause her to be singled out for special abuse by her mistress, who cannot bear to acknowledge the uncanny resemblance between Vyry and her own daughter."[90] The women in the slave quarters recognize Vyry's helplessness, and even before her mother passes away, she has found in Mammy Sukey and Aunt Sally two surrogate mothers. The black community seeks to replace the broken family, to offset the almost inevitable horrors facing the child.

Hetta died on the "changing hour," that time between night and dawn. Her departure at the time when the cocks crow to announce another day and the field hands get up to work suggests that her death hardly altered the order of the plantation. However, "suddenly Granny Ticey gave a bloodcurdling yell, startling all the watchers and making them all sit up wide awake . . . Gathering up all her ample skirts, coarse petticoats, and apron, she threw them over her head, showing her aged nakedness while covering her face, and thus she run blindly and screaming down the road."[91]

Granny Ticey's reaction reveals her utter despair in relation to Hetta's death. Her yell echoes Jake's "terrible groan"[92] and takes the place of the words they cannot articulate. On another level, it dramatizes the absurdity of the slavery system. The image of the old woman with her skirts thrown over her head, her eyes covered, running aimlessly evokes an upside-down world that has lost sense and direction. Walker presents a hellish world in ways that stress the realities that drive an old woman to the brink of madness and despair. Her body, dressed but exposed, expresses the emptiness and the hollowness of her community's condition.

Immediately after Ticey runs out of Hetta's cabin and the expectant slaves are awoken by her scream, Brother Zeke begins the chant of death. The song confers a circular form to a chapter that also began with a song, providing it with unity and coherence. The choice of the spiritual also suggests, as in other moments of the narrative, that there are instances in the slave's life that can only gain expression through religion. Such is the nightmare they inhabit that agreed-upon formulas of response are the only way forward. Thrown on their own resources, the responses are screams and groans—the minister offers form and meaning in the absence of other systems of expression.

This is a chapter comprising images of death and stagnation. The characters are consigned to the immediate surroundings of Hetta's cabin. The almost total lack of movement suggests a lack of freedom, and this is evident also in the "hardened dirt-clay road, more like a narrow path before [the slaves'] doors."[93] This contrasts significantly with the Big Road before the master's house. The slaves' narrow path, which seems to lead to nowhere, evokes the absence of liberty, while the broad road in front of John Dutton's residence suggests a world of possibility—the privilege of the whites. Against the enormity of the power of the slaveholders lies the voice of the minister who draws the immediacy of death into a timeless world of belief and hope.

Slavery and Resistance

Chapter 2 differs greatly from the previous chapter in its descriptions of motion and change. The section opens with a stanza from the spiritual "Go Down, Moses." Throughout the novel, Walker establishes a parallel between the plight of the Hebrews in Egypt and the enslavement of African American people. The biblical analogy between the slavery of the Israelites and African American slavery becomes a leitmotif in *Jubilee*,[94] revealing the central theme of the novel: the journey from slavery to freedom, affirmed in the refrain of the song: "Let my people go." The use of this particular spiritual at this stage of the narrative, when freedom is so far away for Vyry, seems untimely. Nevertheless, the title of the chapter, "Along the Big Road in Egypt's land . . . ,"[95] puts the use of the song in perspective. The heading compares the American South to Egypt, the land of bondage under the Pharaoh, and the reference to the Big Road, the road travelled by Vyry to reach the Big House, marks her passage from the protective realm of Mammy Sukey's cabin to the hostile dominion of the master's house. Vyry is born a slave because, in accordance with slavery laws, the child follows the condition of the mother. However, it is with her move to the Big House that her predicament gains a new dimension as it paradoxically initiates her path to freedom.

In this way, Vyry's walk along the Big Road toward the master's house becomes a metaphor for her journey from slavery to emancipation: "When they started down the Big Road toward Marse John's Big House, nearly five miles away as the crow flies, dew was still on the grass, but the rising sun was already beaming . . . At first the cool, damp grass and the moist earth felt squishy under Vyry's bare feet, but soon they were on a hot dusty clay road. Occasionally she felt pebbles and roots roughen her way so that she stubbed her toes, and sometimes she stumbled."[96] The first time the reader sees Vyry on the Big Road, she is on Brother Zeke's shoulders. Her feet do not even touch the rough ground, and although she is about to see her mother for the last time, Sukey is present to watch over her and carry on her role as Vyry's surrogate mother. This time, Vyry has to walk by herself, and the further away she goes from Sukey's hut, the more difficult it becomes for her to walk without stumbling on roots and rocks. Holding on tightly to the child's hand, Mammy Sukey expresses her anxiety over Vyry's inevitable hard times in the Big House. As a mother, she educated her child for life in the Big House. However, as an old slave who has seen the treatment received by the master's illegitimate children at the hands of the mistress, she knows that there is nothing she can do to prepare Vyry for her new role: "Politeness and cleanliness and sweet ways ain't make no difference nohow. She gone stomp her and tromp her and beat her and mighty nigh kill her anyhow."[97]

As announced by the title, the road is the central space along which the story line will develop in this chapter: "When Marse John rode away from his house, Vyry and Mammy Sukey were well on their way toward the Big House. At the same time the slave driver, Grimes, who was Marse John's overseer on the plantation, was returning home with six new slaves he had purchased two days before at the slave market in Louisville."[98] It is important to note that while all the characters in this passage travel the Big Road, they do not meet each other, suggesting the separate status of master, overseer, and slave. The second aspect of significance is that while Mammy Sukey and Vyry and the overseer and his gang walk toward the house, the master rides away from it. This is consistent with a pattern established in the novel whereby when Dutton is invariably absent when he should be involved in his household.

Dutton's absenteeism leaves his slaves exposed to the malice of the overseer. In several episodes reminiscent of the style of the slave narrative, in which minor characters are incorporated into the plot to illustrate certain aspects of life in slavery, bondsmen lose their lives as a direct result of the master's absence. During the height of picking season, Grimes's mule falls dead due to exertion, and he asks Grandpa Tom to bring two of the master's thoroughbred horses to use in the crisis. When Tom refuses to follow an order that contradicts Dutton's instructions, he is brutally whipped and finally shot by the overseer. Grimes's total lack of respect for the slaves' lives is also illustrated in the episode that relates the deaths of Uncle Plato and Uncle Esau: "They were both so old they walked with a stick . . . Marse John had plainly told them and told Mr. Grimes that they were not to go into the fields any more."[99] However, on a hot summer's day, in need of more hands to harvest the cotton, Grimes orders them to the fields. They soon collapse and are instructed by the overseer to go to one of the empty slave houses: "There was a great mix-up over whether he actually ordered his guards to burn that particular house or another. Anyway they threw a drum of coal oil on the rickety shack and saturated it, then they lighted it."[100] These episodes not only expose the consequences of the master's absenteeism and the cruel and vicious disposition of the overseer but also are fundamental to understanding the precarious nature of life in bondage and in reminding readers of the exceptional uncertainty at the very core of the slaves' lives.

Dutton is also absent when Grimes, after talking to Salina, brands the letter "R" on Lucy's face because of the slave's attempt to escape. It is not clear if the torture was conceived by Salina or Grimes: "Big Missy . . . and Grimes had a whispered conversation between them. Vyry strained her ears, but she could not make out what they were saying."[101] The fact that Vyry cannot make sense of their murmured words is an important gap in information and suggests that Walker did not want to distinguish between Grimes and Salina in this matter. The incident establishes the way mistress and overseer unite their efforts to devise the torments inflicted on the slaves; it revises the image of the plantation mistress as an angelic figure, the very incarnation of virtue, too feeble to help herself and cause harm to others. Grimes's high opinion of Salina is an effective means of characterization, simultaneously demonstrating their separate social status and their similar "moral" conduct: "She's a real Christian woman, a Bible-reading, honest dealing, high-quality lady who knows and acts the difference between niggers and white people. She ain't no nigger lover namby-pamby like that s.o.b. pretty boy she's married to."[102] Grimes's characterization of Salina serves a double purpose. First, it deconstructs the image of the idle Southern lady, who lived a life of leisure and whose household was smoothly run by slave house-servants. More importantly, Walker discards the mythical figure of the black mammy, who, as White puts it, "was completely dedicated to the white family, especially to the children of that family. She was the house servant who was given complete charge of domestic management. She served also as a friend and advisor. She was in short, surrogate mistress and mother."[103] This larger-than-life woman, invariably grotesquely obese, deeply religious, a strict disciplinarian, and the very incarnation of efficiency, managing the Big House with a firm hand is absent from Walker's text. In *Jubilee*, it is the white mistress who presides over the household. Walker undoes the image of the ethereal Southern lady whose grace and fragility prevent her from doing any manual work. Salina is described as a "big-boned girl, tall, and inclined to get fat,"[104] who is both physically strong and resolute in all things concerning her household. Even before historians paid major attention to the history of the female slaveholder, Walker was already revising the cultural construct of the Southern lady.

Subsequent studies based on diaries, letters, travel journals, and slave narratives support the role Walker attributed to Salina. During her visit to the United States, Harriet Martineau did not find many black women in charge of the master's household, remarking that it was the mistress who "is forever superintending, and trying to keep things straight, without the slightest hope of attaining anything like leisure and comfort."[105] In her extensive examination of the history of slaveholding women, largely based on their journals and correspondence,[106] Elizabeth Fox-Genovese discusses the role and profile of the mistress in the American South. In many instances, Fox-Genovese's conclusions are consistent with Walker's fictional representation of the mistress. Like Salina, the mistress of the household keeps, as Fox-Genovese states, "as symbol of her station . . . the keys to the innumerable storerooms as domestic outbuildings."[107] Describing the daily and seasonal routines of the Dutton house, the narrator shows how domestic activities took place under Big Missy's inexorable eye:

> In the morning Big Missy came out with a bunch of keys and opened the cupboards and took out the things she wanted Aunt Sally to cook and then she locked the cupboards again. In one pantry Big Missy kept under lock and key her jars of preserves and jellies, pickles and relishes, canned fruits and vegetables. All her precious china and glass were kept in the Big House and even washed by Caline under Big Missy's watchful eye . . . Big Missy held the keys to the smoke house as well as the cane mill . . . Big Missy supervised all her household of female help in canning and preserving.[108]

The name given to Salina by the slaves, Big Missy, illustrates both her lack of resemblance to the stereotype of the feeble lady and also how the slaves secretly and humorously responded to being the subject of nicknames by, in turn, attributing names to their masters. In a world with few opportunities for self-expression, the slaves find words to resist the powerful mistress—"Big Missy" expresses the seeds of self-affirmation for the black community. However, the repetition of the substantive "keys" throughout the short passage demonstrates how the mistress's bunch of keys functions both as a symbol of her authority and an effective means of controlling most aspects of the household. Notwithstanding the levels of resistance from the black community, Big Missy remains their jailer.

In *Jubilee*, Walker examines the daily tasks of running the household, childbearing, and childrearing that bring mistress and slave together. However, the boundaries of race are the insurmountable walls that keep them apart. The relationship between slaves and slave owners, as Fox-Genovese states, "could range from love to hatred, but whatever their emotional quality, they were more likely than not to include a high level of intimacy. Mistresses whipped slave women with whom they might have shared beds, whose children they might have delivered or who might have delivered theirs, whose children they might have suckled and who frequently had suckled theirs."[109] In *Jubilee*, the mistress's cruelty toward the slaves supersedes that of her husband, owing both to his personality and to his frequent absences from the plantation. This is another aspect of Walker's work that seems to have been carefully researched. In her prologue to *Within the Plantation Household: Black and White Women of the South*, Fox-Genovese declares, "With some pain I am compelled to express my considered opinion that, in some essential respects, [slaveholding women] were more crudely racist than their men."[110] Such racism is a critical aspect of Salina's character—Walker makes that abundantly clear.

Salina's interactions with Vyry expose the violent nature of her bigotry most vividly. Hetta's daughter's arrival in the Big House at the age of seven marks the abrupt end of her childhood. Vyry's sudden transition from the sheltered environment of Mammy Sukey's home to the workforce of the Dutton plantation and her forced separation from "all the mother she had ever known or could remember" leaves her in a state of bewilderment and dread.[111] She struggles to understand and follow the instructions given to her while she tries to avoid Big Missy's ire: "Twice Big Missy slapped her in the mouth with the back of her hand, and once Vyry barely escaped the foot of her mistress kicking her. Once she yelled to the startled child, 'You stupid bastard, if you break airy one of my china dishes, I'll break your face.'"[112] The sequence in the text of "startled child" immediately followed by "stupid bastard" emphasizes the disparity between the narrator's and mistress's perspectives. The omniscient narrator conjures an image of a helpless seven-year-old child, while Big Missy's words and actions illustrate her racism and her hatred of the child of her husband. The crudeness of Salina's words and deeds compels the reader to deal with bigotry as a cultural construct that denies Vyry her humanity and her status as a child.

Vyry's complexion is an effective means of representing race as an ideological concept—the black slave is the fair haired, blue eyed, white Vyry.

However, the disparity between Vyry's and her half-sister Lillian's existence is such that, at times, while reading Vyry's story, the reader struggles not to digress to a mental picture of a child with a dark skin tone. It is interesting to note that on the cover of the Bantam Books edition of *Jubilee*, Vyry, who could be easily mistaken for Lillian's twin, is represented as a distinctly African woman. The recurrent allusions to Vyry's complexion in the beginning of the novel become less prevalent as the narrative progresses, and when the narrator or a character refers to Vyry's "whiteness," the reader's association between slavery and blackness is put in check. The construction of racial identity is dramatized in the scene where Caline combs Miss Lillian's hair into curls, and standing beside her half-sister, Vyry asks if she could have curls too. "But Miss Lillian laughingly said, 'Niggers don't wear curls, do they Caline?' And Caline watching Vyry's stricken face said, 'Naw Missy, they sure don't.'"[113] Walker juxtaposes Vyry's innocence with cultural constructs of race and class, while the reader is left to consider the absurdity of the conventions that governed the peculiar institution—even hair has its decorum.

Critical to Walker's vision are the means of defiance. While she carefully describes a terrible system of abuse, she also creates a complex black community capable of acts of resistance. Such responses within the black community vary, of course. One of the most important is the action of Aunt Sally. In Aunt Sally, Vyry finds the mother twice lost. Aunt Sally's cabin, which becomes Vyry's home after the day Big Missy hangs her by her thumbs in the closet, represents a counterbalance to the hostile world of the Big House, a safe place where the child recovers a maternal figure and a sense of community. Sally teaches her survival skills, "how to live in the Big House and get along with Big Missy,"[114] how to "outsmart" the mistress and ensure she had enough food to eat by hiding it in the countless pockets of her skirt, and how to use humor as a means of dealing with the frustrations of the day: "Once safe in the cabin they would fill their stomachs full of good food, tittering over the thought of how many different kinds of fits Big Missy would have if she knew how she had been outsmarted."[115] By undoing all the rags that were tightly wrapped around Vyry's hair during the day so that her sandy hair would not provoke Salina's anger and combing it into curls, "delighting the little girl's heart beyond measure,"[116] Aunt Sally also teaches Vyry to develop a sense of a private self separate from the identity imposed by hegemonic others. The surrogate mother is also Vyry's link to her own past. From her, Vyry learns about her birthplace, the time of her birth, her mother and father, Granny Ticey and Mammy Sukey, Big Missy's reaction when she first saw her, and Jake's dislike of his wife's white baby. Without Aunt Sally's storytelling, Vyry's personal story would have been fragmented and partially lost. Aunt Sally replaces Hetta not only as the nurturing mother but also as the teller of stories who ensures that the foremother's narrative will be passed on to the next generation. As a mother, Vyry will take on the role of the storyteller to narrate to her children the story of the women who raised her. In many ways, Walker presents this as the site of most significant resistance. In the story lies access to the past and, through that knowledge, the means to survive the present and build the future.

Motherhood and Resistance

Motherhood transforms Vyry's dream of freedom. Carrying the master's unborn slave in her womb makes her desire for freedom gain a sense of urgency she has never felt before. Randall Ware, an experienced worker of the Underground Railroad, is able to give his wife, Vyry, precise directions for the first stage of her escape. She reluctantly agrees to run away and follows all his instructions but one: "Be sure you leave the younguns."[117] With one child by her hand and another in her arms, Vyry walks slowly, leaving behind a trail of footsteps on the muddy red soil of the back woods of Georgia: "Exhausted and hopeless she sat and waited for the men who surrounded her to capture her and her children. She could not have run one step if her very life had depended on it. Despite everything, she felt glad the children were still with her and they were safe. She looked into Minna's sleeping face and smiled, and she patted Jim's hand softly to reassure him of her nearness. Then she pulled him closer to her in a warm embrace."[118] This passage illustrates the difficulties that the slave mother faced when attempting to escape. Caught between a painful separation from her children and the increased risk of capture for taking them with her, she was left with very few choices. In *Runaway Slaves: Rebels on the Plantation*, John Hope Franklin and Loren Schweninger point out that "[d]uring the early period [1790–1816], males constituted 81 per cent of those who were advertised as runaways . . . Exactly the same proportion of slaves was listed during the later period [1838–1860] . . . the precise male-female percentage remaining exactly the same over a period of more than two generations."[119] The factor that probably contributed more to the difference in ratio between female and male runaways was age. "[T]he great majority of runaways," as Franklin and Schweninger state, "were young men in their teens and twenties," and among those who were advertised as runaways, "78 per cent were between the ages of thirteen and twenty-nine."[120] This period, between the late teens and the twenties, coincides with the woman's childbearing years. "A woman of this age," as White observes, "was either pregnant, nursing an infant, or had at least one small child to take care of."[121] Concerned with the welfare of their children, freedom without them seemed to offer poor consolation to slave mothers. This is not to say that slave children were not loved by their fathers. However, the responsibility of childcare was almost totally delegated to the women. Furthermore, as White affirms, "since women and small children were often sold as a group, a father was more likely to be sold away from his children."[122] In this way, male runaways had more assurance, however small, that their children would be taken care of and would stay with their mothers.[123]

Vyry's love for her children will allow her to survive not only her capture but also the 75 lashes on her naked body, which she receives as punishment. The "warm embrace" with which the novelist closes the chapter shows the everlasting bond between mother and child, and the circularity of this gesture also suggests the interdependency of their lives. In this way, in *Jubilee*, the children depend on the mother for love, protection, and guidance, while she depends on them for belief in the future and the means to survive the adversities of life in bondage.

Civil War

In the first section of the novel, the Dutton plantation serves as the setting for almost all the action, focusing on the space that separated the slaves from the world beyond the Big Road. However, to not completely reroute the narrative beyond the boundaries of the plantation, where her protagonist remains during this period, Walker conveys much of the war events via newspapers, read primarily by Big Missy. In the summer of 1961, Walker acquired a collection of reprinted Civil War newspapers, both Northern and Southern, and as she states, "[m]any items in *Jubilee* were lifted from these newspapers with only slight changes of names . . . There were such items as ads for runaway slaves, stories about the munitions workers, Jefferson Davis's speech on the increasing rate of desertions from the Confederate Army, and the failure of the Confederate currency."[124] In the Civil War section, Walker's concern with historical record and accuracy is yet again apparent. The intertwining of primary sources with fictional characters and events establishes a narrative that maintains historical accuracy in broad terms. Rather than invent a past, Walker's intense engagement with historical data consistently underpins the development of her characters.

Walker also examines how the Civil War years represent a period during which the complex and sometimes contradictory nature of the relationships between masters and slaves is exposed. As Leon F. Litwack argues, "The war revealed, often in ways that defied description, the sheer complexity of the master-slave relationship, and the conflicts, contradictions and ambivalence that relationship generated in each individual . . . The humble, self-effacing slave who touched his hat to his 'white-folks' was capable of touching off the fire that gutted his master's house. The loyal body-servant who risked his life to carry his wounded master to safety remounted his master's horse and fled to the Yankees."[125] In *Jubilee*, she dramatizes how the unwavering desire for freedom was tied in with "a strange code of honor, duty, and noblesse oblige which [the slave] could not explain" in relation to her or his master.[126] The close proximity in which slave (in particular the house servant) and master lived bestowed on their relationship a myriad of intricate feelings inherent in contact between human beings. What Walker explores is that the absolute dominion of the master over the slave did not consume the latter's humanity, which in some cases is extended to the hegemonic other in a compassionate gesture. Jim, Dutton's body servant, finds that he cannot leave the young master to die away from home: "*I'll carry him home to his Maw where he can die in peace, but I sho ain't staying there.* If Jim had been a field hand, such a delicate conflict would not have disturbed him. He would have felt no ties to the Dutton household, but he had nursed the old man and he had watched the children grow."[127] Clearly Walker does not promote sentimental situations gratuitously, but she seeks to represent the nature of the relationship, which undermines and transcends the institutional divisions set by slavery.

If Jim temporarily leaves the Union army and returns to his place of bondage to bring the young master home, the newly emancipated Vyry cannot leave the Dutton household until she is assured that Lillian, now demented, will be taken care of: "I can't leave Miss Lillian here by herself. You knows I can't go off and leave her helpless and sick in her mind!"[128] Vyry's feelings for Lillian, the half-sister who lived her life in total conformity to the ideal of the Southern belle and never did anything to help or ease the slave's plight, represent the perplexing and at times conflicting emotions that bound slave and master: "She felt terribly unhappy over Miss Lillian and it seemed so strange that things had turned out this way for the little golden girl she had always adored since she was a slave child herself growing up the Big House."[129] It is difficult to discern if Vyry's affection for Lillian is tied in with the memories of the few happy moments of her own childhood when she went to the Big House to play with the young mistress or if she saw in their remarkable physical similarity a vision of a society that the slave could imagine but never realize. Walker resists the explanation of the slaves' feelings in order not to simplify what is intrinsically complex. Yet she used the chaotic experience of the Civil War years to reveal the limited and ignorant presumptions about slaves, who were supposedly simple and knowable under the terms set by slavery.

Reconstruction

The third section of *Jubilee*, dedicated to the Reconstruction years, opens with Vyry's departure from the Dutton plantation to join the hundreds of thousands of African Americans who were traveling the Southern roads in search of new places to call home. Felix Haywood, a Texas freedman, describes in an interview given in the 1930s how slaves reacted to the Emancipation Proclamation in his community and how many freed men and women started on the move to see the world beyond the confinements of the master's household and to look for a place to settle: "Everybody went wild. We all felt like heroes, and nobody had made us that way but ourselves. We was free. Just like that, we was free . . . Right off colored folks started on the move. They seem to want to get closer to freedom, so they'd know what it was—like it was a place . . . We knowed freedom was on us, but we didn't know what was to come."[130] While Haywood illustrates the almost euphoric sense of hope that emancipation brought, freedom per se, however, hardly prepared the newly freed women and men for "what was to come." In *Jubilee*, Randall Ware articulates this sense of a dream fulfilled and a dream defeated: "Well, I thought once, right after the war, that colored people were going to reach the Promised Land with land, education, and the vote just because the government said so. But I've learned different."[131]

In her treatment of the Reconstruction years, Walker articulates the vital need for the attainment of land, literacy, and the vote while exploring the difficulties that African Americans faced in their acclimatization to a capitalist economy and the compromises they made for the sake of survival. In *Souls of Black Folk*, W. E. B. Du Bois describes the complete destitution of African Americans and how ill prepared they were to enter a competitive economic market and a hostile social system: "To be a poor man is hard, but to be a poor race in a land of dollars is the very bottom of hardships. He felt the weight of his ignorance,—not simply of letters, but of life, of business, of the humanities; the accumulated sloth and shirking and awkwardness of decades and centuries shackled his hands and feet."[132] Vyry's days on the Southern roads, carrying all her possessions in a wagon and looking for a place to settle, become representative of the journey from slavery to freedom undertaken by hundreds of thousands of African Americans in the aftermath of the war. Like other freed women and men, Vyry and her second husband, Innis Brown, feel the weight of poverty and ignorance described by Du Bois. Without any help or direction from the government, the Browns are left to fend for themselves. They hear that the Freedmen's Bureau is "helping Negroes get settled by homesteading or on abandoned lands, but Montgomery was more than one hundred miles away and they knew they could not make that trip in a rickety wagon with one old balky mule."[133] Instead they set up house in the woods of Henry County, Alabama, on the bank of the Chattahoochee River. When the river bursts its banks and their fields and house are flooded, they realize the reason why that land had not been taken by the white man and why they had been left to settle in it: "We right here in the river bottom. Maybe that's how come that white man looked so satisfied when I told him where we was."[134]

From the bottom of the river, the Browns move to a "a steep hill where the ground was rocky all the way."[135] They take a farm over from a white family that was unable to produce any crops out of the barren land and left in order to avoid starvation. In this episode, Walker exposes the exploitation suffered by poor whites at the hands of landowners, and she illustrates the consequences of the ex-slaves' ignorance of life and business. Without realizing it, the Browns did not settle in a derelict house and farm, but they entered into a sharecropping scheme. Innis Brown's mark on a contract, which he could not read, becomes the tangible symbol for the illiteracy and ignorance that kept freed slaves subservient to the old hegemony. With each visit of the landlord to the farm, the contract changed and new bills appeared. The white man presents the written document as evidence of Brown's debt—the purchases he did not make in the proprietor's store and the rent his family owed in an initial rent-free house. Innis Brown's dependency on the oral word and memory to run his farm leaves him helpless in the hands of a dishonest landlord:

> "I disremembers buying airy nickel's worth of stuff from your store."
>
> "Your memory is might short then. I've got it all set down right here and your contract, too."
>
> "But I told you sir, I can't read and write."
>
> "That's your hard luck, and none of my business at all. Ignorance of the law is no excuse. It has nothing to do with the hard cash you owe me."[136]

This passage illustrates how the legacy of slavery still exerted immense power in the lives of black people. All the freedman's records depended on memory. This dependency on memory, as Gates observes, "made the slave, first and foremost, a slave to himself, a prisoner of his own power to recall."[137] It is through the memory of past events that Innis makes sense of his life, conducts his life, and runs his farm. Juxtaposing oral and written traditions, Walker exposes how illiteracy relegated African Americans to the margins of a society that promoted and recognized the veracity and legality of the printed word. The white man's written record, which reconstructed reality to suit his purposes, functions as a synecdoche for the records kept by the hegemonic others and the distorted or effaced black experience.

An oral culture dependent on the repetition of its record, passed on from individual to individual and generation to generation, is for the freed slave a double-edged sword. She or he is caught between the desire to remember and the need to forget painful experiences. In Fred D'Aguiar's *The Longest Memory* (1994), the slave Whitechapel expresses this imperative to forget: "Memory hurts. Like crying. But still and deep. Memory rises to the skin then I can't be touched. I hurt all over, my bones ache, my teeth loosen their gums, my nose bleeds. Don't make me remember. I forget as hard as I can."[138] Innis's memories haunt him during his sleep—he "thought that somebody was running him, lashing him with the whip, or he heard bloodhounds on his heels."[139] "Memory," as Whitechapel puts it, "is pain trying to resurrect itself."[140] In this way, memory performs a ghostly dance, making the slave relive traumatic events again and again. Paradoxically and significantly, memory for the slave also constitutes an almost exclusive thread to her or his sense of being—repression of the past is consistently shown to be a dangerous option in African American experience and literature.

To escape the vicious cycle of debt into which they fell under the sharecropping scheme, the Browns find themselves on the road again looking for land and shelter. With the help of a white industrialist, they build a house and cultivate a tract of land of the "over a million acres of public land . . . in Alabama, and the government says all you have to do is stake your claim and prove up by staying there five years."[141] In *Jubilee*, Walker illustrates that for many freed women and men, like the Browns, the dream of freedom was tied to the aspiration of owning and working their own plot of land. Bayley Wyatt, a former slave from Virginia, articulates this idea: "Our wives, our children, our husbands, has been sold over and over again to purchase the lands we now locate upon; for that reason we have a divine right to the land . . . And then didn't we clear the land and raise the crops of corn, of cotton, of tobacco, of rice, of sugar, of everything? And then didn't them large cities in the North grow up on the cotton and the sugars and the rice that we made? Yes! I appeal to the South and the North if I hasn't spoken the words of truth."[142] If, on the one hand, African Americans' attempt to obtain land, as Wyatt says, represented a means of procuring compensation for their enslavement, on the other hand, farming was the Southern economic basis at the time and constituted a mode of living familiar to many former slaves. However, the old ruling classes, trying to regain their economic power, realized that to sustain a profitable agricultural system they needed land and cheap black labor to work it. As a result, throughout the South, African Americans were intimidated and terrorized into abandoning their farms by secret organizations such as the Knights of the White Camellia and the Ku Klux Klan (KKK).

In *A Red Record* (1895), Ida B. Wells articulates the view of a society characterized by "a system of anarchy, outlawry,"[143] and brutality toward black people that had replaced the peculiar institution in the South: "Vested with unlimited power over his slave, to subject him to any and all kinds of physical punishment, the white man was still restrained [during slavery] from such punishment as tended to injure the slave by abating his physical powers and thereby reducing his financial worth . . . [B]ut with freedom a new system of intimidation came into vogue; the Negro was not only whipped and scourged; he was killed."[144] Wells describes the climate of extreme violence that followed emancipation and how the process of Reconstruction failed freed slaves. Some, like Hannah Tutson from Florida, suffered repeated threats, whippings, and rape, yet held their land. In her testimony in the KKK Investigations, Tutson expresses her courage and her determination to keep her land: "In the red times, how many times have they took me and turned my clothes over my head and whipped me? I do not care what they do to me if I can only save my land."[145] Others left land and crops for the sake of survival. In a joint affidavit, George Underwood, Ben Harris, and Isiah Fuller state that they were left no choice but to leave their land: "[T]hey beat Isiah Fuller, and whipped him, and then we got afraid, and left the place; we got about thirty acres in cotton . . . ; and we have about twenty-nine acres of corn . . . and it is ripe, and the fodder ready to pull, and our cotton laid by; and runned us off from the place, and told us not to come back any more."[146]

In *Jubilee*, Walker illustrates the significance of the land question for African Americans in the Reconstruction years by focusing not on the heroic acts of those like Tutson, who risked their lives to challenge the prevailing order, but on the compromises made by the masses to stay alive. In her treatment of Reconstruction, similar to that of slavery and the Civil War, the novelist's focal point remains the lives of the ordinary African Americans whose daily struggle was so typical of the wider black experience that would remain outside a historical record, which, up to then, tended to value only the lives of a small minority.

The Browns' abandonment of their land and the ripe fruit of their toil after the KKK sets their house on fire, rather than constituting an acceptance of defeat, bears witness to their indomitable will to stay alive and find a safe place for their family. Notwithstanding, the fire leaves an indelible imprint on the Brown family. Walker's protagonist, who in the Reconstruction section emerges as a strong female character—a working woman who not only takes her place in the fields beside her husband but also assumes the leading role in her family—is defeated. The fading figure, kneeling among the rubble and the ashes of her ruined home, bears little resemblance to the woman who overcomes adversity by quickly adjusting to unfamiliar circumstances and resorting to a well of practical knowledge that enables self-reliance. Vyry not only takes on the primary responsibility for her family's diet, clothing, and health care but also emerges as the primary decision maker in matters the reader might reasonably assume to be the preserve of Innis Brown, a former field hand. It is Vyry who decides when to plant their first crop on the bank of the river and what to plant in the rocky soil of their hillside farm; it is by looking at Vyry's "tight face" and seeing "her shaking her head"[147] that Innis Brown "subsided into a mumble"[148] rather than trying to reason with the dishonest landlord; she is the one who makes the decision to leave the sharecropping scheme, conscious of the cycle of debt in which they had fallen; and she is the one who explains to her husband what the KKK meant by setting their house on fire and the need for their urgent departure. In her role as a decision maker, Walker's protagonist does not emerge as a domineering figure; her decisions are taken through a close partnership with her husband and are based on a practical philosophy centered on the welfare on her family. In this sense, Vyry remains a woman of her time: she thinks and acts within the gender conventions and constraints of the late 1800s.

In the spring of 1870, five years after emancipation, the Browns are still unsettled, and although they have found a new farm, this time with the help of the Freedmen's Bureau, Vyry refuses to build a new house. The time spent living in the open, having only an improvised tent as shelter, is an uncertain time for the Browns. This is also a period of intense inner searching for Vyry, who in her sense of despair and displacement tries to find a safe path for her family. Responding to the cries of Betty-Alice and assisting her to give birth to her first child, Vyry not only extends her solidarity to a member of the community in need but also attains a safe place for her family. In *Black Women Writers and the American Neo-Slave Narrative: Femininity Unfettered*, Beaulieu states that "[b]itter and depressed after being routed not once but twice from her home, Vyry has lost her faith in mankind and trusts only her instincts. This time they do not fail her, leading her to assist Betty-Alice Fletcher and, finally, to trust the men who come to offer community and protection."[149] To Beaulieu's sense of "instinct," the Judeo-Christian tradition might be added as a significant influence that shaped and conditioned Vyry (and, indeed, Walker's world vision expressed in *Jubilee*). When Vyry says, "I feels like it's my duty to help anybody I can wheresomever I can"[150] and "I ain't no more'n my Christian duty to help anybody I can,"[151] when she feeds a hungry white family without making them feel uncomfortable,[152] when she helps a white young woman in labor,[153] and when she frees herself of all resentment, she translates Walker's own belief that "[f]reedom, peace, and human dignity are only possible in a world where common humanity supersedes race."[154] In

Vyry's altruistic gestures, Walker maps out her notion of humanistic tradition, which informs her artistic project. It is Vyry's respect for the common humanity of both blacks and whites that not only opens the way for her family to be accepted in the community but also initiates a new course for that community that evolves toward a social order that will overthrow racism. In this way, without making a militant out of Vyry's character, whose actions are a testament to a deeply lived Christianity rather than to a sense of political and social reform, Walker creates a female protagonist who is able to both make a safe home for her family and open a new dynamics in the relationships between blacks and whites in the community. The representation of this community, developing outside color divides, reflects Walker's concern not only with the suffering and discrimination of African Americans but also with the direction of American society as a whole.

The white men helping Innis to build a house for his family and the women good-naturedly talking with Vyry over their quilt making conjures up an image of community where individuals come together for the common good and trust the direction of the group to a disinterested partaking: "It was hard to say who had had a more satisfying day, the neighbors who had built the house of good will with their good deeds, or Vyry and Innis in their humble gratitude of this fine gesture of friendship and understanding from their new neighbors."[155] By the end of the episode, the turn in the narrative is complete. This chapter, titled "We got new neighbors now," suggests that the Browns have finally found not only a plot of land to cultivate and on which to build their home but also a community and, as the epigraph emphasizes, a much desired sense of security: "I got a home in a hard rock / Debbil in hell can't bother me."[156] The solidity of "a home in a hard rock" contrasts profoundly with the precariousness of their previous dwellings: a tent, a house taken away by water, another taken by a fire, and yet another taken by the dishonesty of the white man. The rock functions as a metaphor for the community more than the description of the material of the house itself, since it is the first rather than the latter that make the Browns feel secure and welcomed. This episode yet again reinforces *Jubilee*, as Walker writes, as "a canvas on which I paint my vision of the world."[157]

Conclusion

Since her 1948 outline of *Jubilee*, Walker "knew that the center of [her] story was Vyry and that the book should end with Randall Ware's return."[158] When he returns to Georgia after the war, Ware finds a deserted plantation and a "For Sale" sign on the Dutton property. When he finally meets Vyry again, seven years after his departure, they both realize that the experiences of slavery and the Civil War and its aftermath made their lives separate forever. Their separation has as much to do with the uncertainty of the times as with their very distinct outlooks on life. Ware, as Melissa Walker observes, "has delayed his return to private life to attend the First Convention of Colored People in Georgia. Putting his public responsibilities before private ones, he joins the Georgia Equal Rights Association and determines to take "an active part in the political affairs of his county, town, and state." It is during Ware's delay that Vyry despairs and leaves with Innis. Just as Vyry's exclusively private vision robs her of the power to public action, Ware's public commitments result in the loss of his private world."[159] Vyry's life evolves in an almost exclusively private sphere. Her role as a midwife makes her an important contributor to her community, but this is a role that primarily serves to secure the acceptance and security of her family in the community. In this way, as Walker argues, Randall Ware was not very sensitive to Vyry's personal and family needs, leaving her and two young children to an uncertain destiny at the Dutton plantation at the end of the war. On the other hand, Vyry's ignorance of the African American political struggle, which followed the aftermath of the war, and her lack of understanding for Ware's commitment to the attainment of civil rights caused her to lose the chance to test her relationship with her first husband in a "free" society. "Neither," as Walker puts it, "finds a way to balance public and private responsibilities."[160] When they are reunited, the reader wonders if their relationship would, in fact, stand the test of their differences.

Randall Ware is a militant man. Fully aware of the importance of political representation for African Americans, he runs for the state legislature after the war and is elected for Terrell County. However, when the KKK kills his journeyman and almost beats Ware to death, he is made to sell a part of his land to the old overseer of the Dutton plantation and give up a political career that had hardly taken off. Although he does not give up his right to vote, he abandons the prospects of a life in the public arena. This is an example of the compromises that African Americans had to make for the sake of survival. Ware's awareness of the political direction of the country in 1870 makes him feel little hope for the achievement of full citizenship for African Americans: "Freedom won't mean much more than they can't buy and sell us on the auction block. Even the Confederates abolished the slave trade. But they mean to keep us down under the same kind of different system, controlling our labor and restricting our movements, and not allowing us to vote, and trying to keep us ignorant. The Ku Klux Klan will be just like the drivers and the patter-rollers were in slavery time."[161] What Ware foresees is the segregated system of the Jim Crow laws under which African Americans lived for almost the entirety of the following one hundred years. By the end of the narrative, he is a bitter and frustrated man. Ware, as Walker explains, "did not get want he wanted, and he was conscious of how he had been cheated. He was forced to sell his land; he failed to get his political rights as a free citizen; he was shamed into a kind of cowardice at the cost of his life and manhood, and he was even denied the pleasure of seeing his children grow."[162] His belief that "colored people haven't got any friend in the white man, North or South. Average white man hates a Negro, always did, and always will"[163] places an insurmountable barrier between himself and Vyry. This is a stand that she cannot comprehend and that contradicts the very core of the values that govern her life: "White folks needs what black folks is got just as much as black folks needs what white folks is got, and we's all got the stay here mongst each other and git along that's what."[164]

Vyry believes that specific white people wronged specific black people, but even in this acknowledgment, she reserves no place for resentment: "I honestly believes that if airy one of them peoples what treated me like dirt when I was a slave would come to my door in the morning hungry, I would feed em. God knows I ain't got no hate in my heart for nobody."[165] Toward the end of the novel, Vyry's spirit of forgiveness and reconciliation becomes more than the articulation of the best characteristics of a particular individual; it becomes the expression of Walker's belief that out of the chaotic experience of slavery, African Americans will rise to show the way out of a social organization based on the ideas of racial superiority and enter a new social order based on common humanity:

> She was touched with a spiritual fire and permeated with a spiritual wholeness that had been forged in a crucible of suffering. She was . . . a spark of light that was neither of the earth nor September air, but eternal fire . . . She was only a living sign and mark of all the best a human being could hope to become . . . [S]he was alive and standing in the highest peaks of her time and human personality. Peasant and slave, unlettered and untutored, she was nevertheless the best true example of the motherhood of her race, an ever present assurance that nothing could destroy a people whose sons had come from her loins.[166]

Vyry's characterization conjures up an image that on one hand celebrates the illiterate slave who without the advantages enjoyed by the privileged classes becomes an example of humanity for all Americans; on the other hand, the depiction of the individual character is gradually replaced by a representative figure of mythical proportions. Vyry, portrayed as the mother of all African Americans, not only reinforces the theme of motherhood, which opens and closes the narrative, but also expresses Walker's artistic vision, which reconciles the historical past with the hope for the future. In this way, Vyry's profoundly lived spirituality and her determined humanity are an assurance of the survival and the thriving of the African American people.

Vyry whose "eternal fire" of commitment to the common good was passed on to her by her surrogate mothers and who will pass it on to her daughters, emerges in the narrative as Walker's symbol of reconciliation in both the 1860s and the 1960s—the latter being that decade in which the novelist wrote most of *Jubilee*. In this manner, as Gwin observes, "[I]t is Walker's voice rather than Vyry's which moves us. Vyry herself is a simple woman. She does not come to her decision to forgive past cruelties out of a fullness of consciousness that would make such gesture fictional dynamic. It is Walker's vision of human reconciliation that is complex and significant; its fictional counterpart seems thin by comparison and less developed in *Jubilee* than imposed upon it."[167] Vyry, who, as Walker emphasizes, "reflects the Christian upbringing of the Quarters and the Big House,"[168] could not be represented as revolutionary. Rather, it is Walker's artistic project as a response to the American racial conflict that is revolutionary. In a period during which "the black artist," as William J. Harris puts it, "must teach the black masses to harden their hearts towards the whites,"[169] Walker's voice of reconciliation appears to be significantly isolated.

In *The Black Aesthetic* (1971), the volume of essays edited by Addison Gayle Jr. and that became the manifesto of the Black Arts movement, Hoyt Fuller summarizes the general attitude of the theorists and writers of the Black Arts movement: "[B]lacks and whites are residents of two separate and naturally antagonistic worlds."[170] Larry Neal also emphasizes this separatist strategy: "The motive behind the Black aesthetic is the destruction of the white thing, the destruction of white ideas, and white ways of looking at the world."[171] Poets such as Amiri Baraka, Nikki Giovanni, Sonia Sanchez, and Haki R. Madhubuti, among others, write direct attacks on whites.

In "Black Art," a poem published 1969, three years after the publication *Jubilee*, Baraka presents an unapologetic, violent, and racist rhetoric that envisages art as a political weapon in the creation of a new black world. Although Walker shares with the Black Arts movement the belief that individual freedom and mass revolution cannot be separate, both her answer to America's racial oppression and her vision of a new social order are radically different from that of the artists of the 1960s movement. In a time when some African American artists incite the masses to revolt, Walker's voice in *Jubilee* is conciliatory, not militant; for her, social change has to be rooted in the African American humanist tradition, and her idea of a new social order is based on the acknowledgment of the common humanity that unites people from different diasporas. Walker's notion of social direction is integrationist rather than separatist, and in this sense she promotes a vision of American society as a whole.

The singularity of Walker's voice is also asserted in her distinctly African American perspective of the experience of slavery, Civil War, and Reconstruction in a time when little attention was given to fictionalized narratives of the period: "[F]ictionalized accounts of that period," as Hajek points out, "largely come from either white southerners or white northerners, including women writers such as Harriet Beecher Stowe and Margaret Mitchell. Well into the seventies, the black perspective North and South, male or female, found little expression and even less attention."[172] Walker rewrites the history of the American South from an African American perspective and in doing so she reimagines the most untold story of them all: the female slave's story. "What gives [*Jubilee*] lasting value," as Walker states, "is it's not a story you've ever heard before. It's a different story. It's unique. A lot of people, however, will say, 'That's the same story my grandmother told me. I heard that story.' But nobody had ever put that story down."[173] Telling the story of the silenced female slave and reconstructing her history, Walker fills an obvious gap both in literature and history. Until the publication of *Jubilee*, as Phyllis Rauch Klotman declares, "the perspective, whether of history or of fiction, was almost inevitably white, usually male, and regionally identifiable."[174] Moreover, having as her protagonist a woman, a milky-white and unlettered woman, Walker challenges the historical record of the hegemonic whites while confronting the sexism and the racial prejudices of the Black Arts movement.

By asserting a maternal history rooted in folk customs such as quilting, herbal medicine, cooking, gardening and folk expressions such as sayings, songs, and stories, Walker calls the attention of the subsequent generations of writers to the fact that the experience of slavery did not crush the African American spirit and that out of the chaotic experience it developed a unique culture. "Her confirmation that enslavement did not defeat the human spirit of her protagonist, Vyry," as Pettis states, "is Walker's legacy to later female protagonists of historic fiction, including Jane Pitman, Dessa Rose, and Sethe."[175] Moreover, it is Walker's thorough research, her concern with historical accuracy, and her meticulous representation of the daily life of the ordinary that freed other writers of the constrictions of verisimilitude and allowed them to approach history in ways that are less representative and that enabled them to imagine the extraordinary stories of the female experience.

3

History as Birthmark

Gayl Jones's *Corregidora*

Contexts

The 1960s witnessed a renewed interest in slave narratives and African American history and culture, and the development of an aesthetics that was politically engaged, highlighted a need for social and economic reform, and moreover was distinct and separate from white western traditions. The Black Arts movement, to use Larry Neal's words, "propose[d] a separate symbolism, mythology, critique, and iconology."[1] This move toward a new black aesthetics, the expression of which was an art that reflected a sense of self-determination, meant that the "Black artist," as the poet Etheridge Knight states, had to "create new forms and new values, sing new songs (or purify old ones); and along with other black authorities, he must create a new history, new symbols, myths and legends (and purify old ones by fire)."[2] This concept of a need for cultural "purification" in order to achieve an unadulterated form of African American expression was also articulated by other aestheticians of the movement. Addison Gayle Jr. states that the "Black Aesthetic . . . is corrective—a means of helping black people out of the polluted mainstream Americanism."[3] In an essay titled "Towards a Black Aesthetic," Hoyt Fuller seems to take this idea a step further. For Fuller the break with white culture also meant that the black artist had to disentangle himself from "those who would submit to subjection without struggle [and] deserve to be enslaved. It is one thing," he goes on to say, "to accept the guiding principles on which the American republic ostensibly was founded; it is quite another thing to accept the prevailing practices which violate those principles."[4] Discussing the validity of the blues for the Black Arts movement, Maulana Karenga writes, "We will not submit to the resignation of our fathers who lost their money, their women, and their lives and sat around wondering 'what did they do to be so black and blue.'"[5]

In this manner, the movement, with its misogynist and homophobic undertones and its infamous rhetoric of anti-Semitism, was also dominated by the view that the previous generations of African Americans had not done enough in order to ameliorate their living conditions. For both the black power and the Black Arts movements, revolution not only implied a break from all things identified with "whiteness" but also limited diversity in their definition of "blackness." The proposal of an African American identity based on assumptions about heterosexual urban males was questioned by those whose experiences did not fit this fixed notion of self.

The generational shift of the 1970s was characterized not so much by a radical review of the ideology of the 1960s, but by the clear attempt to diversify African American identity in order to include the experiences of women, gays and lesbians, and immigrants, among others. In this effort to redefine identity, African American writers once again turned to an exploration of the past in order to find explanations and meaning for the present. In an interview given to the *Black Scholar*, Octavia Butler discusses the motivation behind writing a novel about slavery: "I wrote [*Kindred*] because I grew up during the sixties . . . and I was involved with the black consciousness raising that was taking place at the time. And I was involved with some people who had gone off the deep end with the generation gap. They would say things like, 'I would like to get rid of that older generation that betrayed us. I'm not going to do anything because to start, I would have to kill my parents.'"[6] In another interview with Randall Kenan, Butler states that "*Kindred* was a kind of reaction to some of the things going on during the 1960s when people were feeling ashamed of, or more strongly, angry with their parents for not having improved things faster, and I wanted to take a person from today and send that person back to slavery."[7] Taking a contemporary character back to slavery and testing her survival skills with the knowledge of the present was for Butler a means of dealing with the sentiments of shame and anger that affected her generation's view of their ancestry and history.[8]

The ways in which the lives of previous generations influenced those of contemporary characters also constitutes one of the main themes of Gayl Jones's first novel, *Corregidora*. In an interview with Charles H. Rowell, Jones states the following: "History and personality are interests there [in *Corregidora*]—the relationship between history and personality—personal and collective history—history as a motivating force in personality . . . Michael Harper—my advisor and teacher at Brown—asked me a question: What is the relationship between autobiography and history? So, much of the answer for it became a part of the creative process of writing that book."[9] Both Jones's and Butler's explorations of the history of slavery reflect a prevailing interest in the 1970s in a past that will provide meaning for the present. In this manner, the novels of this decade that deal with slavery—*Corregidora*, *Kindred*, and Ernest J. Gaines's *The Autobiography of Miss Jane Pittman* (1971)—focus less on the reconstruction of a fragmented past and more on the effects that it continues to exert over the lives of African Americans in contemporary society.

In the 1970s, with the emergence of black studies departments and the publication of studies on the history of slavery, such as John Blassingame's *The Slave Community* and George Rawick's *From Sundown to Sunup*, both published in 1972, the novelist could be less preoccupied with her or his role as a social historian whose interweaving of fact and imagination attempted to represent a historically accurate account of the past. Thus the novelist in the 1970s, less concerned with social and historical conditions, was freer to enter the more complex psychological landscape of the enslaved subject.

The present chapter focuses on Jones's *Corregidora* and attempts to illustrate how this novelist not only established new paradigms for the recreation of slavery but also forged a new role for the novelist who deals with African American history. In the interview with Rowell published in *Callaloo* in 1982, Jones places her work in the context of the African American historical novel:

> Unless the writer can say something different or explore some new dimension of Afro-American slave experience that hasn't already been done and finely done by Ernest Gaines in *The Autobiography of Miss Jane Pittman* and Margaret Walker in *Jubilee*... it's a genre I think and a truth of the American experience; what are the truths about it that haven't already been told? . . . For instance, Frederick Douglass . . . wasn't free to do [in his narrative] the things that Gaines and Walker do in theirs—Walker's focus on the personal relationships and complexity of Afro-American character; Gaines' range of character and event. Gaines and Walker free new writers to do new things with it.[10]

In attempting to find a different mode of exploring slavery, Jones does not reject previous works that deal with the subject, but rather she roots her own writing in a tradition, which in her view, can be developed and reinvented. Although she considers both Gaines's and Walker's novels as creators of a genre that privileges the enslaved female, Jones is particularly influenced by Walker's dramatization of personal relationships. Gaines's Miss Jane,

Jones states, directs her attention "outside herself, and those events which are described in detail have social, rather than personal or intimate implications. [One does not] have any sense of her relationships."[11] In contrast, the driving forces of Walker's protagonist lie in the context of family and community. For Walker, personal relationships between slave and master or mistress, women and men, women and women, mother and child, and so on are not only a means of recreating history from the perspective of the oppressed; they also constitute the means by which she gives shape and direction to her narrative. This is a pattern followed by Jones not only in *Corregidora* but also in works such as *Eva's Man*, *Song for Anninho*, and *Xarque*. "I see a pattern," Jones states, "in terms of ideas I have been interested in: relationships between men and women, particularly from the viewpoint of a particular woman, the psychology of women, the psychology of language, and personal histories."[12]

Jones follows Walker in an African American female tradition that explores the relationship between story and history in order to create a personal narrative of slavery. The relationship between oral and literary traditions, which Walker articulates in *Jubilee*, is also evident in Jones's work. In the same way that Walker identifies the story that her grandmother told her as the genesis of *Jubilee* and the importance of folk speech as a means of validating oral history, Jones also identifies the spoken word as the primary influence in her work: "I learned to write by listening to other people talk . . . my language/word foundations were oral rather than written . . . my first stories were heard stories—from grown-up people talking . . . So I've always heard stories of people generations older than me. I think that's important. I think that's the important thing."[13]Among Jones's earliest influences were also the stories told and written by the women in her family. Her maternal grandmother, Amanda Wilson, wrote plays for church productions, while her mother created stories to amuse both the future novelist and her brother. "I have to say," Jones states, "that if my mother hadn't written and read to me when I was growing up I probably wouldn't have even thought about it at all."[14]

Walker's usage of African American folk speech and her concern with the recording of oral traditions are also reflected in Jones's work. In an interview with Michael Harper, Jones declares, "it's necessary to make connections between the oral traditions and written documentation, unless you're in an environment that maintains the integrity of oral traditions. When you're not, it's necessary to document the traditions—to counteract the effects of false documentations."[15] In this way, for both writers, the inclusion of the oral in the written work is an integral part of recovering folk speech and culture and validating oral history.

In this manner, *Corregidora* reflects both an acknowledgement of the contribution of *Jubilee* to the African American historical novel and a departure from Walker's model. Free from the twofold task of writing fiction and social history undertaken by Walker, Jones abandons the chronological narration of history, and a recreation of the past based on a detailed and historically accurate depiction of the daily experience of slavery. With Jones the reader enters into a world where history is recreated from memory, a brutally unforgiving memory—the past is a dangerous place. The realistic depiction of time and place is replaced with the psychological, sexual, and artistic landscapes of Jones's characters. In this psychological realm where different time spans coexist, the chronological narrative is abandoned in favor of a narrating mode that is fragmented, and at times seemingly disjointed, in order to mirror the mental processes by which one remembers, selects, and recreates different aspects of personal history.

All in the Telling

Jones's narrative form, which requires a first-person narrator, has major implications for the way in which the author uses folk speech. In order to solve the tension between the third-person narrator's standard English and the characters' dialogue or monologue in black dialect, "the story-teller," to use Jones's words, is "part of the same speech community, the same essential world view, and telling the story of those people who also identify with that language and world view and with those human values."[16] In *Liberating Voices: Oral Tradition in African American Literature*, Jones appropriates John Wideman's concept of "framed story," "a story contained within or bracketed by another story [and at times] the story within the frame is written in a variant language, considered subordinate or inferior,"[17] in order to distinguish different usages of standard English and vernacular in African American literature. In *Jubilee*, Walker frames the usage of folk speech within a standard English third-person narrator's voice. In *Corregidora* Jones breaks out of this "frame,"[18] and by doing so she not only removes the hierarchical relationship between standard and black English but also validates African American oral tradition by creating stories "written in the first person as if an audience were being *spoken to*,"[19] rather than written to. This points to a radical rejection of the white hegemonic discourse with literary and political implications. In this instance, Jones's usage of folk speech in *Corregidora* is closer to Gaines than to Walker.

Free from Walker's reconstruction of what Ashraf H. A. Rushdy calls the "dailiness" of slavery, Jones initiates a new trend in the African American historical novel. Her work moves toward the exploration of those events, which as Rushdy argues, form "a break, a fissure, a tear in the fabric of history"[20] and become almost incomprehensible occurrences in the present, while having perdurable effects on the future. When such experiences become almost unimaginable in the present and are effectively beyond representation, the notion of historical continuity is compromised not because the past remains irremediably cut off from the present, but rather because it remains a ghostly and terrifying presence in the present.

Corregidora explores the ways in which history, revealed in a direct truth-telling form, can entrap individuals in its webs and consume their lives. Jones's narration of history exposes slavery's bare facts and raw realities, and leaves both her characters and her audience with no place to hide. Jones emphasizes the necessity to define boundaries between private and collective history. In this sense, *Corregidora* invites the reader to enter a fictional realm in which history and personal life are closely braided, often entangled.

Ursa Corregidora, the protagonist of the novel and its narrator, starts her autobiography, to use Jones's terminology, in a rather unusual way. There is no mention of her name, her place of birth, or any of the other basic factual information about her origins that usually opens conventional autobiographical narratives. Rather, she commences her story by exposing the two main tensions in her life: her art, and her love for a man who does not understand how her songs are as much part of her life as he is:

> It was 1947 when Mutt and I was married. I was singing in Happy's Café around on Delaware Street. He didn't like for me to sing after we were married because he said that's why he married me so he could support me. I said that I didn't just sing to be supported. I said I sang because there was something that I had to do, but he never would understand that. We were married in December 1947 and it was in April 1948 that Mutt came to Happy's drunk and said if I didn't get off the stage he was going to take me off. I didn't move.[21]

As we can observe from the first lines of the novel, the narrative voice owes so much to oral speech that its casual tone often belies the significance of what is said. Jones begins the text in straightforward and nondramatic mode, and it is quite surprising when, later in the novel, we perceive that what is being described in the opening is the very turning point in Ursa's life, that point that in many ways justifies her need to tell her story. *Corregidora* demands an observant reader, one who is alert to the significance of prosaic events. In this context, the meaning of the excerpt is enclosed in three expressions that without an attentive reading can pass unobserved, given Jones's deliberately subdued tone: "I sang because it was something that I *had to do*," "he would *never understand that*," and "I *didn't move*"(italics mine). The form of the verb "to have" implies, in this context, more than a responsibility or obligation; it denotes that, for Ursa, her music is a crucial element in her life. She feels a compulsion to sing because it is the only way she knows of giving form and expression to her feelings; her songs provide her with a language of her own to communicate her experiences. From the first lines of the novel Ursa defines herself as an artist whose art form is in conflict with her personal life. The adverb "never" suggests the impossibility of change, thus placing Ursa and her husband, Mutt, in opposition to one another. And lastly, the negative form of the verb "to move" does not imply loss of motion or paralysis, but a strong affirmation of the place where she chose to be—the stage. The themes of the novel are apparently revealed: Ursa is a singer who has to solve the antagonism between her public self as an artist on the one hand, and her private self as woman and as Mutt's companion on the other.

The story begins with an ending, since it starts with the separation of the two lovers. However, when we realize that the tension between Ursa's public and private sides is aggravated by her historical legacy as a daughter of the Corregidora women, we recognize that the opening is actually the beginning of an isolation that will render union impossible in a variety of ways. To enter Ursa's psychological universe is to step into an agglomeration of rooms: each room has more than one door, all opening to recollections of Ursa's private memories and the stories of the Corregidora women. All the doors to these rooms seem to be open and we can easily move from one room to the next, travelling in a nonchronological manner from a nineteenth-century Brazilian plantation through the first seven decades of the twentieth century in the United States. Ursa herself incessantly wanders through different time spans. Her quest takes place within her psychological boundaries, and is a process of separating the collective memories of the Corregidora women from her own private memories and finding a role for the past in her life that will allow her to claim a present of her own—a present that will enable her to live her life and pursue her relationship with Mutt on equal terms.

The absence of a distinction between Ursa's life and the past she inherited from her foremothers, between personality and history, is well illustrated in the scene in which Tadpole asks her for her surname. Instead of simply stating her last name, Ursa relates the past that is attached to it as if the two were indistinguishable: "Corregidora. Old man Corregidora, the Portuguese slave breeder and whoremonger . . . He fucked his own whores and fathered his own breed. They did the fucking and had to bring him the money they made. My grandmama was his daughter, but he was fucking her too."[22] Ursa has a surname that corresponds to a well-delineated face, the face of the man that was simultaneously her great-grandfather and grandfather; moreover, this was the face of the man who enslaved her great-grandmother and grandmother and who owned, repeatedly raped, and prostituted their bodies. Unable to utter "Corregidora" without associating it with the face of the Brazilian slave owner Simon Corregidora, Ursa's name, given to her by her ancestors, belongs to a ghost that has a very real dimension in Ursa's life. Corregidora represents the part of Ursa's identity that she has to rescue from the hands of Simon Corregidora, or from the hands of her foremothers, the women from whom she learned the contours of the face and all the hatred allied to it.

Proper names are the first distinct mark of our individuality, a symbol of our uniqueness. Surnames, on the other hand, are our first link to our immediate relatives and our ancestry. Names give us simultaneously our first idea of individuality and community. For African Americans, names can be the vessels of paradox, since many slaves were named after their slave-owners, and they were also frequently named after the place where they were born or worked—both marking them with a symbol of their oppression. Slaves had no right to a name of their own, and thus no right to an identity of their own. After the abolition of slavery in 1863, African Americans were still subject to being misnamed. For example, in Marsha Hunt's second novel, *Free*, the protagonist, a young black man, recalls, "but then it did seem that Mister Kleber had odd names for Dusty Simms [his mother] too, calling her his day girl although she was every bit of thirty-five when she died."[23] Nevertheless, black American's names are important links, facilitating connections to a past so many had simultaneously wanted to know and wanted to erase. In *Repossessing Ernestine: The Search for a Lost Soul*, Hunt presents an autobiographical account of her reunion with her grandmother. Wandering through the rooms of the house where her ascendants had been slaves, the narrator questions, "How was my family related to that house, those owners? We would never know. All that's certain is that we have carried their name."[24] Although Hunt might never find out how the family of her great-grandparent's masters was related to hers, her name took her to the place where they spent part of their lives, and it took her closer to them, probably the closest she will ever come.

In "Hidden Name and Complex Fate," Ralph Ellison writes, "They [our names] must become our masks and our shields and the containers of all those values and traditions which we learn and/or imagine as being the meaning of our familial past."[25] Ellison suggests that the African American past has to be both "learn[ed]" and "imagine[d]." In order to discover the past, black Americans have to, like Toni Morrison's Milkman in *Song of Solomon* (1977), engage in detective work, follow the clues, the footprints of their ancestors in order to unveil their history. However, official and personal records are scarce, in many cases nonexistent, and often have been carefully destroyed. This is the point when the detective search ends and the imagination begins in an attempt to reconstruct the past. Walker's *Jubilee* illustrates this double process of researching the past, seeking ways of verifying the oral history that was passed on to her, and filling the blanks that, even after her study, remained unknowable in conventional terms.

For Ursa Corregidora, her name is more than an emblem of her ancestry; it is a constant reminder of her heritage and her role as a witness to it. As the story of the Corregidora women must be passed to the next generations, so must the Corregidora name itself. Ursa is unable to acknowledge all the complexity contained in her name, as she charges it with all her "hates" but not with her "loves [and] aspirations," as Ellison puts it.[26] She transforms it into the center from which she interprets the world, but she fails to "imagine" in her "familial past" a place from where she can decode her ancestors' past on her own terms. In other words, she cannot disconnect herself from the Corregidora name. Even when she marries Mutt Thomas and has the opportunity to adopt his name, she keeps her own. On the one hand, she was taught that both the name of her ascendants and their memories cannot be left behind—because to forget their legacy, or even to be silent about it and not pass it on to the coming generations would represent a second enslavement of her foremothers. On the other hand, as an artist Ursa knows that there must be a different mode of telling the story of the Corregidora women, a new way of saying, distinct from the words incessantly repeated to her. As an artist she also knows that "*everything said in the beginning must be said better than in the beginning*."[27]

She locks herself in the world of her memories to hear the voice of these women again and again in an attempt to unveil the meaning that lies behind the words and the silences that they never allow themselves: "Great Gram sat in the rocker. I was on her lap. She told the same story over and over again. She had her hands around my waist, and I had my back to her . . . It was as if the words were helping her, as if the words repeated again and again could be a substitute for memory, were somehow more than the memory. As if it were only the words that kept her anger."[28]Great Gram's lap is a locale that conventionally would represent nourishment and love. However, as Dorita's psychological realm is like a rocking chair moving to and fro endlessly between two points, her memories and her necessity to pass them on, first to her grandchild, Ursa's mother, and then to Ursa, her lap is a place that does not recognize any other time besides the past, nor any other feelings besides vengeance. Putting her arms around Ursa, Great Gram creates a circle that delineates the boundaries between her narrative and the world beyond it. Encircling her great-grandchild, Dorita is metaphorically enclosing her in her space, her life, and consequently in her time. It is a sense of time that is always expressed in the past tense since Dorita has let herself become entrapped in her own revenge without considering any possibility for healing and reconciliation, and consequently has denied herself, and those whom she makes vessels of her memories, access to a present and, principally, to a future. Hence, Ursa is a child deprived of the time that belongs to children—the future. Great Gram's enveloping arms create a circle, the symbol of the invisible barrier that Ursa will feel in her adult life prevents her from recognizing a clear frontier between her foremothers' lives and her own.

Dorita and her daughter conceive time as a congealed period that they equate with their time in slavery. For them time is, therefore, what Frank Kermode calls *kairos*, a "season, a point in time filled with significance."[29] However, they reject the time that functions as a balance to *kairos* and gives it meaning; the succession of days, or what Kermode identifies as *chronos*, the "passing time."[30] Great Gram and Gram's present is void of any sense of progression and fluidity. It is a stagnant time. They conceive the present as a period of waiting for a time that will confer the centrality and the significance that they give to their past. Time is the "*time to hold up the evidence*"[31] of their enslavement. Both women make of their postslavery lives a continuum of waiting for a mythical end that will finally judge the deeds of the slave master, and ultimately free them. Being unable to engage in any kind of healing process, both Great Gram and Gram find a new bondage in freedom. Refusing to break away from the past and find any meaning or purpose for their lives, other than keeping the memories of slavery alive, they become the slaves of their own memories, and moreover, they transform the sequence of their days into an unbroken circle in which they daily imprison their descendants. Both Ursa and her mother are enslaved in a time that is not theirs, and in memories that took over the place of their own private memories.

The fear that the present might intrude on their recollections and alter them makes both Dorita and her daughter enclose themselves in this fixed and stagnated time, unable to acknowledge time as *chronos*. In order to keep their recollection of the past intact they repeat the same words unceasingly because they know that if they stop, memories will be not only changed but also lost. This repetition of the past results in a conscious homogenization of their experience. Wanting to both erase the distinction between an event and its recollection, and claim an absolute truth telling, their days become hysterical attempts to stop the flow of time with their words. As Ursa believes, their words are the "*substitute for memory . . . somehow more than the memory . . .* [and are] *only the words that ke[ep their] anger*." As a consequence, everything that defies their story or disrupts the rhythm of their narrative must be resisted and excluded. For example, Dorita's sons, her daughter's sons, and Ursa's mother's intimate memory of Martin are placed in the realm of the unspoken because they have the potential to awaken feelings capable of interfering with their anger and desire for revenge. The women—obsessed with the idea of keeping their story alive and of passing it to Ursa for her to pass to her descendants and so on until judgment day—create a silent daughter.

With Ursa we enter the domain of the memory of what is continually unspeakable. Great Gram, her daughter, and her granddaughter are compulsive speakers, and at the age of five Ursa hears her great-grandmother talking about repeated rape, prostitution, lesbian intercourse, and incest.[32] Ursa is subjected to hearing what is usually concealed from children. The Corregidora women's experiences create a psychological numbness that dulls their feelings and limits their ability to judge what they can say to a five-year-old child. As Dorothy West's Cleo points out in relation to her five-year-old daughter,

> Slavery was too hard a thing to tell a child.
>
> There was time enough for Judy to know that the North and the South were not indivisible, with justice and liberty for all. Let her learn to hold her head up first. Let her learn to walk proud like the Jericho women who had died before her. Like Great-aunt Fanny who hung herself in the hay loft where her master left her running blood after he gave her her first whipping for stepping on the tail of his valuable hunting hound . . . And Great-grandmother Patsy—the time Old Missus scolded her for burning biscuits, the only time she ever burned a pan of bread in forty years . . . Great-grandmother Patsy walked out of that kitchen and down to the river. When they fished her out by her long black hair her soul had got free . . .
>
> When Judy was ready to know about slavery, these were the tales to tell her.[33]

Contrary to Cleo's experience, the Corregidora women fail to understand that it is necessary to prepare children to deal with the history of their ancestors' lives and deaths in bondage. Great Gram, Gram, and Mama do not allow Ursa to grow and be "ready to know about slavery," and Ursa will grow into a woman crippled by the history of her ancestors.

Jones introduces the reader to an ancestral figure, or figures, that diverge fundamentally from those that usually inhabit the pages of black women writers. Joanne M. Braxton writes, "The ancestral figure most common in the work of contemporary Black women writers is an outraged mother . . . [She] embodies the values of sacrifice, nurturance, and personal courage—values necessary to an endangered group . . . Implied in all her actions and fuelling her heroic ones is outrage at the abuse of her people and her person. She feels very keenly every wrong done [to] her children, even to the furthest generations."[34]The female ancestral character that predominates in female African American literature is, thus, the outraged mother that will do anything within her power to shield her children from a particularly antagonistic society. The outrage of this central figure in the black American literary imagination does not promote or condone violent or revengeful actions against the white hegemonic classes, but insists on the sacrifice and self-repression necessary for the survival of her people. The outraged African American mother, generally speaking, does not confront her oppressors directly, but strives to nurture and prepare her community to live in a deeply divided and unjust society.

The Legacy of the Outraged Mother

In *Incidents in the Life of a Slave Girl*, Harriet Jacobs personifies both this maternal archetype and the woman whose survival is dependent on the protection of her grandmother. In a desperate attempt to protect her children from their master, Harriet decides to escape, though she is well aware that her life is at risk. As a runaway slave she finds a safe shelter in her grandmother's house. Her survival depends on this woman to whom Harriet refers as "the good grandmother," or "the kind grandmother,"[35] expressions that illustrate the nurturing and protective role that this woman has in her life. She is one of the very few people with whom Harriet talks during the seven-year period she spends in a garret. Harriet's grandmother provides both the emotional and practical support essential to her survival in such adverse conditions. She brings her "herb teas and cooling medicines"[36] in order to help her cope with the bites of insects during the summer, and "bed-clothes and warm drinks"[37] during the winter, and it is through her that Harriet communicates, advises, and nourishes her children without their knowledge. The sight of her children through a hole that she managed to make with a gimlet contributed as much to her survival as the air and light she gets through it: "At last I heard the merry laugh of children, and presently two sweet little faces were looking up at me, as though they knew I was there, and were conscious of the joy they imparted."[38] It is this self-imagined maternal figure and her will to have a family that she can nurture and protect that makes her rebel and helps her to survive until she finally reaches the North.

Zora Neale Hurston's Nanny in *Their Eyes Were Watching God* (1937) is another example of the outraged mother in African American women's writing. Similar to Harriet, Nanny expresses her outrage by running away from the slave plantation soon after giving birth to prevent her mistress from selling her blond and grey-eyed baby: "Ah knowed mah body wasn't healed, but Ah couldn't consider dat. In de black dark Ah wrapped mah baby de best Ah knowed how and made it to de swamp by de river. Ah knowed de place was full uh moccasins and other bitin' snakes, but Ah was more skeered uh whut was behind me."[39] She leaves with only the determination to protect her child and the wild and venomous place where she finds refuge, though threatening, seems to her less deadly than the one she left behind. As a free woman after emancipation, she tries to create a way of life that will allow her to raise and protect her daughter. However, at the age of 17, Leafy is raped by her schoolteacher, who leaves her pregnant and psychologically and emotionally incapable of bringing up her child. Although Nanny is deeply aggrieved by the spiritual death of her daughter, she welcomes her granddaughter to the world as "another chance"[40] for her to nurture and protect a child, and once more she gathers her force to construct an alternative mode of living to the one she knew as a slave: "Ah raked and scraped and bought dis lil piece uh land so you [the granddaughter] wouldn't have to stay in de white folks' yard and tuck yo' head befo' other chillun at school."[41] Nanny expresses her outrage at postbellum Southern society, not by challenging the status quo, but by constructing a safe environment for her grandchild. This tiny plot of land becomes a place where she can protect her charge from the outside world while simultaneously providing her with the skills necessary to survive in it.

In Maya Angelou's *I Know Why the Caged Bird Sings* (1969), Momma Henderson, the narrator's grandmother, represents the outraged female ancestor. Momma is a self-sufficient woman that provides for her two grandchildren and her disabled son, and, as with Hurston's Nanny, she is a model of dignity, restraint and self-sacrifice. A deeply religious woman, Momma believes that if God protected the Jews from the Pharaoh, He will also protect, and ultimately free, black people. Until that day comes she teaches her children to rely on God and avoid contact with the white community. Mrs. Henderson "didn't cotton to the idea that white-folks could be talked to at all without risking one's life . . . In fact, even in their absence they could not be spoken of too harshly unless [one] used the sobriquet 'They.'"[42] Momma uses her strength to protect her children but not to confront or challenge the white hegemony. However, when there is a need to protect any member of her family or community, she does not vacillate. Risking her own security, she hides a man who, if caught, would have been lynched.

In one of the central episodes of the narrative, when her granddaughter, Maya, needs badly to go to the dentist, Momma takes her to the only dentist in Stamps, Dr. Lincoln, a white man. Even though he is in debt to Mrs. Henderson for a loan, he refuses to change his policy and treat the child: "I'd rather stick my hand in a dog's mouth than in a nigger's."[43] Unable to cope with the humiliation of the dentist's bigotry, Maya imagines that her grandmother becomes "*ten feet tall with eight-foot arms*"[44] and orders

Lincoln to "*leave Stamps by sundown*"[45] and "*never again practice dentistry.*"[46] Though Maya's fantasy had no resemblance to the actual exchange of words that took place between the dentist and Momma, it brought her an image of justice. Momma becomes a giant figure with enough physical strength "*to set* [the white man's] *head and arms to shaking loose on the ends of his body,*"[47] with the power to decide his future, and the authority to change the course of his life exclusively according to her will. Her newly acquired mythical powers allow her to express her outrage by using the very language of abuse to which she is subjected. The imaginary scene that unfolds before Maya's eyes constitutes an opening in the narrative of racism and oppression through which black Americans can express their rage, yet still avoid the horrors of vengeful and violent actions. In *I Know Why the Caged Bird Sings*, fantasy functions as an outlet for the hatred and resentment felt by African Americans, which allows them to survive and strive. At least in an unreal world Mrs. Henderson could show all her anger at the abuse her family endured and break the legacy of silence that burdened the African American community in the 1930s.

Morrison presents us with a more controversial ancestral figure, Eva Peace, the matriarch in *Sula*. She is the dominating presence in the Peace house sitting "in a wagon . . . directing the lives of her children, friends, strays, and a constant stream of boarders."[48] Ironically the presence of this strong and domineering woman is characterized by the loss of her left leg. After five years of an unhappy marriage, her husband left her with $1.65 and three children, and less than a month later Eva left her children with a friend and moved out of Medallion for eighteen months. When she came back to claim her children, she did not have her left leg. The loss of her leg originates fearful stories told by Eva herself and other members of the community and the pocketbook full of money that she brought with her when she returned to the Bottom: "Somebody said Eva stuck it under a train and made them pay off. Another said she sold it to a hospital for $10,000."[49] How Eva lost her leg during the time she spent away is not disclosed, but we can imagine that her journey was one of self-mutilation to save her children from dying of hunger. Her mutilation works as a dramatic physical expression of the tendency for sacrifice and self-repression evident in these four narratives.

Mutilating her own body, Eva carries out the ultimate maternal gesture for the sake of her children. However, her presumably deliberate act transforms her into a problematic mother who claims absolute control over her offspring. Adopting a godlike attitude with power to create and destroy, Eva burns her son to death because he is a war veteran whose addiction to heroin caused him revert to infancy. Throughout the novel, Eva fails to justify the killing of her son. However, she remains an ambiguous character, and we perceive that the killing of Plum was as driven by arrogance and overconfidence, as well as an inexplicable but deep love: she "held him close first. Real close."[50] Both the killing of her son and the mutilation of her body indicate a desire to protect her family and remove pain. In the 1920s, Eva has no means of confronting the white hegemonic classes largely responsible for her socioeconomic conditions, for sending her son to war, for returning him broken, and for turning him into a helpless man, "thinking baby thoughts and dreaming baby dreams and messing up his pants again and smiling all the time."[51] Hence, her outrage gains expression in the form of violent acts that invariably occur within the sphere of her family and personal life. When Eva realizes that she cannot make her son reborn, and nurture him to be a man whose sense of manhood comes from within him and not from a society that will always deny it to him, she kills him.

Eva burns her only son, and she is later to see her daughter steamed to death, as if nature took revenge on her most unnatural act. Before he dies, Plum sees his mother as a "the great wing of an eagle pouring a wet lightness over him."[52] However, when this same "eagle" tries to fly out of her bedroom window to cover her daughter's flaming body with her own, she misses her and "com[es] crashing down some twelve feet from Hannah's smoke."[53] By the end the novel the reader is not certain if Eva has learned that if she disposes of her limb to offer her children a dignified life, she cannot dispose of them as if they were her limbs, mere continuations of herself. It is difficult to judge the intentions that underlie the gestures of this despotic mother who kills one of her children and promptly risks her life to save the other. Nevertheless, like Harriet, Nanny, and Mrs. Henderson, she is an outraged mother, who embraces self-sacrifice for the good of her family.

The female ancestral presence in these texts incarnates, even when misguided, the values of altruism, sacrifice, courage, wisdom and spirituality. Those outraged and brave women constitute the maternal myths that, as Braxton puts it, play an important role in "sustain[ing] a struggling [and endangered] people."[54] The Corregidora women clearly diverge from this archetype of motherhood. The image of the woman as a protector, recurrent in female African American literature, is not sustained in Jones's work. Throughout the slave narrative genre and in the postemancipation accounts of female former slaves, or in the fictional work of black women writers who attempt to portray the female experience of those periods, there seems to be a common preoccupation on behalf of female slaves: how to free their children. When they plan their escape, they either try to take their children with them or release them first. This pattern is evident in, for example, the cases of Harriet Jacobs, Hurston's Nanny, Walker's Vyry and Morrison's

Sethe. This point is emphasized by the conscience of Alice Walker's Meridian, descendant of slaves, who feels guilty when she decides to leave her son in order to attend Saxon College because she "knew that enslaved women had been made miserable by the sale of their children, that they had laid down their lives, gladly, for their children, that the daughters of these enslaved women had thought their greatest blessing from "Freedom" was that it meant they could keep their own children."[55]This image of the woman protector occurs so often in the works of black female writers that it may be considered a norm. Jones's work, however, does not subscribe to that norm. In *Corregidora,* Great Gram chooses to stay with her master after the abolition of slavery in Brazil at a time when "black people could go anywhere they wanted to go, and take up life anyway they wanted to take it up."[56] When she eventually flees from the plantation, not only does she leave her baby daughter behind, but it also takes her approximately 18 years to come back for her. By the time of her return, her daughter has been repeatedly raped by Simon Corregidora and is pregnant. Leaving her daughter at the mercy of her former master, Great Gram fails to protect her from a fate very similar to her own and, even more surprisingly, throughout the novel she never tries to justify her actions.

Once in the United States, mother and daughter fuse their memories in such a manner that allows them to *remember* episodes of each other's lives as though they were experienced by both of them in exactly the same way, as if they were one person. Great Gram and Gram's memories once formed two separate circles that now intersect each other as the women are reunited. Differences between them are dissolved: "*Naw, I don't remember when slavery was abolished, cause I was just being born then. But Mama do, and sometime it seem like I do too,*"[57] Gram says, and she goes on narrating the abolition of slavery to Ursa as if she had experienced it herself when, in reality, she is telling her mother's story. Mother and daughter homogenize their experiences and pass on a single story to their descendants with almost no distinctions, no gaps or silences. It becomes a story that is to be transmitted along an uninterrupted generational cycle. The only thing that these women want from their descendants is for them to continue to transmit their bitter narrative to future generations. It is this defined story that clearly sets Jones's characters apart from the "the outraged mother" in that the only thing they want for their daughters is for them to preserve that same narrative. Great Gram and Gram do not seek a better or alternative way of life for their children, and furthermore they do not allow them the freedom to pursue a life distinct from theirs. Both Ursa and her mother are marked at birth with their ancestors' history and a predetermined future: to "*mak[e] generations.*"[58]

Excluded from free access to the written word, living outside the walls of literacy, Great Gram and Gram understand that the transmission of a personal and cultural memory can only be achieved with the spoken word. In their text, the rupture of the familial lineage has an unavoidable consequence; it is not only an interruption of their narrative but also the announcement of its cessation. Perceiving speech as the only vehicle of communication over which they have control, the Corregidora women respond with their words to the absence of a written history that includes them, and in the face of the destruction of incriminating records by slave owners, who burnt words in order to erase deeds. For Dorita and her daughter, only the spoken word kept in memory, sculptured in the individual's consciousness, cannot be effaced by fire: "*The important thing is making generations. They can burn the papers but they can't burn conscious, Ursa. And that what makes the evidence. And that's what makes the verdict.*"[59]

With their words, Great Gram and Gram weave an oral history that bears witness to their crushing past. Karl Marx noted, "men [and women] make their own history, but not spontaneously, under conditions they have chosen for themselves; rather on terms immediately existing, given and handed down to them."[60] In this way, the Corregidora women's historical text is uttered with the purpose of objecting to and replacing a master's narrative that tried to erase them from the memories of human kind. However, since their bondage determined the terms on which history was "handed down to them," the text of Dorita and her daughter also embodies and reproduces the tyrannical and oppressive gestures of the hegemonic discourse it wants to replace. On one hand, as Sally Robinson puts it, the Corregidora women are convinced "they must speak through their bodies in the form of producing children to whom they can pass on the story of Corregidora"[61]; reproduction is, for them, a means of transforming their bodies, the primary site of enslavement, into a locale of resistance not liberation. On the other hand, the dynamics of Corregidora's sexual abuse continue beyond the abolition of slavery, and both Great Gram and Gram internalize the slave master's representation of the black woman as a trade article with no control over her body or sexuality. Furthermore, the Corregidora women are incapable of breaking the knot firmly tied by slavery that matches black female identity with sexuality.

Unable to displace their selfdom as women from the body, and caught in a definition of the self based on a biological determinism, the Corregidora women are precisely what their name connotes—Corregidora's women. Powerless to break away from an identity that was forced on them, they remain imprisoned by Corregidora, and thus, their story reproduces the master's narrative it attempts to amend and replace. As Robinson writes, "[Great Gram and Gram] allow Corregidora to retain control over the place of enunciation by keeping him firmly in the center of their reconstructions . . . [they] have no control over their pasts and their discourse, despite what they see as their power to 'give evidence.' . . . The Corregidora women are all trapped within a narrative that can only represent them through the lens of the master's desire."[62] When we first hear Great Gram, it is her voice that penetrates us, but it is Simon Corregidora's figure that starts gaining form in our imagination: "*He was a big strapping man then. His hair black and straight and greasy . . . He looked like one a them coal Creek Indians.*"[63] Dorita commences her first-person narrative, not by asserting herself as the center on which her enunciation will develop, but with a physical characterization of the main character of her story. This fact demonstrates the contradictory nature of Dorita's autobiographical gesture. Although she wants to compose her autobiography, Great Gram produces a text that does not have herself at its core. As she unrolls her account we gradually perceive that Simon Corregidora is the force that gives shape to her story.

In her narrative, Dorita occupies the same passive and secondary place that she had in her master's house, as the manner in which she constructs her sentences attests, "*he took me out of the field . . . He would take me hisself first and said he was breaking me in. Then he started bringing other men.*"[64] Great Gram's discourse is punctuated by this imperious "*he*" that signals the beginning of most her sentences and does not allow her to affirm an "*I.*" Gram's narrative reflects her mother's. The first time that Gram speaks in the novel, she, like her mother, begins with a description of Simon Corregidora: "*His* hair was so dark and greasy straight you could a swore *he* was pure Indian . . . Naw, but *he* wasn't though. *He* was from over there somewhere in Portugal . . . *He* was a seaman. Naw, a sea captain. That's why the king gave *him* lands and slaves, and things, but *he* didn't hardly use nothing but the womens."[65] Like her mother, Gram keeps the master at the center of her utterances, making use of the masculine third-person personal pronoun to commence most of her sentences. Although Gram's first speech runs almost for an entire page, she only uses the pronoun "I" once, and then only to say that she did not know her master's birthplace.[66] In this way, as Robinson suggests, the master is at the center of Dorita and her daughter's discourse and his presence functions as a filter through which they represent themselves. However, contrary to what Robinson indicates, neither woman chooses to "allow" Corregidora to keep control over their text because they are in a position where, as Marx observes, they are not allowed to choose. Gram and Great Gram are clearly unable to break away from their master and the means he used to represent them. Articulating their story in his terms, mother and daughter give voice to feelings, fears, and desires that express a history "given and handed down to them."

Using their words almost as an echo of Simon Corregidora's actions, Dorita and her daughter confiscate their female descendants' bodies for their own ends, and present to them a world that, just like slavery, offers no choices. In this way, Great Gram and Gram produce and enforce a fixed identity on their daughters in the same manner that Corregidora constructed their perception of themselves. Although the Corregidora women want to redefine their selfhood, they are unable to go beyond the confines of the body. Great Gram and Gram, as Amy Gottfried puts it, "first defined as 'pussy', they are now *self*-defined as womb. The function of a woman's body, therefore, is single-minded still: No longer a sexual commodity, it has become a political commodity."[67] The bodies of their descendants become a means through which the first two women of the Corregidora lineage can carry out their political agenda, to "make generations" and keep their legacy alive. Reflecting the master's ideology, Great Gram and Gram entrap their daughters' identity within their bodies.

This concept of an identity that cannot expand beyond the boundaries of the body, conditions the life of the third woman of the Corregidora family line. Her identity acquires the exact contours of her body, and it cannot be dissociated from it. When she meets Martin, her husband, she cannot assume any other role besides the one attributed to her as the descendant of the Corregidora women, and she is incapable of recognizing any form of sexual desire that might divert her from the path set for her, "to make generations": "But still it was like something had got into me. Like my body or something knew what it wanted even if I didn't want no man . . . But it was like it knew it wanted you. It was like my whole body knew it wanted you, and knew it would have you, and knew you'd be a girl . . . Just knew what it wanted, and I kept going back there."[68] Irene's desire to have a child is expressed solely in terms of her body. The third woman of the Corregidora family line, Irene uses the pronoun "it" to refer to her body, and by doing so she confers on her own body an almost separate existence from herself, and expresses the lack of control that she has over it. For Irene, to bear a child had very little to do with sexual desire, love, or even a partner. In the same manner that she did not have control over the day that her body chose to give her her first menstruation, it would give her the only child she could have: a long-haired girl. In Irene's veins ran the blood of the Corregidora women and the historical legacy that could not be dissociated from it, and both of these compelled her to deliver the fourth generation of the Corregidora lineage.

On the one hand, Irene knows that she was trapped in the concept of womanhood that she inherited from her foremothers, which induced her to believe that men were rapists and women were their defenseless prey, but that women had to continue "making generations" in order to keep their legacy alive. On the other hand, she recognizes that Martin offered her an opportunity to redefine her identity and engage with companionship, sexuality, and love: "I wouldn't even believe you could get along that well with a man."[69] The language with which she chooses to depict him is sensual, but between her and her would-be lover was the hurricane of Great Gram and Gram's words, and an embrace was impossible because Irene failed to realize that "making generations is making love," as Janice Harris notes in relation to her daughter, Ursa.[70] Unable to reconcile the reproductive desire that her ancestors insist on, and the sexual desire for Martin, she abandoned both her new name, *woman*, without unveiling its significance and the man who gave it to her. Although Irene says that Martin "married [her] and then . . . he left [her],"[71] she comes to realize that she was the one who left him in the first place by never allowing him to get close to her. The previous quote marks a shift on Irene's narrative. Uttering what was probably locked inside her for so long makes her recognize that she is not being truthful to herself or Ursa's father. After this moment, she attempts to do what her grandmother and mother never taught her to do: to see that everything in life is like the trade beads that Ursa is wearing, everything has several patterns and colors that form naturally—"no one paints them on."[72] There is no straightforward or homogeneous truth.

Irene begins to reveal the truth and the complexity of her private memory to her daughter. She progressively breaks away from her mother's discourse and tries to find a language that will enable her to express her own past. Delving into the furthest recesses of her memory, while telling her story to her daughter, she realizes that saying that the only thing that Martin wanted from her was to get in between her legs is an easy statement that reveals almost nothing about her relationship with Ursa's father.[73] Thinking back and gradually unlocking the doors of those memories that time had shut away, as if they were to be kept that way forever, Irene remembers "all that hurt there"[74] in Martin's eyes. She remembers the way that a past, not totally hers, occupied the site where love could have found its place, and recalls "all that hurt there" in Martin's eyes. She finally sees that she wove a mask with no features or lines—a uniform face for the man that was to give her a longhaired baby girl, and that she put it on to Martin's face and tightened it with a firm knot so that it would not be easily unfastened, and "all that hurt there" in Martin's eyes. Even when he asked the first two Corregidora women the question she never dared to ask: "'How much was hate for Corregidora and how much was love,'"[75] the question that could have helped her to see that in Great Gram and Gram's story contradictory desires coexisted, and that their words contained more than one layer of truth, Irene cannot escape the Corregidora's women legacy. Mama is unable to reconcile her divided desires and, therefore, remains in a realm where she cannot possess a lived life, only a heard one. Irene is enclosed in the past, while Martin claims a present and desires a future.

Irene and Martin's relationship ends in violence. By beating his wife Martin delivers her back to where he thinks she belongs and where there never was a place for him: to the world of the Corregidora women. Abusing her physically was not enough for him—if Irene was not able to leave her mother's for him, he wants her to feel what it is to actually be one of them, and he tells her to "go on down the street, lookin like a whore."[76] However, as Melvin Dixon observes, "Mama was virtually made into a whore not by Martin but by Great Gram and Gram, who needed generations to continue their rage against Corregidora more than they needed men as stable family partners."[77] Great Gram and Gram created their narrative around one man, Simon Corregidora, and consequently, they excluded all men from their world. The image of this domineering man will reproduce itself in other men's faces as if they all were mirrors of Simon Corregidora. In this way, Martin makes Irene look like a whore because she made him look like Simon Corregidora. A relationship that offered to both lovers a possibility of love and mutual understanding ends up falling into a mirror image of the past, showing the tremendous hold the slave master has on the women of the Corregidora family.

Irene is Martin's victim, but he is also her victim, trying to free himself from an imposed identity as rapist and breeder. Jones's work constantly defies fixed identities—victims and agents of victimization reverse their roles at different times in order to expose the complexity of human nature. Her characters are driven by irreconcilable forces that contain them, and those forces unhinge men and women alike. Seeking control of the past, and the means to heal the wounds of the past, becomes the near-impossible task set for Jones's characters. She presents us with the stories of the women, but she implies that the stories of the men are not excluded from the challenges she describes.

Irene leads us to another sphere: Great Gram and Gram's memories. She heard their stories, learned every single one of their words, savored them like fruit, sensed their aroma, and felt their contours in order to reproduce the exact tone and accent of her foremothers' utterances. And when she tells their story, she does not simply sound like the old Corregidora women, she *becomes* them: "[S]he [stopped being] Mama . . . she was Great Gram talking."[78] Leaving Brazil for Bracktown, Great Gram and Gram left the lived life and carried on with a spoken one. All they seem to do is sit on the porch of a house that is in a town that is "set back from the highway,"[79] as they are "set back" from life itself. Their words only take them to more of their words, and almost still, on the chairs from which they tell their stories, they perpetually circumnavigate their own vicious circle.

Breaking with the Past

Ursa's trip to her hometown constitutes part of the route she has to travel in order to break her foremothers' vicious circle. In her youth she left Bracktown in order to make a life for herself. Now past the age of forty, she returns for that part of the Corregidora women's memory that she did not carry in her own memory. In *Corregidora*, the theme of the journey, similar to other contemporary African American works, such as Morrison's *Song of Solomon* and Paule Marshall's *Praisesong for the Widow* (1983), is associated with the discovery of the ancestral past. From her mother Ursa learned that "Corregidora [was] responsible for that part of [her] life. If Corregidora hadn't happened that part of [her] life [her relationship with Martin] never would have happened,"[80] and presumably she would not have "carried him to the point where he ended up hating [her] . . . That's what [she] knew [she]'d do with any man."[81] In other words, Ursa learns that female and male relationships in her family are conditioned by her foremothers' past. Moreover, she discovers that she was not alone in having to deal with the consequences of the Corregidora women's lives in bondage. Those who get close to her, close enough to hear the ghosts that appear without warning and haunt her days and nights, are also caught in the whirlwind of her foremothers' past. As her father suffered the effects of loving a woman whose life had been taken by the memories of other people's lives, her husband also had to deal with the Corregidora women's legacy.

However, when Ursa achieves this level of understanding about her ancestral past, and the consequences it had both on her and the people who surround her, she has already travelled far and in her journey she had encountered many losses. One of those was Mutt Thomas: "When I first saw Mutt I was singing a song about . . . this a train going in the tunnel, but it didn't seem like they was no end to the tunnel, and nobody knew when the train would get out, and then all of a sudden the tunnel tightened around the train like a fist. Then I sang about this bird woman, whose eyes were deep wells. How she would take a man on a long journey, but never return him."[82] The imagery of the tunnel, the train, and the bird in Ursa's songs suggest a death of sorts: one by strangulation and suffocation and the other by kidnapping and abandonment. The train and tunnel as sexual metaphors imply infertility—it is mere entry, just as the suffering bird woman ("whose eyes were deep wells") can seduce but not relate—both metaphors express profound loss. Ursa's songs draw the landscape of her relationship with Mutt. It is a dark, distant place from which there is very little chance of returning and where lovers fight to gain supremacy over each other. The themes of journey and related sexuality merge to give expression to contradictory desires. The train and the tunnel function as metaphors for the male and female sexual organs, respectively, or as a synecdoche for man and woman. Entering the tunnel, the train enters the darkness, a conventional symbol for what is unknown and somewhat dangerous. Although the train is endowed with the ability to move and enter the tunnel, and it has, thus, an apparently domineering position, once it is inside the tunnel the train is controlled by its surroundings. Only the tunnel possesses the knowledge of its own boundaries, its beginning and its end, and thus has the train completely at its mercy. However, knowing that the singer's psychological realm is a place of no definite boundaries where her own memories and the memories of her foremothers wander freely, where past and present, personal and familial, are almost interchangeable with no dividing lines between them, we also know that the woman Ursa portrays in her songs is unable to limit frontiers, beginnings and endings. In this way, going into the tunnel, the train enters a corridor of death. Incapable of setting the train free, the tunnel has no alternative but to strangle it. In doing so, it occasions its own destruction—the train, moving in a "tunnel [that] tightened around [it] like a fist," will make its walls split and finally collapse.

The bird woman of the second song appears to be as domineering as the tunnel woman of the first. It is easy to imagine this gigantic woman taking a man in her claws to a foreign and even exotic place. However, the bird woman forgets that human beings who attempt to fly like birds end, like Icarus, by falling. Making the journey into a flight without return, the bird woman not only shows her inability to set limits to her enterprise but also violates the definition of journey: the distance travelled between two points, the last point being related to the point of departure, either as the home we leave or as the home to which we return. Once more the commencement and the end are undetermined. In this manner, it is not difficult to envisage the struggle of two forces: one pushing forward toward the unknown ("train and bird") and the other one pressing backward in the direction of home ("tunnel" and "man"). Woman and man express paradoxical and seemingly irreconcilable desires. Both songs seem to portray two very distinct experiences for the woman: the tunnel representing confinement, and the flight of the bird woman suggesting freedom. This distinction, however, is superficial since, as we have seen, both chants convey captivity and loss. This intimation of imprisonment functions as a prologue to a profound sense of devastation.

Ursa's songs illustrate that the journey in *Corregidora* is metaphorical rather than physical. Being the dark tunnel of the past, or attempting to escape it, as the flight of the bird woman seems to suggest, are both actions marked by pain and loss. Unlike Butler's Dana, Ursa does not have to be physically transported to the past in order to unveil its significance. In Jones's work, the journey to the past depends on memory, and the imagery of the songs signals the dangers and horror facing her protagonist when such journeys are attempted. Ursa's past lives deep in her as if it was part of her own blood: "Their past in my blood. I'm a blood."[83] However, every time she revisits her foremothers' words in her memories, dreams, and songs, she undertakes a symbolic journey back in order both to engage with the significance of her ancestral past and the central role it has in her life. In this way, Ursa's journey to the past, similar to Dana's, is an act of self-discovery.

Ursa comes to Mutt with her restless art and unsolved past, but he is only willing to embrace Ursa as his "no hard woman."[84] Mutt, as Harris observes, "would have Ursa leave her history outside on the porch, love him, live with him in the present"[85] and ultimately be his wife. As her man, he thinks that he has to be positioned at the very core of her being. Nevertheless, he finds himself lost on the all-too-large canvas of her life where he sees his image in the penumbra of the faces of Great Gram, Gram, Mama, Simon Corregidora, and the innumerable men that go to Happy's Café to fall under the spell of her music. Perhaps Mutt could have found a way of living with the rhythm of the Corregidora women's words and learned that, as an artist, Ursa needed her audience, if only in the intimacy of their room he felt that he could wholly embrace her. However, in their lovemaking he feels that she does not give herself to him, and like the bird woman of her songs she cannot stop wandering. She is always on her way to the past and never flying toward him. Mutt fails to see that for his union with Ursa to take place, she has to fly toward her "self." Ursa has to come to terms with the legacy of her foremothers and her identity.

Mutt does not know what makes Ursa fly away from him because he does not care to listen to what she has to say. He does not listen to the songs that Ursa sang for him after they first made love, "songs that had to do with holding things inside you. Secret happinesses, a tenderness."[86] In this way, he fails to recognize the love that his wife feels for him. He feels rejected and jealous because he does not realize that Ursa did not feel comfortable about singing "any song that had anything to do with opening up,"[87] not because she does not want to have a life with Mutt and engage with him sexually, but because she is still enclosed in the circle of Great Gram's arms. It is worth noting how the bird and tunnel imagery of Ursa's songs reflects her sexual and historical identity and the way the latter conditions the former. Mutt tries to read Ursa, but he is unable to go beyond the surface to discover that "*the explanation* [of her behavior lies] *somewhere behind the words*"[88]:

> "The thunder sounds like it's talking, don't it"? [Ursa] asked.
>
> "That's because you got music all in your head. The thunder ain't doing nothing but thundering."
>
> "Naw, Mutt, it's talking. If you listen, you can hear it too."[89]

For Mutt, Ursa's past and her songs, like the thunder, do "nothing but thundering." His failure to enter the figurative world reflects his inability to interpret his wife's art, and understand the language she uses to communicate her inner self. When she tries to tell him the lyrics of so many of her tunes, the words that she did not dare to sing or say to anybody, he silences her: "Whichever way you look at it, we ain't them [the slave ancestors]."[90] He does not allow her to explain the significance behind the Corregidora women's words, establishing a void between himself and his lover that will leave her cry for help unheard: "I didn't answer . . . because the way I'd been brought up, it was almost as if I was [the slave ancestors]."[91] Mutt yells that he is "tired a hearing about Corregidora's women. Why do you have to remember that old bastard anyway?"[92] His refusal to engage with her past makes it impossible for Mutt to see that what prevents her from giving herself to him and joining him in sexual pleasure has nothing to do with the fact that she does not love or desire him, or that she has other men. Ursa does not "*feel anything*"[93] sexually because Great Gram and Gram taught her to see her body exclusively in terms of the production of the next generation. Hence, Ursa, like her mother, centers her sexuality in her womb, and though she knows how to "make generations," she has yet to learn how to make love. Her capacity for orgasm is lost in the contradiction that her foremothers' legacy produced, and that made reproductive desire and sexual desire mutually exclusive.

In this way, the woman singer, who on stage seems to personify sensuality, has to learn to how to be comfortable with her body and sexuality; this is something that Mutt fails entirely to recognize. Ursa's inability to feel sexual pleasure hurts her husband's pride and makes him wonder who is in possession of his wife if it is not he: "*Are you mine, Ursa, or theirs?*"[94] Ursa responds to Mutt's question with silence. Her foremothers silence her with the continuous sound of their words, and Mutt leaves her in muteness by failing to see that her family past is as much part of her as her own blood: "Their past in my blood. I'm a blood."[95] Ursa's assertion of the self as a nonself reflects her inability to separate her identity from the stream of her foremothers' memories. This synecdoche that equates Ursa's identity with blood, and the latter with the past, is highly symbolic. Like blood, the Corregidora women's legacy runs through Ursa's veins intoxicating her body with their memories to the extent that she is incapable of establishing a distance from it that would allow her to claim a place for her own memories and develop a sense of selfhood. On the other hand, the metaphorical use of blood suggests that, in the same way Ursa cannot live without it, she cannot live without her past. This seemingly impossible situation, however, offers possibilities of change and reconciliation of opposites since blood is also a symbol of renewal, something Ursa has yet to discover.

Refusing to acknowledge the past, Mutt has no access to Ursa's psychological topography; he does not know the routes to her nightmares, the paths that lead her to her songs, or the itinerary of her desires. He is like the lost train in the tightening tunnel of Ursa's tune. Like the train, he struggles to find a way out, a way of defining the boundaries of the woman he loves but who keeps escaping him. All his anger and frustration seem to lead him to one answer: "You one of them [one of the Corregidora women] . . . If you wasn't one of them you wouldn't like them mens watching after you."[96] Calling his wife a whore and threatening to go to Happy's and sell her body to her audience is, for Mutt, a means of legitimately claiming ownership over her since he feels that there is no other way he can call her his.

Although Mutt threatens to sell Ursa as "a piece a ass,"[97] he is unable to do it because he remembers that his great-grandfather "bought his wife's freedom. But then he got in debt to these men, and he didn't have any money, so they come and took his wife . . . and [he] just gone crazy after that."[98] This episode shows that Mutt himself is also conditioned and influenced by his ancestral past. His behavior reflects the dynamics of slavery and he tries to claim Ursa, as the slave owners claimed his great-grandmother, as "his property, his slave."[99] However, the memory that he retains of his ancestors prevents him from selling Ursa and replicating the master's gesture. In this way, Jones makes all her characters in *Corregidora* feel the nets of history constantly being thrown over them. What differs from character to character is the level of awareness of their condition as descendants of slaves.

As the train cannot stop pushing toward the exit of the tunnel that "tightened around [it] like a fist," Mutt cannot control his desire to possess Ursa, and she keeps resisting him. We already know that the expression of contradictory desires in the song of the train and tunnel ended in their mutual destruction. Mutt and Ursa will do the same to each other just as if their story is the chorus of the song: Ursa is not prepared to live in the present with Mutt and keeps pushing him to her ancestral past; he pushes her down a flight of stairs.[100] Her injuries result in the loss of a baby Mutt knew nothing about and Ursa's hysterectomy.[101]

Memory Recreated: "Let Me Give Witness the Only Way I Can"

Ursa's physical impairment accounts for the dramatic shift that occurs in her life. She loses the ability to "make generations," and therefore, she loses the ground on which her whole identity was constructed. The hysterectomy signals a moment of deep loss, pain, and fear, that will lead her to take rushed decisions. However, it is this state of confusion and hurt that will allow her to evaluate her life and progress. She will revise her identity and history from the perspective of a woman artist who, through her songs, has the power of creation, but whose body no longer has the power to bring forth life. Thus the loss of the womb reveals other levels of creativity.

In the hospital, Ursa undergoes a period of unconsciousness during which she "curs[es] him [Mutt], *and* the doctors and the nurses out."[102] The words, the feelings, and the anger that she had kept to herself since she was a child seated on Great Gram's lap, hearing her speak the unspeakable, finally come out, but come out in tongues that nobody seems to understand. As Tadpole, the owner of the club where Ursa works, points out, the hospital staff "said they didn't know *what* you was."[103] When Ursa recovers from delirium she returns to the silent world of her memories. She is lonely and afraid, and she has to find out who she is and who she wants to be. When she leaves the hospital her steps are conditioned by her fear of what will become of her: "*Afraid only of what I'll become.*"[104] Ursa is afraid, but whatever will happen from this moment on cannot be a continuation of the past. The tunnel and fist song, an imaginary world of despair and destruction, begins to lose its power.

"Out of fear"[105] she asks Tadpole to take her to his place when it is time for her to leave the hospital. While convalescing at Tadpole's house, Ursa lets him take care of her, cook her meals, help her with her bath, accompany her to the doctor, deal with her divorce arrangements; moreover, she lets him love her. Although she cannot "help feeling that [she] was forcing something with Tadpole . . . Something [she] needed, but [she] couldn't give back,"[106] she needs to be close to a man. She searches in Tadpole for someone who can assure her that having lost her womb, and consequently her ability to "make generations," she did not lose her female identity. "Out of fear" and driven by a blind selfishness, she accepts everything that Tadpole is willing to give her without giving him anything in return. Her friend Cat tries to help her see what is happening with her: "Right now's not the time for you to be grabbing at anything . . . Out of fear . . . Ask yourself how did you feel about Tadpole before all of this happened . . . He's looked at you and seem like you scared somebody else won't."[107] Reluctantly she moves in to Cat's house, but "out of fear" that she will surrender to a lesbian affair with her friend, she goes back to Tadpole and marries him. Ursa needs to know that she is still desirable as a woman, that she can still make love to a man. Her marriage is unsurprisingly short-lived. On the one hand, Mutt has joined the gallery of ghosts that haunt Ursa, and a mixture of love and hate, of wanting and not wanting him, prevents Ursa from establishing a relationship with any man. On the other hand, the Corregidora women's legacy, which prevents her from having sexual pleasure with Mutt, corrodes her second marriage in ways similar to those that ended the first.

Ursa is confused because she has suffered a great deal of pain, but advances little in her search for the self. Yet she understands that she has to come to terms with forces that wail inside her in a pugnacious strain: her identity and sexuality, the history that conditions them, and her feelings toward Mutt. In a dream, Ursa has her hands on her lover's body, on "the mark of his birth."[108] This image of apparent physical and emotional closeness is soon dissipated by the realization that Mutt's birth left him the mark of his vinculum with his mother in the same manner that Ursa's birth also left her with the mark of her tie with her mother; however, the locale of their birthmarks is disturbingly different: "I have a birthmark between my legs."[109] The discomfort Ursa experiences comes not from a sudden realization of that reality but because she challenges that same reality for the first time: "[P]ussy. The center of a woman's being. Is it"?[110]

Having her womb removed, and consequently losing her ability to "make generations," makes Ursa feel, for the first time, separated from her foremothers in a very definite way: "I *am* different now . . . I have everything they had, except the generations. I can't make generations."[111] Before the hysterectomy, Ursa had her destiny marked as the descendant of the Corregidora women; after the operation she also feels that her "life's already marked out for [her]—the barren part."[112] However, feeling a degree of separation from her foremothers that she never felt before makes her realize that she has to pursue not only a new identity for herself but also a way to make "the barren part" bear fruit. It is crossing the line between physical fertility and infertility that makes Ursa aware of the creative power of her song. It is worth noting here how the body imagery is sustained in these moments of profound change and liberation for Ursa, illustrating how the history of the African American woman is imprinted on her body. Thus, for Ursa, to address her ancestral past is also to address how female identity is shaped by the objectification of the black body.

After her hysterectomy, Ursa cannot forget the past, as the Corregidora women's master "still howls inside [her],"[113] and she cannot escape the reality that her "veins are centuries meetings,"[114] but she needs to claim a life for herself, a present and a place for her own memories. Ursa longs for a way of expressing all the opposing dimensions of her life: "I wanted a song that would touch me, touch my life *and* theirs. A Portuguese song, but not a Portuguese song. A new world song. A song branded with the new world."[115] The creation of Ursa's new world implies the disruption of the vicious circle of the Corregidora women's words. However, this does not put an end to their legacy, thereby enslaving them in forgetfulness. Instead it offers a transforming vision that reveals a new truth, "a kind of 'knowing' . . . that expresses itself, not in description, repetition, or imitation, but in making, making new." Now Ursa knows not only that "*everything said in the beginning must be said better than in the beginning*" but also that there must be a new medium through which she can say it.

Art of Memory: "I'll Make a Fetus Out of Grounds of Coffee"

In a dream in which Ursa's imagination and memories seem to fuse in order to produce a ritualistic request, she asks her ancestors to acknowledge her mode of telling their history as a valid way of bearing witness to it: "*Let me give witness the only way I can. I'll make a fetus out of grounds of coffee to rub inside my eyes. When it's time to give witness, I'll make a fetus out of grounds of coffee. I'll stain their hands.*"[116] After having lost her womb, and consequently being unable to bring forward the next generation of the Corregidora women, the "only way" Ursa can bear witness to her family's past is through her songs. Ursa's pledge has the force of a promise that she will not fail to carry out and her words invoke the commencement of a new order. She will get handfuls of coffee grains, rub them against each other in order to hear their music, she will give them form, "a fetus out of grounds of coffee," a "fetus" that, rather than symbolizing the delivery of the child that Ursa cannot have, signals the birth of her own notion of history. Jones's use of the coffee beans is highly symbolic. The plantations of coffee in the Brazilian context correspond to the fields of cotton in the United States where so many slaves worked and lost their lives. Thus making music with brown beans, Ursa evokes the ancestors' history, their work and their hardship, and the music that they created and sang while coffee beans rolled out of their hands. This is clearly a cultural practice that sustained them, a musical and verbal expression of their humanity. However, Ursa's music is not mimetic, it is inclusive and transformative: a musical expression that demands a new approach to history.

Her sense of history requires the transformation of her foremothers' absolute truth-telling narrative mode into a blues language that will allow Ursa to break the cocoon of silence, made out of the continuous sound of the Corregidora women's words, and to choose words of her own in order to utter what is unspeakable. Moreover, every time Ursa sings the blues she is bearing witness to her familial past and passing on her testimony to her audience in each song. She is no longer yearning for the birth of a longhaired girl to whom she can tell the Corregidora tale. Neither is Ursa living in a congealed time waiting for the mythical "*time to hold up evidence.*" Although she recognizes the importance of Great Gram and Gram's conception of time as *kairos*, a moment in time filled with temporal permanence, which they equate with the period they spend in slavery, Ursa realizes the need to engage *chronos*, the "passing of time," so that her present can acquire the fluidity and sense of progression that will enable her to transcend the imprisoning past.

Empowered with the ability to deal with and tell history on her own terms, Ursa will have the power to "stain *their* hands," the hands of those who want to keep them clean from history. Primarily she will "stain [the] hands" of her audience, the daughters and sons of slaves, through her voice that is "like callused hands. Strong and hard but gentle underneath . . . The kind of voice that can hurt you . . . Hurt you and make you still want to listen,"[117] she will make them feel her blues feelings, and encourage them to sing her songs, and pass on her testimony and their own to the coming generations. Ursa refuses "*a life always spoken, and only spoken*,"[118] but she also rejects a life always sung and only sung. She "want[s] a song that would touch [her], touch [her] life and theirs," and the plural of the third-person of the personal pronoun includes not only her foremothers but also those that go to the bars where she works to listen to her sing. Ursa's songs urge her audience to act, learn their history, bear witness to their past, gather evidence of their heritage, and, above all, to continue the oral tradition that has kept it alive in the African American memory. Ursa's blues constitute her call to action. As Sherley A. Williams observes, "the internal strategy of the blues is action, rather than contemplation . . . And while not all blues actions achieve the desired result, the impulse to action is inherent in any blues which functions out of a collective purpose."[119] With her songs, Ursa wants to establish a new language that will lead to new ways of dealing with the history of slavery. It is the discovery of the power of the blues that enables her to enter the cycle of healing and reconciliation that she longed for so much.

By reconstructing in her songs the collective memory of black America, Ursa will, along with her community, "stain [the] hands" of those who directly or indirectly contributed to its horrors, of those who tried to erase it, and of those who tried to ignore it. In this way, Ursa's blues are a new way of saying, her means of bearing witness not only to her ancestors' past but also to the history of the whole African American people. "Rather than a rigidly personalized form," as Houston A. Baker Jr. writes, "the blues offer a phylogenetic recapitulation . . . of species experience. What emerges is not a filled subject, but an anonymous (nameless) voice issuing from the black (w) hole."[120] The blues as a form of testimony not only will allow Ursa to share her legacy with the audience and, by telling her story, ease her pain and alleviate her burden but will also help her to acknowledge that her personal history is part of the history of her community. "The particularized, individual experience," as Williams notes, "rooted in a common reality is the primary thematic characteristic of all blues songs."[121] Understanding that individual experience can be contained in a broader "common reality" will enable both Ursa and her audience to feel that, while their stories are simultaneously particular and anonymous, they all belong to the "species experience."

In this manner, Ursa wants to create possibilities both for herself and her audience to use history as a creative and regenerative force, and the blues as a "robust matrix,"[122] as Baker puts it. Her new world is branded with the Corregidora women's old world. She will make music out of the coffee grains Great Gram picked in the master's Brazilian plantation, she will sing their lives, hum their pain, and finally "*explain it, in blues, without words, the explanation somewhere behind the words*."[123] On one hand, Ursa needs to separate herself from the Corregidora women's history and find a way of bearing witness to their lives in bondage that will allow her to claim a life and a present of her own; on the other hand, as an artist she needs her music, and she knows that without her foremothers' past there would be no songs to sing. The blues allow Ursa, as Marilee Lindemann notes, to "make the necessary claims of kinship with her past as well as achieve a degree of separation from it."[124] The blues do not solve the antagonism that exists between the past of the Corregidora women and the present that Ursa wants for herself. Nor does it solve the conflict between her personal memory and her foremothers' collective memories, or indeed the love and hate that she holds for Mutt. However, Ursa's songs form a creative synthesis in which these forces can be contained and expressed. As Baker states, "the [blues] singer's product, like a railway junction itself . . . constitutes a lively scene, a robust matrix, where endless antinomies are mediated and understanding and explanation finds conditions of possibility."[125] Ellison similarly writes, "The blues is an impulse to keep the painful details and episodes of brutal experience alive in one's aching consciousness, to finger its jagged grain, and to transcend it, not by the consolation of philosophy but by the squeezing from it a near-tragic, near-comic lyricism. As a form, the blues is an autobiographical chronicle of personal catastrophe expressed lyrically."[126] The blues also allow Ursa to make the audience finger the "jagged grain" of the past, and sense that the past can be expressed by way of cultural practice. The blues singer acts like a force, an invisible electric-like "impulse," carrying the African American experience along the circuit of her or his community. However, in blues call-and-response structure, the singer, who might be the primary impelling force initiating the musical dialogue with the audience, soon becomes the one that has to respond to it. The alternation between solo singer and audience confers on the blues a circular structure. Using the blues as a means of bearing witness, Ursa overcomes her foremothers' linear concept of history. Ursa's blues, as Lindemann points out, "are more than a mere substitute for her lost ability to make biological generations; they are a profound transformation of the linear passing on of history and 'conscious' . . . into a larger, circular notion of time and human consciousness in which there is space for the 'private memory.'"[127]

Ursa's songs originate from the tension that exists between Ursa's "private memory" and the memories of the Corregidora women. It is Ursa's urge to contain her foremothers' words in her own words and, as Hélène Cixous would express it, "turn [them] around, seize [them]; to make [them] hers . . . taking [them] in her own mouth, biting [their] tongue with her own teeth to invent herself a language to get inside of."[128] By singing the blues, Ursa devises a language of her own to forge and express the record of her own life. The blues, as Ellison notes, are "an autobiographical chronicle of personal catastrophe expressed lyrically," and like the autobiographical gestures of the black women before her, Ursa's is a revolutionary one. It represents a movement from the margins of discourse to a center where she can claim her selfhood. The Corregidora women made use of the master's language to represent their experience. They constructed their autobiographies using the same representational devices that the master used to define them, and thus they failed to "invent a language of [their own] to get inside of." Recreating herself in the language of the blues allows Ursa to break the boundaries of the cultural practices that attempted to silence both her specific identity and her mothers' heterogeneous history.

Ursa took to herself the words of Great Gram, Gram, and Mama and reinvented them to serve her own purposes. In the same manner, her audience will appropriate her lyrics and, as Mikhail Bakhtin writes, by "populat[ing them] with [their] own intention, [their] own accent . . . adapting [them] to [their] own semantic and expressive intention,"[129] they will make Ursa's words their own in order to describe their particular contexts and serve their own intentions. This is the legacy of Ursa's songs—once she sings them to her community of listeners, they are no longer hers, no longer do they stand for her specific history, they become representative of the experience of the whole African American community.

Disclosing the past wrapped in music enables the last Corregidora woman to go beyond the linear passing of history revealed in an absolute truth-telling form and draw frontiers between the past and present, and the personal and collective, that will enable her to gain control of her own life. In this way, singing the blues enables Ursa to transcend the past, and ultimately achieve the freedom her ancestors never attained. Now Ursa is, as her second husband once called her, her "own woman."[130] Through her songs she discovered a means of separating history and personality and she learns a new way of saying her name: "*I am Ursa Corregidora. I have tears for eyes. I was made to touch my past at an early age. I found it on my mother's tiddies. In her milk. Let no one pollute my music. I will dig out their temples. I will pluck out their eyes.*"[131]

Reunion

In the closing episode of the novel, Ursa sings for Mutt again. Although she still hates him, "not as bad as then, not with that first feeling, but an after feeling, an aftertaste, or like an odor still in a room when you come back to it, and it's your own,"[132] he is still her chosen audience of one. After having been separated for 22 years, they go back to the Drake Hotel, where they lived during their marriage: "It wasn't the same room, but the same place. The same feel of the place,"[133] Ursa says. The room functions in the novel as a finite physical place where resolution will occur. In the final scene of *Corregidora*, Jones makes the different time spans and spaces meet and merge in the same locale, illustrating simultaneously the cohesion of the structure and content of a seemingly fractured narrative. In the room of the Drake Hotel, Ursa simultaneously returns to the Corregidora women's past and her own, to the Brazilian plantation where her ancestors were slaves, and to the place where herself and Mutt came together and drew apart.

For the first time, Ursa performs fellatio on Mutt. Biting him in the "split second"[134] before orgasm, "split second of love and hate . . . A moment of pleasure and excruciating pain at the same time,"[135] Ursa not only announces her return to Mutt, but she also discovers and exercises the power that Great Gram had over Simon Corregidora: "I knew what it was, and I think he might have known too. A moment of pleasure and excruciating pain at the same time, a moment of broken skin but not sexlessness, a moment just before sexlessness, a moment that stops just before sexlessness, a moment that stops just before it breaks the skin: 'I could kill you.'"[136] During the sexual act, Ursa loses the perception of "how much was [her] and Mutt and how much was Great Gram and Corregidora."[137] This scene constitutes a play within the play of Ursa's life. It enables Ursa to crawl under Great Gram's skin, *be* her, *be* as close to Corregidora as she was. This absolute identification with her ancestor allows her to go beyond her words and discover the meaning that the continuous sound of her voice had attempted to obscure. In this way, Ursa and Mutt's sexual act becomes, like Avey's dance in *Praisesong for the Widow* or Milkman's song in *Song of Solomon*, a ritual, a means of discovering the significance of the past via cultural practice. Mirroring Great Gram's act enables Ursa to concurrently exercise the power that Great Gram had over Corregidora and unveil its potential. Consequently, Ursa is both performer and spectator of her own play; she has come full circle.

When Ursa unites with Mutt, she is no longer a silent listener of her foremothers' words, and she is no longer a passive victim. Singing the blues, Ursa goes beyond her foremothers' understanding of history; moreover, she overcomes the identity that they established for her as their descendant, and she is empowered by her ability to define herself in her own terms. The blues enables Ursa to invent a language of her own, a form through which she can communicate her experience. "From language," as Dixon states, "comes control," and it is the achievement of control that enables Ursa to gain authority over her life and prevents her from fully exercising her newly discovered power: "I could kill you." Ursa's discovery of what she could do to Mutt is enough for her to move forward and reconcile with him:

> "I don't want a kind of woman that hurt you," he said.
> "Then you don't want me."
> "I don't want a kind of woman that hurt you."
> "Then you don't want me."
> "I don't want a kind of woman that hurt you."
> "Then you don't want me."
> "I don't want a kind of man that'll hurt me neither," I said.
> He held me tight.[138]

Ursa and Mutt's dialogue takes the form of a blues stanza. Ursa sings the blues for Mutt again, and this time he not only has to listen in a way he never did before, but he has respond to her on her terms, using her blues language. The symmetry of the six line call-and-response structure conveys a sharing of power, a recognition of past cruelties, and a mutual understanding that will lead to the healing and reconciliation announced in the final line of the novel: "He held me tight." Ursa lets him embrace her, but she also wants him to feel she will return to him with her past, her songs, her love and her hate. Ursa and Mutt perform a blues song, a duet, announcing the end of Ursa's living solo.

4

"The Undocumentable Inside of History"

Sherley Anne Williams's *Dessa Rose*

Contexts

The notion of the recreation of a past to which the historian has limited or no access informs the African American historical novels of the 1980s and subsequent decades. Toni Morrison's *Beloved* (1987), for example, considers the implications of infanticide, while Charles Johnson's *Oxherding Tale* (1982) dramatizes the sexual exploitation of slave men. The emphasis of the works from this period is on the heterogeneity of the experience of the enslaved self, along with the exploration of facets of that experience, which, in both slave narratives and nineteenth-century literature, remained in the realm of the unspeakable. This also reflects the historiography of American slavery from the 1970s and 1980s, which emphasizes the slave's experience of and perspective on the peculiar institution. The historical studies of this period reflect, as Thomas C. Holt states, "a consensus that despite the harshness of the system, slaves were able to create communities beyond their master's total control. They fashioned institutions and a cultural ethos that were functional to their needs, that enabled them to survive the rigors of slavery and bequeath a legacy of resistance to their posterity."[1]

As in the aforementioned novels, Sherley Anne Williams's *Dessa Rose* (1986), the main focus of this chapter, recreates what Robert Penn Warren calls the "undocumentable inside"[2] of history. Williams's novel explores the history of African American resistance in the antebellum South. While Margaret Walker's *Jubilee* explores the details of the daily experience of slavery and Gayl Jones's *Corregidora* presents characters that, denoting an inability to claim themselves, remain under the master's domain long after emancipation, *Dessa Rose* considers resistance as an integral part of the African American experience of slavery.

Williams acknowledges that *Jubilee* "presaged the modern era in the written history"[3] of black people from an imaginative perspective. However, Walker's concerns for historical accuracy, verisimilitude, and, more significantly, her meticulous representation of the institution of slavery are relegated by those who followed her to a second plane so that a more personal history could emerge. Unlike Walker, Williams does not see the role of the writer of historical novels in parallel to that of the social historian. Her concern lies with the creation of a personal history that is not limited by documented factual information but is constructed around the "inside of [the] characters, the undocumentable inside,"[4] to return to Warren's concept. In her article "The Lion's History: The Ghetto Writes B[l]ack," Williams explains that in their preoccupation with the portrayal of slavery as an institution, slave narratives, "despite their often impassioned language, have always seemed impersonal to [her], shorn of those telling relationships, that sense of network that give vibrancy and depth to autobiographical portraits."[5] Williams goes on to quote the well-known passage from Frederick Douglass's narrative—when after his successful escape to New York, he alludes to his wife-to-be, Anna, whom he failed to mention before in his text, in order to illustrate that the slave narrative, with its focus on the institution of slavery, is a text that reveals the public rather than the private self.[6]

In Williams's attempt to reimagine history from a personal or intimate perspective, the recreation of the voice of the slave becomes a critical issue in the process of writing *Dessa Rose*. As Williams herself states, "The histories of slavery available during the late sixties and early seventies . . . focused on issues that could be traced through archival material in which the slave's voice was largely missing, his or her person treated as mute commodity."[7] Like Walker, Williams makes use of those African American traditions that were communicated via word of mouth and allowed slave communities to develop a culture that survived and developed beyond the printed word in order to ungird the ancestor's voice: "Nineteenth-century black oratory, the lore, songs and stories created by what were then American slaves, gave me a key to unlock the intimate history that had escaped the attention of formal historians."[8]

In order to recreate a more personal history, Williams has to create both a narrative context and form in which the slave subject could express her or his humanity under an institution that saw black people as chattel. In

Corregidora, Jones broke Walker's framed narrative by dismantling the hierarchical relationship between standard English and black vernacular. Williams's novel, in turn, moves away from Jones's autobiographical narrative. *Dessa Rose* introduces shifts in point of view in order to represent slavery from a number of perspectives. This approach exposes the distortion of African American history and the cultural constructs of race that define and condition the relationships between blacks and whites in the text while opening spaces in the narrative in which the slave both claims and recreates her sense of self.

Williams's use of vernacular is also different from that of the novels previously discussed. Jones's *Corregidora* authenticates African American oral tradition through the figure of a first-person narrator who is essentially a storyteller, while Walker's usage of black vernacular denotes her preoccupation with authenticity and her underlying concern with the portrayal of an African American culture that existed and evolved out of the chaotic experience of slavery. Williams shares Walker's concerns in a text in which the lore of the Quarters, its stories and songs, and the survival skills passed on from generation to generation provide the slave protagonist with the necessary means to come to terms with and express her experience. The enslaved subject's control over her narrative is also a critical issue in Williams's novel, which gradually evolves into a first-person account, employing some of the narrative devices used in *Corregidora*, such as the usage of italics to indicate dreams and past memories and the telling and retelling of the story to the next generations as a means of securing historical continuity. In this way, if Walker portrays a whole and rich culture that survived by word of mouth, and if Jones authenticates the African American vernacular by reconstructing history through the voice of the storyteller, then Williams makes use of the vernacular in order to establish frontiers between black orality and white literacy. African Americans, Williams writes, "having survived by word of mouth—and made of that process a high art—remain at the mercy of literature and writing; often these have betrayed us."[9] *Dessa Rose* exposes the boundaries between African American oral culture and the supremacy of the hegemonic written discourse over the black self by exploring slavery via a series of viewpoints drawn from sources beyond the norm, real or imagined.

"I Really Say That?"

In the first of the three primary sections of the novel, the focalization shifts between Dessa, the condemned pregnant slave, and the white amanuensis who attempts to record the story of her insurgence on a slave coffle. These shifts of focalization—"a principle according to which elements of the fictional world are arranged from a certain perspective"[10]—emphasize the discrepancies between the black woman's oral history and its reconstruction in the white man's written record. In order to clarify the multilayered quality of Williams's novel, however, it is necessary to distinguish between focalization, the perspective from which certain situations and events are presented, and narration. Ruth Ronen defines the latter as "the mode of verbalizing the perceiving process and the objects of perception; it is the principle according to which elements are textualized in particular manners of expression carried out from a narrativing stance."[11] In the first part of *Dessa Rose,* while the focalization alternates between Nehemiah and the female slave protagonist, the narration shifts between the first-person accounts of the two characters and that of a third-person narrator.

The distinction between focalization and narration is thus significant in order to understand Williams's use of a third-person narrator. First, the omniscient narrator functions as a mediator between the character of Nehemiah and the reader, emphasizing the white amanuensis's unreliability as both a recorder and a narrator of Dessa's story. The reader's interpretation of Nehemiah's first-person account in his journal entries is conditioned by the third-person narrator's observations about his character, background, and motivations in writing his book, *The Roots of Rebellion in the Slave Population and Some Means of Eradicating Them.* As Williams acknowledges, "The decision . . . to subsume Nehemiah's voice under my own third person narration put me under an unenviable relationship with a character I didn't like."[12] In this way, the third-person narrator disrupts the white man's control over the narrative, cautioning the reader against the perspective he presents about Dessa and African American people in general. For example, after Nehemiah's journal entry on June 26, 1847, in which he enumerates "the facts of the darky's history," the narrator comments on his thoughts while writing the entry: "Nehemiah hesitated; the 'facts' sounded like some kind of a fantastical fiction."[13] I will return to this excerpt at a later stage to explore its significance in the context of the production of the historical record. What is important to consider here, however, is that without a third-person narration and limited to Nehemiah's journal entries and observations about "the darky," his perspective would not have been entirely revealed to the reader. It is the omniscient narrator who discloses the white man's hesitation and thoughts about his own text. Without the third-person narrator, the ambiguity between the word "facts" printed on the page of Nehemiah's journal and the thought of "a fantastical fiction" that crept into his mind would have not been exposed to the reader.

Second, the presence of the third-person narrator is important in signaling Dessa's journey from being a character in a white man's narrative to becoming the creator of her own text. In this way, the presence of this narrator is stronger in the first part of the novel and gradually fades away to give place to Dessa's first-person narrative. The third-person narrator also intervenes in order to clarify Dessa's actions or emotions for the reader. For example, it is through the third-person narration that the reader becomes aware that Dessa is using the interviews with Nehemiah to make sense of her experiences and to try to find out more about the other slaves involved in the coffle revolt.[14] Dessa tells Nehemiah that when she realized that she was pregnant, she discussed the possibility of running away to the North with Kaine. Yet it is through a third-person narration that Dessa's understanding of the "North" is presented:

> "Dessa, run away where?"
>
> "North," she whispered. She'd never heard anyone talk about *going* North. North had been no more to her than a dim, shadowed land across a river, as mythic and mysterious as heaven: rest, when the body could bear no more. But, and she understood this even as she breathed the word, if there was rest for the body, there must be peace for the heart . . . "North."[15]

From this excerpt it is clear that, at this stage of the narrative, if the reader had only access to Dessa's utterance, what she chooses to tell the white interviewer, her story would be partially lost. In this way, the third-person narrator has the role of recovering the meaning and the emotional depth of Dessa's long silences in the presence of the white man. It is important to state here that, in narrative terms, the boundaries between the narrator's text, to use Mieke Bal's terminology, and the character's free indirect discourse are not always clear. Bal argues that free indirect speech has, among others, the following elements: "a personal language situation" characterized by the use of first and second personal pronouns, demonstrative pronouns such as "this/these," adverbs of place like "here/there," adverbs of time like "today/tomorrow," emotive words and aspects, modal verbs and adverbs that indicate uncertainty in the speaker, and a "strikingly personal style" attributed to the character.[16] From this it is possible to argue that the third-person narration of Dessa's thoughts is related by a third-person narrator, especially if we consider that the character's idiom, the distinct features of her enunciations, is absent from the passages discussed.

The omniscient narrator has another crucial role in the first and second sections of *Dessa Rose*—that of unifying a seemingly disjointed narrative. From Dessa's silences to her half-told stories, the fabric of the narrative leaves many loose threads to be picked up at a later stage. The act of reading becomes one of following the retelling of certain episodes until a more complete picture emerges. In a text in which memory is a central issue not only because Dessa's recollections shape the structure of the narrative but also because it is crucial to the reconstruction of an unwritten past, the linear mode of narration is largely replaced by one that is informed by the way one remembers, reflecting blues patterns of repetition and variation. In this context, the third-person narrator has the critical role of maintaining the narrative flow until Dessa is ready to assume full control of the telling of her story in the third section of the novel.

Williams's multivocal representation of slavery is critical to a work that aims to revise the African American past while exposing the cultural constructs that objectified black people, or rendered them invisible in American history. In this way, *Dessa Rose* not only represents the different ideologies at play in the construction of racial and historical identity but also reworks the African American historical novel by showing the production of the historical record in the making. In the first part of the novel, Williams dramatizes the misrepresentation of African American history by exposing the differences between the fragmented pieces of information Dessa chooses to relate to the white man and his journal entries. The slave's utterance is, when not lost, distorted in the white man's written record: "He hadn't caught every word; often he had puzzled overlong at some unfamiliar idiom or phrase, now and then losing the tale in the welter of names the darky called. Or he had sat, fascinated, forgetting to write. Yet the scene was vivid in his mind as he deciphered the darky's account from his hastily scratched notes and he reconstructed it in his journal as though he remembered it word by word."[17] Although the white amanuensis sits opposite Dessa with pen and paper in hand, her words are clearly lost in his writing. Vocables such as "puzzled," "unfamiliar," and "deciphered" emphasize the white man's inability to understand what is being conveyed to him while drawing attention to Dessa's distinct culture and idiom, whose terms of reference are clearly unknown to Nehemiah. It is interesting to note that the white man's hesitations in relation to Dessa's "unfamiliar idiom," which he struggles to "decipher," are not noted in his journal but are conveyed by the third-person narrator. In this way, as an author, Nehemiah does not clarify to his readers that his text is an interpretation of what the slave related to him, rather he "reconstructed [Dessa's speech] in his journal as though he remembered it word by word." The usage of the past subjunctive, "remembered," preceded by the expression "as though" suggests that the memory is flawed and indicates that Dessa's story is as good as "lost" in his text.

The third-person narrator also calls the reader's attention to Nehemiah's methodology and ability as a historian, writing history from "hastily scratched notes" of his interviews with Dessa, which he "abbreviate[ed] with reckless abandon, scribbling almost as he sought to keep up with the flow of her words."[18] If the use of words such as "hastily" and "reckless" undermine Nehemiah's aptitude as a record keeper, the verb form "scribbling" is rather significant in order to understand the role of literacy in the novel. "To scribble" can indicate hurried or careless writing, or meaningless drawing. In this manner, Williams clearly inverts the hierarchy established by the white hegemony between orality and literacy. Nehemiah's writing is seen in the text through Dessa's eyes. Being illiterate, the printed word is for Dessa no more than insignificant doodling. Thus it is hardly surprising that Dessa does not recognize the account of her experiences in the white man's text:

> "You be writing down what I say?" . . .
>
> Instinctively he held it away from her eyes . . . "I do indeed write down much of what you say." On a happy impulse, he flipped back through the pages and showed her the notes he had made on some of their previous sessions.
>
> "What that there . . . and there . . . and that, too?" He told her and even read a little to her, an innocuous line or two. She was entranced. "I really say that?" When he nodded, she sat back on her haunches.[19]

Nehemiah's gesture of showing the slave woman his journal is devoid of meaning since, owing to her illiteracy, the white man's text is a realm to which Dessa has no access. When Nehemiah reads to her, Dessa does not recognize her utterance in the white man's discourse, further emphasizing the practices that distorted African American history. Nehemiah's subtle reaction of averting his eyes from Dessa's makes clear to the reader that in Williams's novel the misrepresentation, if not falsification, of the history of black people was an intentional act. Dessa's recoiling in silence, in turn, stresses the lack of control of the slave over her personal narrative. Sitting outside the walls of literacy, Dessa's history remains like her chained body, in the "depth of the . . . shadow"[20] and under the rule of the white man's writing. In her status of chattel, she cannot overtly do anything but listen to the white man reading and interpreting her life as he "read and interpreted for her selected Bible verses."[21]

In her discussion of Williams's short story "Meditations on History" (1980), which many critics identify as the genesis of *Dessa Rose*,[22] Stefanie Sievers observes that "[t]he story exposes claims to historical truthfulness as ideological fictions by explicitly thematizing that what gets passed on as 'fact' is often only assigned the status of 'truth' by those who have privileged access to public discourse."[23] The same can be argued about the novel:

> These are the facts of the darky's history as I have thus far uncovered them:
>
> The master smashed the young buck's banjo.
>
> The young buck attacked the master.

> The master killed the young buck.
> The darky attacked the master—and was sold to the Wilson slave coffle.
> Nehemiah hesitated; the "facts" sounded like some kind of fantastical fiction. Had he but the pen of a novelist—And were the darkies the subject of romance, he thought sardonically, smiling at his own whimsy.[24]

Dessa Rose emphasizes the cultural dynamics at play in the production of the historical record. Williams emphasizes how the ideological constraints of the figure of the historian, and issues of publication and readership shape the historical text. What distinguishes *Dessa Rose* from other texts, from *Incidents in the Life of a Slave Girl* to *Corregidora*, which draw the reader's attention to the fact that the telling of history depends on the teller, is that Williams shows the process through which African American history is lost or distorted. The aforementioned quotation illustrates that Nehemiah considers it both possible and acceptable to write a coherent narrative of Dessa's history from his disjointed, if not incoherent, scraps of information. The indentation on the page of the "facts" outlined by the white man not only calls the reader's attention to the inarticulate nature of Nehemiah's text but also establishes a parallel between his discourse and the infantile, or unintelligible language that he attributes to Dessa. Thus Williams's text plays with the reader's preconceived ideas about literacy and orality.

It is interesting to note that Nehemiah's role as a historian is, in some ways, similar to that of the writer of historical fiction. In a conscious effort to challenge the gaps and distortions of the American annals, the novelist combines scattered pieces of information with her or his imagination in order to produce a narrative that both reconstructs and reclaims the African American past. Williams's novel is an example of this process. In the "Author's Note" to *Dessa Rose*, Williams explains that her novel is based on two historical episodes. From Angela Davis's article published in *The Black Scholar* in 1971, "Reflections on the Black Woman's Role in the Community of Slaves," Williams learned about an 1829 uprising led by a pregnant woman on a coffle in Kentucky. Reading Herbert Aptheker's *American Negro Revolts* (1947), she came across the second incident: in North Carolina in 1830, a white woman living in a remote area offered refuge to runaway slaves. In reality these two women never met, but their encounter in Williams's imaginative world provides a space where accepted versions of history established by white hegemonies can be challenged. In this way, similar to Walker, Williams creates fiction from fact in order to transform fragments of the African American past into a coherent narrative.

Williams is aware of these ironic similarities between her and a character who, as she admits, "contain[s] too many qualities I recognize as my own—for Nehemiah is, after all, a writer."[25] There are, obviously, fundamental differences between *Dessa Rose* and Nehemiah's *The Roots*. William's novel, as its title significantly indicates, privileges the life of the slave woman, racially discriminated and socially disenfranchised, who existed outside the pages of history. Behind the production of Nehemiah's book, there is no intention of recording Dessa's story per se. *The Roots* is a text for the consumption of the slaveholding readership, reflecting and reinforcing its ideologies and history. It is important to note here that, although the narrator emphasizes the arbitrariness that characterizes the relationship between fact and fiction in the white man's text, there is a marked distinction between the contemporary reader's interpretations of the words "fact" and "fiction," and what they mean for Nehemiah. The contemporary reader recognizes the irony implied in the usage of these words. Having access to Dessa's memories, thoughts, and dreams, the reader is aware that Nehemiah's record is far from "fact" in the sense that it does not correspond to what occurred in Dessa's life. What appears to be like "fantastical fiction" to the white man is not his text but rather the *fact* that both Dessa and her lover reacted violently to their master, using the master's very means of keeping them as chattel. "Master had smashed the banjo because that was the way he was, able to do what he felt like doing. And a nigger could, too."[26] In this sense, *Dessa Rose* attempts to illustrate not only that African American history was obliterated by the hegemonic other but also how, for those who had control over the production of the historical record, African American resistance seemed "a bit of the sensational."[27] It is significant that, although Nehemiah refers to the rumors of uprisings in the Southern newspapers and leaves the Hughes Farm to pursue an encampment of runaway slaves believed to be in the vicinity of Linden, he is stunned by Dessa's revelations of violent behavior toward the master.

The Distortion of Her Story

The distortion of African American history is also emphasized by the manner in which Nehemiah's beliefs of white supremacy shape his interpretation of the slave woman's story. Unable to understand that the banjo represented for Kaine a part of his African heritage, a land where "[n]obody . . . belongs to white folks, just onliest theyselfs and each others,"[28] or, in other words, a part of him that was seemingly outside the master's control, Nehemiah attributes the slave man's act of violence toward the master to the latter's sexual involvement with Dessa: "It's obvious the buck shared the mistress's suspicion about the master with this wench. Why else would the darky attack a white man, his master?"[29] The slave's humanity—his sense of an absolute lack of control over his life and the life of his unborn child—are lost in Nehemiah's record.

Williams exposes the white man's deliberate decision to misrepresent what Dessa tells him. Astonished and somewhat bewildered by Dessa's admission of violence toward her mistress, Nehemiah chooses to discredit her: "[R]emembering the darky's playfulness that afternoon, he found himself rather unwilling to credit her confession."[30] This highlights the white man's control not only over the slave's narrative but also over her identity. Dessa's confession confirms that women are as capable of acts of violence as men. However, Nehemiah dismisses her account on the basis of his preconceived notions of gender. When he considers the possibility that "the female of this species is as deadly as the male,"[31] he believes that it is necessary to adopt a terminology (note the usage of the word "species") that clearly differentiates Dessa from white women, establishing for her a category outside the boundaries of the human race, reflecting the period's influential social Darwinist ideas.

Hence, the way Nehemiah perceives and constructs Dessa's identity plays a crucial role in his interpretation of the bondwoman's history. In *Ar'n't I a Woman? Female Slaves in the Plantation South*, Deborah Gray White points out that "[t]he uniqueness of the African-American female's situation is that she stands at the crossroads of two of the most well-developed ideologies in America, that regarding women and that regarding the Negro."[32] African American female identity is filtered by the doubling effects of gender and race, remaining in the public discourse, as Barbara Johnson declares, "the other of the other."[33] When Nehemiah writes in his journal that "I must constantly remind myself that she is but a darky and a female at that,"[34] he clearly establishes the position that Dessa occupies in the patriarchal order, twice removed from the phallic center. The adverb "but," suggesting "no more than," indicates that Dessa is seen as less human, less rational, and less able than her interlocutor. "Africanism," as Toni Morrison puts it, "is the vehicle by which the American self knows itself as not enslaved, but free; not repulsive, but desirable; not helpless, but licensed and powerful; not history-less, but historical; not damned but innocent; not a blind accident of evolution, but a progressive fulfillment of destiny."[35] What Williams shows in *Dessa Rose* is that in establishing an identity that depends on *the other*, the white man inscribes his own ideology and history on the enslaved female's history.

If race, as Morrison argues, "becomes metaphorical—a way of referring to and disguising forces, events, classes, and expressions of social decay and economic division,"[36] then gender, which patriarchy confines to the woman's body, can also be seen as a symbol of male's superior intellect. "From this belief that the body is the Other," as Judith Butler states, "it is not a far leap to the conclusion that the others are the body, while the masculine 'I' is the noncorporeal soul."[37] Dessa's black body, which Nehemiah sees as grotesque and deformed by pregnancy, functions in his narrative as a tangible manifestation of her inability to articulate her history and produce a coherent narrative: "Her movements, always slow, were even slower, her walk not stumbling but heavy as though her feet were weighted. She eased her bulk onto the ground beneath the tree."[38] Nehemiah's description of Dessa's body and demeanor as bovine-like in its heaviness and gracelessness substantiate both his ideas in relation to her lack of intelligence and his superiority.

In this manner, for Nehemiah, Dessa's identity is strictly defined and confined by her race and gender. White distinguishes two prevailing images of black womanhood in the antebellum American, that of the "mammy" and that of the "Jezebel." The latter, as White explains, was seen as "a person governed almost entirely by her libido, . . . the counter-image of the mid-nineteenth century ideal of the Victorian Lady."[39] These constructs of black female identity are present in Williams's text and are evoked in the second section of the novel, significantly titled "The Wench." In the first part of the novel, however, it seems more relevant to analyze how Dessa "come[s] to represent [an] extreme example of otherness," as Farah Jasmine Griffin puts it.[40] In Nehemiah's eyes, Dessa's "extreme otherness" is established by her identity as an African American female, and, more significantly, as her perceived distinctiveness as a violent woman. It is Dessa's expression of violence that contributes to her image as the "fiend" woman,[41] the evil and the brute.

"[S]lavery by its very nature," as John Hope Franklin and Loren Schweninger state, "created a milieu for interracial conflict. Slaves on occasion refused to work, demanded concessions, rejected orders, threatened whites, and sometimes reacted with violence. Verbal and physical confrontations occurred regularly, regardless to time and place."[42] Slaves, as Franklin and Schweninger argue, reacted to severe punishments suffered by them or by loved ones, being traded, or having family members sold. Most of these acts of open defiance were desperate attempts to assert their selfhood and had serious consequences for the slave. On the other hand, what terrified the slaveholding class were the conspiracies and the uprisings led by both enslaved and free, black and white, which were not only a reaction to the conditions endured by certain individuals but a concerted effort to overthrow the peculiar institution and the prevailing social order.

It is interesting to note that, although Williams based her novel on two historical incidents that took place in 1829 and 1830, she sets her novel in 1840s. This is significant for a novel that seeks to represent resistance and defiance as an integral part of the slave experience. By 1847, the opening date of Nehemiah's first diary entry, the most legendary slave revolts had occurred. The insurrection led by Gabriel Prosser and Jack Bowler occurred in 1800, and Denmark Vesey's and Nat Turner's revolts took place in 1822 and 1831, respectively. Moreover, several conspiracies were uncovered in the 1840s. "In 1840," as Franklin and Schweninger state, "Kentucky antislavery leader James G. Birney ran for president on the Liberty Party ticket. During the campaign, the debates about halting the expansion of slavery into the territories . . . filtered into slave quarters . . . and may well have contributed directly to several conspiracies."[43] In this way, the 1840s provide a fitting background against which to recreate an atmosphere of actual and rumored plots, a sense of unrest in the quarters, and fear among the white population, all of which characterize the setting of *Dessa Rose.*[44] The insurrections of the previous decades, especially the one led by Turner, remained in the collective memory of both blacks and whites, reminding both that organized insurrection could take place. What draws Nehemiah's attention to the coffle revolt in which Dessa was involved was the fact that "slaves killed white men. He had not heard nigras doing that since Nat Turner's gang almost thirty years before."[45] This illustrates the interweaving of the historical and fictional in Williams's novel and her intention to have Dessa's story set in the wider context of African American resistance, resistance that was, at times, localized and personalized.

Notwithstanding the fact that open defiance of the master's authority was an integral part of the slave experience, as Franklin and Schweninger point out, "[n]either age nor gender was a determining factor in predicting who might resist in such a manner."[46] However, the role of women in organized rebellion seems to be less prominent, or at least less documented. What is important to notice in the context of the present discussion is that Dessa's role as one of the ringleaders in the coffle revolt was, for Nehemiah, culturally unsettling and historically unprecedented. On one hand, as a "darky" she is, in his eyes, the beast-like creature that "fell asleep much as a cow would in the midst of a satisfying chew"[47] and is "subject to the same chills and sweats that overtake the veriest pack animal."[48] On the other hand, as the killer of white men, who "roused other niggers to rebellion," she is the "devil woman."[49]

Nehemiah's perception of Dessa as either subhuman or evil makes it impossible for him to understand her experience. For example, it is his inability to recognize that bonded women and men established significant relationships that makes it impossible for him to understand Kaine's central role in Dessa's life: "Nehemiah stopped writing. More of that business with the young buck. He scowled, looking at the darky in exasperation."[50] There is a certain irony implied in the fact that Nehemiah is writing a book titled *The Roots of Rebellion in the Slave Population and Some Means of Eradicating Them*, yet when Dessa gives him an indication of the reason why slaves resist and rebel, he dismisses it. In his fixation with the recording of the action of the uprising on the coffle, he fails to identify that "the roots of rebellion" lie in the dehumanizing experience of slavery.

The loss of the black female's history is further highlighted by the white man's inability not only to understand Dessa's experience, but also the language through which she expresses herself:

> But she continued to herself, in a deeper dialect than she had heretofore used, really almost a mumble, something about Emmalina's Joe Big telling Kaine something and going, but where he could not make out. "They caught—"
>
> "What?" he asked again.
>
> The black sullen look returned to her face; the humming started again.[51]

"[T]he nigra's own dialect,"[52] as Nehemiah calls it, emphasizes the cultural boundaries between blacks and whites, and between illiterate and literate. If the white man fills in the gaps with his own words, distorting Dessa's narrative, her vernacular functions as a site of resistance. The black vernacular, the humming, the vacant smiles, and the silences with which Dessa resists the white man's questioning illustrate that, for Williams, the act of resistance becomes synonymous not only with survival but also with keeping a part of oneself to which the hegemonic others do not have access. In this manner, as Mary Kemp Davis argues, "Dessa weaves a rich tapestry of her life which conceals, rather than reveals, her essential history."[53] Dessa uses coping strategies rooted in her experience of enslavement in order to evade the white man's questioning. For Williams, singing, humming, silence, and evasion are not passive acts; they function in text as vehicles of active resistance. Although Nehemiah interprets these actions as inanity, they allow Dessa to conceal her defiance and preserve her sense of self.

During the interviews, Nehemiah occupies the position of power. Sitting on his chair, notebook and pen in hand, he asks the questions, while on the ground with her limbs chained, Dessa is supposed to answer them. Nonetheless, in this power struggle, which also represents the conflict between hegemonic literacy and black orality, Dessa resists with silence, with song, or by talking about Kaine and her life in the quarters. "Answer[ing] questions in a random manner, a loquacious, roundabout fashion—if, indeed, she can be brought to answer them at all,"[54] or "greet[ing] his statement with a flick of her eyes—almost as though he had been a bothersome fly and her eyes a horse's tail flicking him away,"[55] Dessa frustrates Nehemiah's attempt to record the events around the coffle revolt.

Ignoring the white man's questions, Dessa, as Jane Mathison Fife remarks, "prevents him from easily constructing a linear narrative from her 'ramblings'".[56] Dessa's narrative springs from memory, from the association of diverse thoughts that lead her to verbalize fragments of her experience, and to return to the same recollection at a later time in order to reveal other unspoken details. In this way, her narrative interferes with Nehemiah's effort to produce a narrative that is linear and meant to be written and read rather than spoken and listened to. In listening to Dessa, the reader enters a spiraled narrative where story depends on memory and the narrative line depends on the return to the same event, image, or feeling. The reader has to follow Dessa's memory trail, while the circles of the spiral widen and a more complete account of her story emerges.

Song

The spiraled configuration of Dessa's narrative is mirrored and reinforced by the patterns of repetition and variation in her songs. Her tunes, like her story, are misinterpreted by Nehemiah who cannot enter the double signification of Dessa's language. Thus the bondwoman's songs, as Jacquelyn A. Fox-Good declares, "construct a surface in which the master sees only his own reflection, only his own rigid constructions, beneath or within which the complexity of what the slaves produce can move. This doubleness of language is, then, the duplicity of the mask, beneath which is 'contained, as well as reflected, a coded, secret, hermetic world, a world discovered only by the initiate.'"[57] I would argue that the projection of Nehemiah's ideology on Dessa's song is a more gradual process than Fox-Good implies. This is significant because it allows Williams to explore not only diverse white attitudes toward slavery but also how direct involvement in the peculiar institution altered white people's perceptions about African American people and culture: "He and Hughes had heard upon approaching the cellar a humming or moaning. It was impossible to define it as one or the other. Nehemiah had been alarmed, but Hughes merely laughed it off as some sort of 'nigger business.' The noise had sounded like some kind of dirge to Nehemiah, but Hughes chuckled when he suggested this."[58] As an outsider, "who had never owned a slave—nor wished to,"[59] Nehemiah is unable to distinguish between black music and "a humming or moaning." On the other hand, Hughes's familiarity with the peculiar institution does not grant him a greater understanding of Dessa's song. Assuming that "singin and loud noise" keep slaves happy, Hughes's stance illustrates how black music is "a coded, secret, hermetic world" to which whites have no access. Although Nehemiah is somewhat skeptical of the view that "a loud nigger is a happy one—expressed again and again while doing research for the *Guide*,"[60] he is unable to identify why Dessa's songs make him feel uneasy, "remind[ing] him unpleasantly of Wilson's 'Raise a song there, Nate,' and Wilson's empty sleeve."[61] Something about either the similarity between the black man's name and that of the rebel Nat Turner or the rhythm of the bondwoman's tune makes Nehemiah associate the sound with black violence, suggesting that initially he thought that there was more to Dessa's song than just "loud noise."

However, Dessa's "humming and moaning," which had "alarmed" Nehemiah, gradually becomes "an absurd monotonous little tune in a minor key"[62] and later a sound he is "so accustomed to [that] these tunes . . . seem like a natural part of the setting, like the clucking of the hens or the lowing of the cattle."[63] Fox-Good argues that "Nehemiah's sense that Dessa's sounds are attuned to 'nature' . . . invests them with the sirenic or orphic power they exert over him, their capacity to attract and soothe him, even as they induce sleep and near immobilization."[64] If it can be said that Dessa's songs induce drowsiness in Nehemiah,[65] his equation of the slave woman's songs with other sounds around the farm has wider implications in *Dessa Rose* than those presented by Fox-Good. In associating black music with nature, the white man fails to acknowledge the cultural significance of the songs. It is his failure to recognize the fact that African Americans have a culture, whole and distinct, which makes Nehemiah overlook Dessa's song as a cultural text and ultimately miss the coded signs that announced her escape.

If Nehemiah cannot hear the appeal of the sound and rhythms of Dessa's song, the lyrics are equally lost to him. He cannot penetrate the vernacular in which Dessa sings, and when she sings to him in a way that allows him to decipher the words, he can only grasp the surface of what is being chanted. Listening to the "Gold Band," Nehemiah dismisses it as "a quaint piece of doggerel which darkies adapt from the scraps of Scripture they are taught," as he discounts "Tell me, sister; tell me, brother," which functions as a signal of Dessa's escape, as "something about the suffering of a poor sinner."[66] Writing off Dessa's spirituals as purely mimetic, in associating either their tonal structure with the sounds of the natural world or their lyrics with a simplified interpretation of the Bible, Nehemiah fails to acknowledge the value of the cultural text before him. In the sacred folk music sung by the slaves, as Houston A. Baker Jr. puts it in *Long Black Song*,

> Pharoah [*sic*] was a very real person: he was the white master who sat on the porch, whip in hand. The River Jordan was not a mystical boundary between earth and heaven: it was the very real Ohio that marked the line between slave and free states. And to "steal away" was not to go docilely home to God but to escape from the Southern land of bondage. The slow and beautiful rhythms spoke not only of another world but of the real sorrow in this world; they spoke of the bare consolations offered by the American slave system, and they rejoiced that an otherworldliness was possible for men [and women] trapped in that degrading institution.[67]

The lyrics of the songs sung by Dessa demonstrate that, masked by the biblical references, the slaves had another message to communicate. When Dessa sings "Lawd give me wings like Noah's dove / Lawd give me wings like Noah's dove / I'd fly cross these fields to the one I love,"[68] the subject of affection can be interpreted as God, as a significant other, or perhaps more likely, as freedom. The reference to the Christian journey from earth to heaven that constitutes the leitmotiv of all of Dessa's songs is, in fact, an allusion to another journey: that from slavery to freedom. In this light, when Dessa sings her first call—"Tell me, brother; tell me, sister, / How long will it be / That a poor sinner got to suffer, suffer here?"[69]—the adverb "here" refers to both slavery and earthly life. Thus Dessa's call is really an expression of her hope for freedom rather than death. In response she hears, "Soul's going to heaven, / Soul's going to ride the heavenly train / Cause the Lawd have called you home."[70] This response "[s]tartled [her and] drew away from the window" because she understood the references to the Underground Railroad veiled by the "heavenly train" and to freedom concealed in the usage of the word "home." When moments later she hears the beginning of another song, "Dessa joined in, suddenly jubilant, her voice floating out across the yard: 'Good news, Lawd, Lawd, good news. / My sister got a seat and I so glad; / I heard from heaven today.'"[71] This coded message that announces Dessa's flight to freedom is only understood by "the initiate," facilitating her escape.

In this way, music fulfills several purposes in *Dessa Rose*. For Kaine, it is not only a creative outlet but also a link to Africa—a way of preserving, as Angela Davis observes, the slaves' "ethnic heritage, even as they were generations removed from their original homeland and perhaps even unaware that their songs bore witness to and affirmed their cultural roots."[72] The spirituals also offer some release from the hardships of slavery and comfort to Dessa. In *Incidents in the Life of a Slave Girl*, the narrator comments on the fact that song provided some momentary relief to the slave: "The congregation struck up a hymn, and sung as though they were free as the birds that warbled round us . . . If you were to hear [the slaves] at such times, you might think they were happy."[73] Song in Williams's novel is also "functional," to make use of Davis's terminology: "Tubman's spirituals were functional not only in the sense that they provided concrete information about the struggle of the liberation, they were also functional in the sense that they assisted in the forging of a collective socio-historical consciousness . . . [For the slave] the spiritual played a fundamental role in communicating the ingredients of that collective consciousness to masses of slaves."[74] In *Dessa Rose*, song functions not only as a means of transmitting information about Dessa's imminent flight but also as a way of illustrating how "the struggle of liberation" of one individual is mirrored in the community's hopes and aspirations of attaining freedom. Song also becomes the sole means of contact between Dessa and the slave community. Confined in a dark cellar, Dessa is completely isolated from the quarters. With the exception of Jemina, the house servant who brought her meals, "no one else came near her."[75] Although Nehemiah's interviews under the shadow of the tree allow her to step out of her cell, he functions as a barrier between Dessa and the slave community of the Hughes Farm. From the white man's shoulder she can see "men or women going about some errand in the yard. Once, [she saw] two wide-eyed, bare-bellied children."[76] The usage of the plural of substantives, such as "men," "women," and "children," illustrate Dessa's inability to recognize the individual members of a small slave community, highlighting her sense of isolation. While vocables such as "once" and "twice" give an indication of the lack of contact between the condemned slave and the quarters. In this way, it is through the vehicle of song that Dessa and the other slaves communicate and announce her return to the African American community.

It is interesting to note that, while on the Hughes Farm, Dessa's loneliness is only relieved by Jemina,

> [t]he big, light-skinned woman [who] came to see her almost every night, often bringing some special fixings from the white folk's supper table . . .
>
> At night, Jemina hunkered down beside the window for a few moments' whispered conversation, meaningless words of encouragement that Dessa appreciated, nonetheless.[77]

Jemina is in *Dessa Rose* the ancestral mother figure that Joanne M. Braxton identifies as a prevailing character in the work of African American women writers.[78] Similar to Linda Brent's grandmother, Jemina provides Dessa with the extra nourishment vital to a pregnant woman and emotional support. The house servant also represents Dessa's link to the world beyond the cellar. It is through Jemina that Dessa is made aware that Nehemiah is writing a book and of other "news that she had overheard in the conversation of her white folks."[79] Moreover, Jemina demonstrates that she "embodies the values of sacrifice, nurturance, and personal courage"[80] when she puts herself at risk by assisting in Dessa's escape. Throughout the novel, the relationships established between the women constitute not only a way of exploring those bonds of family and friendship that sustain individuals through times of peril but also a means of challenging the social order and the preconceived notions of blackness and whiteness in the antebellum South.

The first part of the novel, significantly titled "The Darky," seems to be dominated by Nehemiah's views on Dessa. However, as the novel's prologue had signaled that this is Dessa's narrative, her dreams and recollections of her lover, family, and friends, which are sometimes italicized and extend to several pages, disrupt the white man's narrative and claim space in the text for the black woman's expression. The italicized sections illustrate that despite the dehumanizing experience of slavery, African Americans developed their own culture and established significant family and community bonds. "These sections [in italics]," as Ann E. Trapasso states, "stand suspended outside the action of the novel, outside its chronological time. They assert the humanity and survival of the African American people despite the violence of the slave system."[81]

Coloring White and "'Mammy' Ain't Nobody Name"

In the second section of the novel, titled "The Wench," the narrative alternates between two points of view, Dessa's and that of the white woman whose farm becomes an accidental safe harbor for fugitive slaves. Williams uses this device effectively to explore notions of blackness and whiteness, and particularly to racialize the latter. The critical texts on *Dessa Rose*, in focusing on how the black body is represented in the novel, overlook this rather innovative aspect of Williams's narrative. In "Textual Healing: Claiming Black Women's Bodies, the Erotic and Resistance in Contemporary Novels of Slavery," for example, Griffin presents a discussion of how women writers revise historically constructed images of the black female body but fails to notice how Williams racializes the white body in order to explore how fixed notions of whiteness shape the way the enslaved self sees herself and the hegemonic other. In an article titled "Marking the Body, Demarcating the Body Politic: Issues of Agency and Identity in *Louisa Picquet* and *Dessa Rose*," Shelli B. Fowler points out that in "a culture, an academy with a grand tradition of historical amnesia with reference to . . . systemic imbalances of power between racial groups and with a general reluctance to racialize whiteness . . ., Williams provides a critique of . . . the dominant ideology that supports the production and critical acclaim"[82] of a novel like *Dessa Rose*. However, if in her article she demonstrates that Williams "challenges the historical privileges of whiteness,"[83] then she fails to address how the white body, under the gaze of black female self, is redefined in the novel.

African American women writers have explored the ways in which white standards of beauty affect the self-image of their black female characters. In *I Know Why the Caged Bird Sings*, Maya Angelou dramatizes the effect that idealized white definitions of beauty have on African American girls: "Wouldn't they be surprised when one day I woke out of my black ugly dream, and my real hair, which was long and blond, would take the place of [my] kinky mass . . . ? My light-blue eyes were going to hypnotize them . . . [b]ecause I was really white."[84] In *The Bluest Eye* (1970), Morrison explores how African American girls' identities are shaped by white models of beauty. Pecola's sense of inadequateness is manifested in her desire to have blue eyes, while Claudia had "not yet arrived at the turning point in the development of [her] psyche which would allow [her] to love [Shirley Temple] . . . [She hated] all the Shirley Temples of the world."[85] Confused by the notion conveyed by "[a]dults, older girls, shops, magazines, newspapers, window signs—all the world had agreed that a blue-eyed, yellow-haired, pink-skinned doll was what every girl child treasured,"[86] Claudia dismembers white dolls in an attempt to unveil the essence of desirability that made white women admired, light-skinned girls receive preferential treatment, and made her feel unattractive and unloved.

In *Dessa Rose*, the black body represents more a site of healing than ineptness and it is the white body that is redefined to the reader. Looking at the white woman through Dessa's eyes, the white body becomes the locus of strangeness and unattractiveness conventionally identified with the black skin and physiognomy, dislocating whiteness as an archetype for the familiar and appealing: "The white woman's 'hair was the color of fire; it fell about her shoulders in lank whisps. Her face was very white and seemed to radiate a milky glow; her mouth was like a bloody gash across it.'"[87] The established standards of Western beauty, the straight long hair, the pale skin and the contrasting red lips, are perceived as lifeless and somewhat repulsive. In forcing the reader to look at the white body through Dessa's eyes, Williams is neither merely reversing the supremacist discourses that equated physical difference with lack of intellectual ability and used it the justify the dehumanization of people of African descent, nor simply reversing stereotypes. Rather, she uses the image of the white body, an image that "filled [Dessa] with terror,"[88] in order to dramatize what bell hooks calls "a response to traumatic pain and anguish that remain a consequence of white racist domination, a psychic state that informs and shapes the way black folks 'see' whiteness."[89] It is Dessa's traumatic encounters with white people that color her view of Rufel. In her febrile state Dessa struggles to make sense of what happened to her, where she is, and who the white woman is. However, either dreaming or awake, she identifies Rufel as an antagonistic figure,[90] a deathly presence, and "[s]ometimes it seemed to Dessa that she was drowning in milky skin, ensnared by red hair."[91] In this way, the physical differences between Dessa and Rufel are emphasized in order to unveil the cultural discourses, which produced fixed notions of black and white identities.

These preconceived views of blackness and whiteness are sustained by clearly defined social roles. However, when social positions become somewhat blurred, it becomes increasingly problematic to hold in place the structure of the slave society. Motherhood is one of the critical issues through which boundaries between blacks and whites are redefined. Rufel nurses Dessa's baby, not only reversing the role of the black "Mammy" but also destabilizing the slave and mistress relationship by acknowledging the infant's humanity and refusing to reduce him to chattel. The child was hungry and Rufel could and did feed him:

> Rufel had taken the baby to her bosom almost without thought, to quiet his wailing while Ada and the other darkies settled the girl in the bedroom. More of that craziness, she knew; but then it seemed to her as natural as tuneless crooning or baby talk. The sight of him so tiny and bloodied had pained her with an almost physical hurt and she set about cleaning and clothing him with a single-minded intensity. And only when his cries were stilled and she looked down upon the sleek black head, the nut-brown face flattened against the pearly paleness of her breast, had she become conscious of what she was doing. A wave of embarrassment had swept over her and she had looked guiltily around the parlor . . . he's hungry and only a baby . . . Whatever care she might have had about the wisdom of her action was soon forgotten in the wonder she felt at the baby.[92]

In her sociological study of the relationships established between black and white women in the antebellum South, Elizabeth Fox-Genovese, explains that these women lived their lives quite closely. Black and white women assisted each other in childbearing and rearing, and if slaves frequently nursed their mistresses' children, the opposite, though more sporadic, was also a part of the life of the slaveholding household.[93] However, as Fox-Genovese illustrates, this did not mean that the relationship between female slave and mistress was not tainted with racial prejudice. The daily tasks of running the household brought mistress and slave together but the boundaries of race clearly defined and conditioned their relationships.

The above excerpt illustrates that, for Rufel, the imperative to care for the needs of the child takes precedent over her racial prejudice, as highlighted by expressions such as "almost without thought," "as natural as tuneless crooning," and "a single-minded intensity." However, the white woman's recognition of the vulnerability of the "tiny and bloodied" infant in her arms does not denote that she is above racial discrimination. She is aware that nursing a black baby is an act of transgression. It is interesting to note that when "she become[s] conscious of what she was doing," "she looked guiltily around the parlor." If she were to be seen, she would have to confront the reality of her transgression, illustrating that Williams's text emphasizes the sociocultural roots of racism. The act of nursing the black baby functions in the text as a way of dramatizing race as a social construct.

When Rufel takes the baby to her breast, she is responding to the infant on a human and compassionate level, while the contrast created by "the nut-brown face flattened against the pearly paleness of her breast"[94] serves to emphasize the established racial boundaries.

The routine of suckling Dessa's baby is accompanied by small gestures that bring him closer to Rufel's children. She spoke to him "aloud as she often did when she nursed [her] babies alone"[95] and she "stroked his silken curls" as she used to stroke "the bald heads of her own newborns."[96] However, when the exterior world interferes with this private space, the racial and social divisions between the infant and his wet nurse are exacerbated. The relationship that Rufel establishes with Dessa and their brief but intense exchanges make the white woman look at the child in a different light, even if only temporarily: "[S]he shrank from the thought of nursing him, a *pickaninny*, seeing this for the first time as neighbors might—*would*—see it. His dark skin might as well be fur."[97] The use of "would" is significant in order to convey the improbability of Rufel's statement. In this way, the isolation of the Sutton's Glen, the fact that she is the only white person on a plantation run by escaped slaves, creates an unfamiliar social realm in which racial and socially assigned roles might not be overlooked, but have the potential to be renegotiated. Rufel recognizes that breastfeeding Dessa's child gave her "some real power over the wench,"[98] but facing the fact that "[s]he had used the baby's hunger to spite the wench [made her feel] shamed by the knowledge."[99] This knowledge not only makes Rufel feel "a sudden wave of protectiveness and remorse [and] she climbed back in bed and bared her breast to [the baby's] searching"[100] but also foretells her acknowledgment of the humanity of people of African descent. "Ruth's acceptance of Dessa's baby," as Elizabeth Ann Beaulieu observes, "prepares her for her impulsive response to Nathan's sexual advances and prefigures her later involvement with a man of color."[101]

The atypical realm of the Glen functions as a microcosm where social change can take place because of the fact that its members are displaced from the wider social context. Thus Rufel is freer to confront the ambiguous feelings felt toward the slaves, and more importantly she is able to act on those feelings by helping the runaway slaves and saving Dessa's child's life. Had her husband not been absent, or had she not been estranged from her family, the presence of a white male in the Glen, as Valerie Martin portrays in *Property* (2003), not only would make her powerless but also would have curtailed her possibility of self-growth: "She would have no more rights than they when Bertie came back."[102] This is an admission that makes Rufel recognize that her attitude toward the escaped slaves has changed. Bertie "drove them hard and stinted on their food and clothing. Rufel knew this without ever having really seen it . . . And she had accepted this as long as she didn't hear the screams ... Could she be that blind again?"[103] Her increased understanding of the slave experience also makes Rufel consider, for the first time, the similarities between her social and economic status and that of the African Americans. The acknowledgement of the *other's* humanity results in the recognition of her economic destitution and her social alienation, and the profound realization that she has to assume control of her life, prompting her participation in the escapees' fraudulent plan to raise money in order to attain her own freedom.

In this way, in *Dessa Rose*, social awareness springs from personal experience and growth. Nevertheless, even in the world of possibility created by Williams in the isolation of the Glen, the past lingers over black and white characters alike, making their feelings toward each other ambiguous, if not contradictory. Dessa is grateful for the fact that the white woman nurses her child, but this generous gesture not only defies all that Dessa knows about white women but further exacerbates the contradictory nature of her feelings toward Rufel: "And the white woman let them stay, nursed ... It went against everything she had been taught to think about white women but to inspect that fact too closely was almost to deny her own existence."[104] The usage of the verbal form of "to teach" emphasizes notions of race as sociocultural constructs and draws attention the difficulty that characters face when "all [they] knew" is destabilized. In this manner, this second section of the novel signals how past knowledge conditions the present and the imperative to learn new coordinates in order not to "deny [one's] own existence," but to gain a new perspective over oneself and the *other.*

From Monologue to Dialogue

As in the first part of *Dessa Rose*, the distinction between fact and fiction becomes a critical issue. However, if in the second section Dessa's body is unshackled, her voice gradually becomes engirdled. Thus in this part of the novel there is a struggle to attain what Keith Byerman calls "discursive power in which the fictions take the form of quests for voice, for authority over the narration itself."[105] Rufel's social status allows her to hold discursive power. Williams dramatizes this in the scenes in which, while sewing, Rufel talks about her youth more to herself than to the drowsy Dessa. It is interesting to note that, although the latter is too weak and confused to respond, Rufel keeps talking. It is obvious that the white woman's loneliness prompts her monologue. However, this is also the only way she knows how to communicate with people of African descent. She expects an expression of interest, perhaps a brief comment, or a facial expression to reinforce her views. When talking about fashion with Annabelle, Rufel reacts furiously to the girl's lack of interest.[106] Treating the enslaved as an extension of herself, she expects her interlocutor to echo her, rather than engage her in dialogue. Even when Rufel remembers those moments when Mammy disagreed with her, she, as Ashraf H. A. Rushdy insightfully points out, "attempts to reconstruct Dorcas's voice so that it echoes her own."[107] For example, Rufel dismisses Ada's story of sexual abuse at the hands of her master and anticipates Dorcas's conformity. Yet the slave frustrates her expectation: "'Miz Rufel!' Mammy had said sharply. 'You keep a lady tongue in your mouth. Men,' Mammy had continued with a quailing glance as Rufel opened her mouth, voice overriding Rufel's attempt to speak, 'men can do things a *lady* can't even guess at.'"[108] However, unable to conceive Dorcas as a separate individual, Rufel recreates the slave's words and emotions in a way that reflect her own: "Mammy had probably not believed Ada's story herself, Rufel thought now, but had not wanted to antagonize Ada. No, Rufel had concluded, hurrying now lest she be trapped in grief and fear, 'the cruel master' was just to play on her sympathy."[109]

In "Reading Mammy: The Subject of Relation in Sherley Anne Williams' *Dessa Rose*," Rushdy argues that the manner in which Rufel appropriates Dorcas's voice and narrative represents "her own family inheritance,"[110] the way the white woman learned to interact with slaves, and it is her exchange with Dessa about "Mammy" that triggers "a state of crises,"[111] causing Rufel to seek Dorcas's history. However, it was worth noting that, while the white woman reconstructs Dorcas's utterance and sentiment so that they do not differ from her own, she is not unaware of her act of appropriation. "Hurrying," she strives to make the memory recede, "lest she be trapped in grief and fear." If the vocable "grief" points toward Rufel's sense of loss, the word "fear" evokes the seed of doubt that Dorcas's thoughts and feelings may have not been similar to those of Rufel. In this way, Williams seeks a level of ambiguity and complexity that Rushdy's analysis seems to overlook. This uncertainty is crucial in a text that aims to portray round, rather than flat, characters. Williams's novel not only reveals an intricate history but also illustrates how the personal influenced the political arena of the antebellum South. Individuals made choices that contributed to the dehumanization of people of African descent. Rufel's position in the patriarchal order was weak, but she could not escape the fact that all she knew about Mammy was what both herself and her family imposed on their slave's identity—a fabricated name, date of birth, and history.

Through her brief but tempestuous exchange with Dessa, Rufel is forced to acknowledge that she hardly knew the woman she called "Mammy" and in whom she confided and implicitly trusted. Rufel has to come to terms with the fact that her memories of Mammy reveal very little about the woman she became accustomed to think of as an extension of herself:

> "Wasn't no 'mammy' to it." The words burst from Dessa. She knew even as she said it what the white woman meant. "Mammy" was a servant, a slave (Dorcas?) who had nursed the white woman . . . But, goaded by the white woman's open-mouthed stare, she continued, "Mammy ain't made you nothing!"
>
> "Why, she—" The white woman stopped, confused . . .
>
> Seeing it, Dessa lashed out again. "You don't even know mammy."
>
> "I do so," the white woman said indignantly, "Pappa give her—"
>
> "Mammy live on the Vaugham plantation near Simeon on the Beauford River, McAllen County." . . . The white woman gaped like a fish, Dessa thought contemptuously, just like a fish out of water . . .
>
> "My, my—*My* mammy—" the white woman sputtered.
>
> The words exploded inside Dessa . . . "Your 'mammy'!" No *white* girl could ever taken [Carrie's] place in mammy's bosom; no one. "You ain't got no 'mammy,'" she snapped.
>
> "I do—I did so." [. . .]
>
> "'Mammy' ain't nobody name, not they real one."
>
> "Mam—"
>
> The white woman's baby started to cry . . . Dessa's voice overrode the tearful wail, seeming to pin the white woman in the chair.[112]

Dessa "knew even as she said it what the white woman meant. 'Mammy' was a servant, a slave (Dorcas?)" and Rufel also "knew they were talking about two different people."[113] Hence, this confrontation is based not on a misunderstanding, since both women are aware of the fact that they are talking about distinct persons, but rather on "quests for voice, for authority over narration itself." Dessa's response is rather distinct from the vaguely engaged way in which she used to address Nehemiah. Vocables such as "burst," "lashed out," "exploded" point not only to the impetuous nature of the exchange but also to Dessa's newly found voice. On the other hand, when instead of a nod, Rufel gets a reply, her voice falters. When the terms that governed the interaction between mistress and slave are subverted, Rufel is "just like a fish out of water." The silence left by "the white woman's open-mouthed stare" creates the necessary gap in the narrative from which the history of the black female can emerge through Dessa's voice:

> Dessa heaved herself to her knees, flinging her words in the white woman's face. "Mammy gave birth to ten chi'ren that come in the world living." . . . The first one Rose after herself; the second one died before the white folks named it. Mammy called her Minta after a cousin she met once. Seth was the first child lived to go into the fields. Little Rose died while Mammy was carrying Amos—carried off by diphtheria . . . Remembering the names now the way mammy used to tell them, . . . lest her poor, lost children die to living memory as they had in her world . . .

> Even buried under years of silence, Dessa could not forget. She started on the names of the dead before she realized that the white woman had gone . . . Dessa's voice continued . . . [114]

Dessa recites her mother's history, a narrative shared and learned between her mother's knees when hair was being braided and the familial past weaved in her memory.[115] Calling "the names now the way mammy used to tell them," Dessa evokes a history passed on in the quarters via word of mouth in a realm outside the master's gaze. In this way, Dessa's narrative has only been "buried under years of silence," ignored by the pages of the hegemony's history, which silenced the slave's voice.

Rufel has to come to terms with the fact that, although Dessa is not telling Dorcas's personal story, she could be doing so in the sense that she is narrating the history of the African American female—a history silenced by Rufel, since she constructed Dorcas's life story so that it would supplement her own. Dorcas was not born on Valentine's Day, the date Rufel had chosen for her birthday,[116] nor had her father "given her Mammy as a birthday present as Rufel sometimes claimed,"[117] nor was Dorcas's name Mammy; the Carsons "called her Mammy because Mrs. Carson thought the title made her seem as if she had been with the family for a long time."[118] The creation of Rufel's life record as the epitome of the Southern lady required the erasure of her slave's history. Ultimately, it was not Dorcas who "didn't know a thing about history,"[119] but Rufel, who "had never asked."[120]

Dessa asserts her "authority over narration" because she recites a history that was entrusted to her in dialogic practice. Rufel's continuous monologue, on the other hand, left only silence where the other's voice should be. The white woman, as Rushdy observes, "denies the dialogue of voices in her imagination and thereby loses the opportunity for communal connection."[121] Left with only her memories, Rufel only has her part of the story: "Had Mammy minded when the family no longer called her name? Was that why she changed mine? . . . Was what she had always thought loving and cute only revenge, a small reprisal for all they'd taken from her? How old *had* Mammy been? Why had they gone to France? . . . Had she had any children?"[122] Seeking out Dorcas's identity, Rufel begins to realize that African American history is one of destitution—Mammy was even stripped of her name, of resistance, the slave duplicated the mistress's gesture by renaming her, and a history of ambiguity because the love and care that Dorcas devoted to her charge was tainted by her status as commodity.

Attempting to "recall the familiar face [Rufel] see[s] the familiar features . . . altered so the face seemed that of a stranger."[123] To Rufel "it was as if the wench had taken her beloved Mammy and put a stranger in her place."[124] In order to reconstruct Dorcas's face in her memory, Rufel has to engage in dialogic practice with the other slaves. Seeking Mammy's history, she finds those of Harker, Dessa, and Nathan. When the latter tells her Dessa's story, "Rufel could see the scene described as he described it . . . She could almost feel the fire that must have lived in the wench's thighs."[125] Yet, if her first reaction is one of empathy, she promptly reconstructs Dessa's story so that it fits her distorted image of slave women: "I bet she was making out to the master; that's why the mistress was so cruel. I bet that's what it was."[126] Being familiar with the ways in which the slaveholding system justified the subjugation of African American people, Nathan asks Rufel, "The mistress have to see the welts in the darky's hide, eh?"[127] Her shame weakens her reply and she is only able to utter a weak "Ye—."[128] However, her answer illustrates that in attempting to interpret African American history using the terms of reference that render it silenced, Rufel, comparable to Nehemiah, misses the meaning of the oral text before her. In this way, resembling Nehemiah, the counterfeit mistress's distrust of her interlocutor is established not only on the basis of his skin color but also on the lack of value that she attributes to orality.

Although Rufel barely resists uncovering Dessa's body in search for tangible evidence of her history, she engages in dialogue with the fugitive:

> "What's your name, gal?" Rufel asked sharply.
>
> "Dessa. *Dessa Rose*, ma'am," she said in a raspy voice.
>
> . . . "I mean, why your mistress use you so?"
>
> "Cause she can," the wench said on a long shuddering breath as she turned her face away.
>
> Rufel was stunned for a moment by the ring of utter truth in the statement.[129]

Moving from a monologic to dialogic practice, Rufel becomes aware of an African American history that does not exist simply as an appendix to her own personal record. Williams, however, carefully avoids a single epiphany as a means of negotiating notions racial identity. While Rufel does not name Dessa, as the above excerpt illustrates, she assumes that the runaway slave does not know the correct pronunciation of her own name and refers to her as Odessa. Rufel also "call[s] Ada 'Auntie' like they was some kin"[130] and considers that "as mistress of the place, she ought at least to have been advised"[131] in relation to the naming of Dessa's child. It is interesting to note that Rufel claims an entitlement to name the infant not because she saved his life by nursing him but on the basis of her social status as mistress of the Glen, illustrating that despite Rufel's awareness of the *other's* humanity, she has yet, as Nicole King states, to find "her role as a white woman in the antebellum South, not according to tradition but to the particular relationships in which she participates."[132]

The "utter truth" of Dessa's statement owes not to the fact that Rufel was told something she did not previously know but to the fact that the slave's words made Rufel confront what she already knew. What she knew is that the master's control over his slave was absolute and that "[i]t didn't take much"[133] to provoke the wrath of what Martin calls the "soul-deadening system."[134] "And Mammy—Had anyone ever whipped her? . . . [Rufel thought] remembering Mammy's tart answers, her way of forgetting to do what she didn't want to do . . . Often it had taken no more with Bertie than a broken plowshare . . . or a darky who didn't move fast enough."[135] Thus, in Williams's novel, the acknowledgment of the *other* depends not on an epiphanic moment but rather on the choice to no longer ignore what one had always known. *Dessa Rose* illustrates how slavocracy depended on rigid binary concepts such as superior versus inferior, rational versus irrational, and good versus evil. However, when a level of uncertainty about the *other's* inferior, illogical, or depraved nature creeps in, it becomes increasingly difficult to hold the social structure of the slave society in place.

"True to her trade as a caricaturist," as Deborah E. McDowell observes, "Rufel has an exaggerated and distorted image of Dessa and the other escaped slaves."[136] However, after her exchanges with Dessa and Nathan, Rufel can no longer ignore the disparity between the representations of African Americans propagated in nineteenth-century antebellum South and the human faces before her: "She had seen coffles; they were a common enough sight on the riverboats, the men loaded the chains, the women with scarcely enough rags to cover them decently, all of them dirty and desolate. She found it hard to reconcile that memory with the presence of [Nathan]. They seemed to personify wretchedness; he glowed with life."[137] Rufel's impression of Nathan is clearly influenced by the fact that she is attracted to him. In this way, striving to represent how the personal conditions the political, Williams illustrates that Rufel has difficulty in recognizing the escapees' heterogeneous history. While she moved away from the time when "[n]either she nor Timmy would ever recognize [the Glen slaves],"[138] she still associated "even Ada with the stock cuts used to illustrate newspaper advertisements of slave sales and runaways: pants rolled up to the knees, bareheaded, a bundle attached to a stick slung over one shoulder, the round white eyes in the inky face giving a slightly comic air to the whole."[139]

The slaves' stereotypical representation as flat figures on the page indicates the loss of their multifaceted history. Although Rufel learns that the slavery experiences of Ada, Nathan, Harker, and Dessa are varied, she nonetheless distrusts the oral histories that are related to her and takes refuge in the textual representations of the peculiar institution, which reflects and reinforces the slaveholding ideology.

In this way, it is only when Rufel sees that "[t]he wench's loins looked like a mutilated cat face" and that "[s]car tissue plowed through her pubic region so that no hair would ever grow there again"[140] and reads the imprint of Dessa's painful history on her skin that Rufel can acknowledge the black woman's experience and the authority of her oral record: "'Your mammy birthed you, and mines, mines just helped to raise me. But she loved me,' she couldn't help adding, 'she loved me, like yours loved you.'"[141] In this admission, the white woman also recognizes Dorcas's history as separate from her own; a history that cannot be retrieved and that might have been similar to that of Dessa's mother. Rufel will never find out the answer to the question that seems to haunt her: "And the children, Mammy's children—girls or boys? Had Mammy been taken from them? How did they bare such a pain? she wondered, thinking then of a branding iron searing tender flesh."[142] It is worth noting that Williams establishes motherhood as the necessary common ground for Rufel's understanding of the female slave experience. She may not know the hardships of fieldwork, or the trials of sexual abuse, what it feels to be whipped or branded, but she can imagine the pain in the loss of her children.

Dessa is willing to accept Rufel as long as she adheres to the social role assigned to her as the mistress of the Glen. When the white woman transgresses social and racial boundaries by establishing a sexual relationship with Nathan, Dessa not only perceives the threat that such a relationship poses to the group but also is perturbed by the fact that her history becomes intrinsically linked to that of Rufel. In order to make sense out of her chaotic experience, Dessa attributes one single identity to white people and makes a concerted effort to obliterate them from her life record. For her, Rufel is included under the category of "[w]hite woman . . . everything [she] feared and hated,"[143] a collective character that "had taken everything in the world from [her]."[144] It is worth noting that in the italicized text of Dessa's dreams and recollections, white people occupy a quasi-marginal role. In fact, the Vaugham master and mistress are no more than faceless agents of evil in Dessa's memories: "[T]hese wasn't peoples in my book."[145] Seeing "Nathan sprawled in whiteness, white sheets, white bosom," Dessa views him as "nothing but than a mark . . . That's what we was in white folks' eyes, nothing but marks to be used, wiped out. Hadn't I seed it in Mistress, in that white man's eyes under the tree?"[146] What she does not realize is that in refusing to see Rufel beyond the mask of "white woman"—a mask imposed by Dessa—she also makes the counterfeit mistress a mark to be "wiped out" from her autobiography. Harker tries to deconstruct that image: "You know, Dess, Ruth ain't the one sold you; her husband ain't killed Kaine—."[147] However, it is not until he points out to Dessa that hers and Rufel's history are already linked, that the black woman commences to redefine Rufel's identity, while she reviews her own: "We *been* trusting her all along, just like *she* been trusting us."[148]

Avoiding, as argued, a single epiphany as a means of redefining notions racial identity, Williams opts for the creation of situations where the political is negotiated through personal experience:

> The white woman was subject to the same ravishment as me; this the thought that kept me awake. I hadn't knowed that white mens could use a white woman like that, just take her by force same as they could do with us.
>
> . . . Cause they could. I never will forget the fear that come on me when Miz Lady called me on Mr. Oscar, that *knowing* that she was as helpless in this as I was, that our only protection was ourselfs and each others.[149]

Comparing the sexual politics of the antebellum Northern and Southern states, John D'Emilio and Estelle B. Freedman argue that the rural character of the social and economic organization of the slave states "prevented the development of the urban, commercial and industrial economy that gave rise to social—and sexual—transformation in the northern states. In contrast . . . the Southern planter family remained a patriarchy in which a man ruled over the women, children, and slaves within his household."[150] In the South, the construct of white female purity resulted in a greater control of white women's sexuality due to the belief in their "moral weakness, rather than [their] moral superiority"[151] and the sexual abuse of black women promoted by their image as sexually licentious in a system that tied sexual exploitation to the preservation of racial supremacy. Living most of her life away from the master's house, Dessa ignored the extent to which the white male controlled white women's sexuality. While the regulation of marriages according to issues of property and family connection, decisions on family planning, and the strict limitation of women's movements—single or married women could not travel or socialize without a chaperon without risking their reputations—was socially accepted,[152] the women who deviated from this rigid control suffered serious consequences.

If the sexual politics of the South depended on the idealization and protection of the white female while using black women as sexual outlets, it does not necessarily mean, as Dessa discovers, that the white woman's apparent privileged position was always secure. For over a period of two years, politician James Henry Hammond, as D'Emilio and Freedman state, sexually abused his four teenage nieces. When one of the girls revealed the abuse to her father, her uncle was merely temporarily estranged from his wife and social status, and his political career recovered from the scandal, with Hammond later becoming a member of the Senate. However, "the reputations of the four nieces were ruined . . . As one observer explained, 'no man who valued his standing could marry one of the Hampton girls.'"[153] This episode illustrates that, in terms of the sexual privilege of the

Southern planter, the much cherished purity of the white woman was not always a deterrent. Dessa's assumption that the "white woman was subject to the same ravishment" as the black female does not have historical resonance, but Williams makes use of the Southern sexual dynamics in to order to create a context in which fixed notions of identity are reshaped through common personal experience. In Dessa's realization, that "our only protection was ourselfs and each others," is implied both a sense of mutual reliance and a degree of parity with a figure that, thus far, she defined in opposition to herself.

Voice

In *Dessa Rose*, Williams continually plays with issues of identity in order to expose it as a fluid, rather than a fixed concept, as illustrated by the titles of the three primary sections of the novel. While the first and the second parts of the text, "The Darky" and "The Wench," respectively, denote the black woman's entrapment in an identity established by the hegemonic *other*, the third section, significantly titled "The Negress," which, as Dessa's future lover explains to her, is French for "black woman,"[154] signals her newly found sense of self.

The novel establishes stereotypical representations of race only to reveal characters that do not conform to a standardized sociocultural image. Looking into Nathan's face for the first time, Rufel "blinked, expecting to see the bulbous lips and bulging eyes of a burnt-cork minstrel. Instead she looked into a pair of rather shadowy eyes and strongly defined features that were—handsome!"[155] Nathan's facial features do not coincide with Rufel's idea of a black man and "[s]he looked again,"[156] beginning to distinguish the individual from the caricature. Similarly, it is in the chasm between Dorcas, the slave's name, and "Mammy," the fabricated designation, that Rufel commences to enquire about the black woman's identity. Ironically, it is under the disguise of skilled and faithful slaves on the auction block that showed the escapees, as Dessa puts it, that "slavery didn't have no hold on us no more . . . This, I told myself, this what we come to get."[157]

In this way, it is interesting to observe that in the novel's closing scene, Dessa and Rufel reach a sense of understanding by revealing their private selves to each other while using the disguise of the helpless white lady and of the dim-witted slave in order to deceive the peculiar institution personified by Nehemiah: "Friend or not, best she could do for me then was to prove that I wasn't nothing but her slave."[158] In this final episode, Williams brings together the prevailing motives of the text, the tension between orality and literacy, the boundaries between individuality and caricature, masking and unmasking, and the blurred frontier between fact and fiction, in order to grant Dessa's freedom by employing the master's tools of oppression. Nehemiah yet again turns to the written word as a means of establishing Dessa's identity: "White man say I had to be locked up and started reading from that paper. 'Hundred-dollar reward. Scaped. Dark complexed. Spare built. Shows the white of her eyes—.'"[159] The sheriff's reply illustrates how Williams subverts the institutionalized caricature of African Americans in order to conceal, rather than reveal Dessa's identity: "Nemi, that sound like about twenty negroes I knows of personally."[160] Although Dessa "match[es] the description in the poster,"[161] the characterization is too general for the sheriff to associate it with the woman before him. Defeated by a poster that renders Dessa almost faceless, Nehemiah turns to another written text, the letter R branded on the black woman's thigh. This is the text that when read by the white man would confirm that Dessa was "something so terrible . . . wasn't even human."[162]

While the conflicting stories unfold in the sheriff's office, almost like in a play within the narrative, the outcome seems to depend on the credibility of Rufel's custom and performance as "a respectable white lady."[163] The white man's unkempt appearance—"his shirt didn't even have a collar; his ankles dirty . . . with no hose on his feet," while beads of sweat formed in his forehead—did not match the figure of the cultivated man of science that he wanted to project. On the other hand, Rufel's dress and demeanor with a child in her arms matches both figures of the plantation, mistress and helpless woman, easy prey for men like Nehemiah. The white woman rises to her role, and even when the predicament in which she finds herself causes her to stutter, both men present "thought that she was stuttering about Nemi being so crude up in her face, talking under a darky's clothes."[164] Williams's usage of the artifice of the mask yet again highlights the fluidity of notions of identity based on racial and social status. Rufel's disguise confers on her the reliability and authority over Dessa's life record, which the fugitive lacked and a poor white was not expected to have: "it was the word of a crazy white man against a respectable white lady."[165]

Nevertheless, it is an old black woman who is summoned to give the final word on the text printed on Dessa's flesh. The arrival of Aunt Chole in the jail, almost like a deus ex machina, functions as a way of conferring African Americans authority on their history. The positive intervention of this character initially seems to point toward the figure of the elder who will bear witness to the history of the community. Running her hands over the young woman's back, however, Aunt Chole finds the smooth surface of a *tabula rasa*. While refusing to see the "corduroyed welts cross [Dessa's] hips,"[166] the old woman not only returns to Dessa the authority over her history but also allows her to heal by leaving untouched "the place Harker had kissed, had made beautiful with his lips."[167]

Rejecting the "the word of some nearsighted mammy,"[168] Nehemiah turns to his own text as proof of Dessa's identity in a desperate attempt to make her captive with his written text:

> "I know it's her," Nemi say. "I got her down here in my book." . . . Clara reached for the book and knocked it out of his hand. The pages wasn't bound in the cover and they fell out, scattering about the floor. [. . .]
>
> "Nemi ain't nothing but some scribbling on here," sheriff say. "Can't no one read this."
>
> Miz Lady was turning over the papers in her hand. "And these is blank, sheriff," she say.[169]

The woman captured in the white amanuensis's book is a barely human, a sexually promiscuous slayer and a "lying sow."[170] Thus there is a sense of irony implied in Dessa's words later echoed by Rufel: "I knew he'd mistook me for somebody else name Dessa."[171] Dessa pleads with Rufel to reveal who she is: "Tell them who I am, Mistress."[172] It is obvious that Dessa is referring to her persona as Rufel's servant and Clara's mammy. However, it is the series of masking and unmasking in this scene that leads to its closing when both women tell each other their names and Dessa hugs the white woman's child, implying also Ruth's embrace. In this way, in *Dessa Rose*, motherhood facilitates both the reshaping of racial and social divisions and a means of self-expression that society precluded.

Oral and Written History

In the closing scene of her novel, Williams seems to put her protagonist in "an unenviable [position] with a character [she] didn't like," to quote the novelist. The scattered pages of his notebook not only cause the chaos that render his text incoherent but, in fact, lead to its erasure. If the sheriff cannot decode Nehemiah's writing, Rufel actually sees the pages blank, denoting that past experience taught her to overlook the version of African American history in the nineteenth-century white annals. It is significant that it is Clara who, in Dessa's arms, knocks Nehemiah's book in a gesture that suggests a sense of hope for the future. Hence, the alliance that the white man attributes to womanhood—"You-all in this together . . . womanhood? . . . All alike"[173]—seems also to cross generational lines. In passing on her history to her child and grandchildren, Dessa wonders, "*Do* [Rufel] *call my name to Clara?*"[174] The black woman's history is now as smooth as her back, a *tabula rasa* to be printed with the sound of her own voice.

In *From Behind the Veil: A Study of Afro-American Narrative*, Robert Stepto observes that in *Their Eyes Were Watching God*, Zora Neale Hurston's decision to have "Janie's tale—her personal history in and as a literary form—told by an omniscient third person narrator, rather than by a first-person narrator, implies that Janie has not really won her voice and self after all—that her author . . . cannot see her way clear to giving Janie her voice outright."[175] In this way, Hurston creates a hierarchic relationship not only between authorial narrator and protagonist but also between standard and black English. Containing Janie's first-person narrative within a third-person narrative in standard English, is Hurston's way of validating the African American voice and vernacular. In *Corregidora*, as discussed in the previous chapter, Jones breaks out of this framed narrative, and by doing so she not only removes the hierarchic relationship between standard English and black vernacular but also confers authority to the African American oral tradition by creating a narrative "written in the first person as if an audience were being *spoken to*,"[176] rather than written to.

Williams, in turn, offers a third narrative model. Her usage of the omniscient narrator in the first and second main sections of the novel is not a matter of establishing the legitimacy of the African American voice, but a way of representing several perspectives of slavery while exposing the hierarchic relationship between literacy and orality that has conditioned the modes of representation of African Americans in the hegemonic text. In Williams's exposure of the ideologies that conditioned race relations in the antebellum South, the narrative form developed by Jones would not allow the necessary space for the hegemonic voices of Nehemiah and Rufel to emerge, while Hurston's framed narrative would not have utterly freed her protagonist from the white man's text.

The third-person narrative, as we have seen, is essential in *Dessa Rose* for reasons other than those exclusively related to the establishment of the legitimacy of the black vernacular and the folk narrator. First, the omniscient narrator alerts the reader to the white amanuensis's unreliability, both as a recorder and narrator of Dessa's story, disrupting the white man's control over the narrative and cautioning the reader against the perspective he presents about Dessa and African American people in general. Second, the omniscient narrator has another crucial role in the first and second sections of *Dessa Rose*—that of unifying a seemingly disjointed narrative. Williams's usage of the omniscient narrator and standard English is not a matter of validating the African American vernacular, but a way of representing several perspectives of slavery and linking them in a cohesive narrative line. Finally, the presence of the third-person narrator is crucial in signaling Dessa's journey from being a character in a white man's text to finding her own voice as the narrator of her own history. Hence, it is important to note that the presence of this narrator is stronger in the first part of the novel and gradually fades away to give place to Dessa's first-person narrative. The narrative device of the omniscient narrator is crucial in creating the necessary time and space in the narrative to prepare the protagonist to assume control over the narration. Dessa goes from feverish digression in the first section of the novel to struggling to claim her free self and voice in part two, and finally achieving first-person control over her narrative in part three. This is something that partly happens years after the events took place, when she finally finds a means of giving expression to her thoughts and emotions.

The difficulty of constructing a coherent narrative line at the time the events took place illustrates the necessary usage of the omniscient narrator so that the protagonist would have the time to order her chaotic experience and find a voice that could express it. This difficulty becomes apparent, for example, when Dessa cannot articulate what she felt in relation to the sexual relationship established between Rufel and Nathan, recognizing, years later, her struggle for self-expression: "I couldn't put into words all this that was going through my head. I didn't have the words, the experience to say these things. All I could do was feel and it was like my own flesh had betrayed me."[177] Years later, the black woman also communicates her state of confusion and her difficulty in expressing her thoughts and emotions: "I didn't have no words to make sense of what my eyes was seeing, much less what I'd been doing."[178] What Williams illustrates is that the slave's history is compromised not only by the lack of literacy but also by the difficulty inherent in claiming the words that could express the experience and creating a linguistic order out of the chaos of the slave experience. This process is essential in a novel that strives to expose the falsification of African American history and identity when the voice of the black woman, or man, is silenced.

It is worth noting that Williams establishes a narrative tension between Dessa's voice and those of Rufel and Nehemiah—a tension between orality and literacy, vernacular and standard English—that informs both the content and the form of the text. Thus Dessa's voice is present throughout the text and given emphasis by italicizing the text of the prologue and her dreams and recollections. These sections in italics create a diegetic level that is separate from the hegemonic narrative, affirming the black woman's experience and voice. Hence, when the folk voice assumes narrative control in the third section of the novel, this is a significantly familiar, rather than a strange voice to the reader, stressing both the chronological and the psychological time essential for the untangling of emotional knots and the establishment of Dessa's first-person oral narrative.

Dessa's chronicle acquires the form of a folk tale, a narrative mode learned between her mother's knees: "*This is where I learned to listen, . . . where I first learned to speak, from listening at grown peoples talk.*"[179] While plaiting Dessa's hair, the mother interweaved the loose strands of the family history, passing to Dessa oral tools that allowed African Americans to assert their humanity, history, and a distinct culture that emerged despite the degrading experience of slavery. Thus, in constructing Dessa's first-person narrative, Williams molds the written text so that African American orality and its tale-telling tradition are sculpted on the printed page.

The novelist makes use of some of the features that Jones attributes to the oral story in *Liberating Voices: Oral Tradition in African American Literature*. Time, for example, is condensed and acquires the fluidity of the folk tale, as illustrated by the use of expressions such as "This was another evening, maybe a day or so later"[180] and "This was another time."[181] Williams also recreates what Jones calls "the dynamics of real conversation" that punctuate Dessa's narrative, conferring a sense of proximity to the narrated events. However, it is interesting to observe that Williams does not create the illusion that her character can remember verbatim what was uttered: "This is not exactly what [Nehemiah] say, you understand; what none of them said. I can't put my words together like they did."[182] Rather, the writer exposes how her character appropriates the hegemonic discourse and "populates it," as Mikhail Bakhtin puts it, "with [her] own intention, [her] own accent . . . adapting it to [her] own semantic and expressive intention."[183] In this way, the hegemonic other's standard English is transformed in Dessa's oral text in order to serve her own narrative purposes. In *Dessa Rose*, this process of translating the hegemony's standard English into vernacular is not a simple satirical inversion of the white man's appropriation and falsification of the African American narrative; rather, it serves to dismantle the cultural constructs that equated literacy with intellectual ability and the aptitude to create one's own historical record. In *Dessa Rose*, Williams illustrates how the lack of literacy does not curtail African Americans' ability to construct their history.

Dessa's oral history, composed as a folk tale, "as if an audience were being *spoken to*," rather than written to, requires the presence of an interlocutor. Jones's observations about *The Autobiography of Miss Jane Pittman* are also valid in relation to *Dessa Rose* in the sense that in both novels, "there are direct comments to the listener; the listener is as present as the storyteller."[184] The presence of Dessa's audience becomes more pronounced as her narrative evolves. From the usage of the substantive "honey"[185] to expressions such as "you know" and "you understand,"[186] the faceless listener acquires more distinct contours toward the end of the third section, where Dessa refers to it as "child" and "children,"[187] and the reader finally realizes in the epilogue that she is speaking to her grandchildren. Although Dessa passes on her history to the children while braiding their hair, as her mother had done, and Mony listened to her story so many times that he "tell it to his babies like the memories was his, stead of things he heard when he was coming up," the grandchild can write it down: "[*I*] *t wrote down . . .* [and] *the child say it back*."[188] The telling and retelling of Dessa's memories as a means of ensuring historical continuity evoke the means of transmission of personal and cultural memory in *Corregidora.* In Jones's work, the passing on of history for Ursa's ancestors can only be achieved via the spoken word. For Great Gram and Gram, only the spoken word cannot be destroyed by the hegemonic written text: "*The important thing is making generations. They can burn the papers but they can't burn conscious, Ursa. And that what makes the evidence. And that's what makes the verdict*."[189] In contrast, Williams has her protagonist entrust her history to her grandchild's written word, significantly discarding the figure of the sympathetic white abolitionist, who could make a written record of Dessa's life. When "*the child say it back*" she recognizes the narrative that came out "*from [her] own lips*,"[190] an experience rather different from the time when Nehemiah flicked through the pages of his note book and read to Dessa, who bewildered asked, "I really say that?" As Dessa comes to terms with the fact that white people also figure "in [her] book," she comes to understand that orality is not in binary opposition to literacy. The novel's closing suggests the tensions inherent in the works of African American historical fiction that while reclaiming and emphasizing the black oral tradition, fix the organic tale in the silent confines of the written text.

5

"Her Best Thing, Her Beautiful, Magical Best Thing"

Toni Morrison's *Beloved* and Phyllis Perry's *Stigmata*

Contexts

Recent portrayals of the slavery era are dominated by two main trends: the genealogical novel and narratives that use fantastic and magical realist elements in order to represent history. Linda Beatrice Brown's *Crossing Over Jordan* (1995), Connie Briscoe's *A Long Way from Home* (1999), and Lalita Tademy's *Cane River* (2001) all explore the lives of several generations of African American women of the same family dealing with issues of racism, sexual exploitation, miscegenation, and passing, which not only blur racial boundaries but also depict the complexities of African American history. In these multigenerational narratives, the mother-and-daughter relationship emerges as an essential conductor of history. In this sense, these are novels that continue the African American tradition established by the novels discussed in previous chapters, *Jubilee, Corregidora*, and *Dessa Rose*. J. California Cooper's *In Search of Satisfaction* (1994) and *The Wake of the Wind* (1998) are also narratives told across generational lines in order to reconstruct African American history by drawing on family chronicles.

Cooper's *Family* (1991), Phyllis Perry's *Stigmata* (1998), and Bertice Berry's *Redemption Song* (2000) are novels that combine the real and the magical in order to evoke the past. In *Family*, African American history is told by the spirit of Clora who, after escaping slavery by committing suicide, chronicles the lives of her children in the years before the Civil War and in its aftermath. In *Redemption Song*, the past is evoked by the encounter between Fina and Ross who meet in Miss Cozy's bookshop in contemporary Cleveland to read together the only known copy of the diary of Iona, a slave who never learned to read or write but seemed to have suddenly gained the gift of literacy. The journal depicts the dehumanizing experience of slavery, while Fina and Ross come gradually to realize that the story that they are reading is actually the narrative of their own past lives, a novel in which the knowledge of the past becomes a spiritual journey.

In the present chapter I will concentrate on the more innovative of these two trends, the magical realist narrative, focusing on *Beloved* (1987) and *Stigmata*. These novels mark a departure from realistic modes of representing history and, therefore, signal an important development of the African American historical novel. In both Toni Morrison's and Perry's works, the magical emerges as an essential narrative strategy to represent a lost history while reworking the genealogical narrative tradition. Both *Beloved* and *Stigmata* share with the novels discussed in previous chapters the preoccupation with the gaps in the historical record, both emphasize how the dynamics of slavery condition the lives of the bonded women and men, and their descendants, and both also represent the difficulties of narrating a traumatic history, presenting quests for voice and authority over personal and collective experiences. More importantly, Morrison and Perry pursue ways to "say something different or explore some new dimension of Afro-American slave experience that hasn't already been done and finely done by Ernest Gaines in *The Autobiography of Miss Jane Pittman* and Margaret Walker in *Jubilee*,"[1] as Gayl Jones puts it. Hence, the artistic projects of Perry and Morrison are inspired by the desire to portray slavery, while reworking the narrative trends established by previous novels. Behind *Beloved* and *Stigmata* there is a question similar to that which Walker, Jones, and Sherley Anne Williams pose for themselves while developing their own novels: "what are the truths about [the African American experience] that haven't already been told?"[2]

In the 1970s, novels such as Ishmael Reed's *Flight to Canada* (1976) and Octavia Butler's *Kindred* (1979) were already experimenting with form and content, introducing fantastic elements in narratives that attempted to explore distinct modes of representing slavery, developing and reworking the African American historical novel. *Flight to Canada* presents a parody of Harriet Beecher Stowe's *Uncle Tom's Cabin* in a text that revises the conventions of the slave narrative. Reed's usage of the fantastic in the form of anachronistic elements such as a slave's escape by a jumbo jet and the television broadcast of Lincoln's assassination blurs the boundaries and draws parallels between slavery and Civil War and the present of the bicentennial anniversary of the United States. In *Kindred*, Butler uses time travel to transport her protagonist from contemporary California to a nineteenth-century plantation where her grandmother was born, testing her survival skills. The most influential precursor of this development in the African American historical novel, however, is undoubtedly Toni Morrison's *Beloved*. Similar to the novels previously discussed in other chapters, the mother-daughter relationship in Morrison's novel is the focal point of African American history. Yet Morrison's transformative narrative represents not only the passing on of the familial history from mother to daughter across generational lines, but it also intersects broader notions of identity, time, and reality.

Beloved: Magical Realism and the Recovery of History

In the magical realist text, the real and the fantastic come together in narratives in which extraordinary occurrences are woven into the ordinary traits of the quotidian and varied cultural and literary heritages are combined in order to reflect the hybrid nature of works that are, generally speaking, rooted in a dual tradition. "In the case of the writer of African descent," as Henry Louis Gates Jr. states, "her or his texts occupy spaces in at least two traditions: a European or American literary tradition, and one of the several related but distinct black traditions."[3] In "Rootedness: The Ancestor as Foundation," Morrison discusses this dual tradition, identifying some of the distinct elements of African American literature: the dynamics between orality and literacy, the presence of the ancestor and a chorus, and the participatory nature of black writing, which requires the reader to actively engage in the construction of meaning.[4] In this article, the novelist also emphasizes the role of the magical in black culture. According to Morrison, magic has a central role in the African American cultural tradition, since it is a way of not only representing but also perceiving the world, or what Morrison calls "another way of knowing things" [5] in the black community. As P. Gabrielle Foreman states in relation Morrison's use of the magic in *Song of Solomon*, "Solomon, the flying African, is not simply a fantastic figment of a single author's imagination; rather, he springs from her imagination *and* black cultural traditions."[6] This merging of the real and the magical, as the novelist states, has origins in the "acceptance of the supernatural and a profound rootedness in the real world at the same time with neither taking precedence over the other."[7] The merging of the real and the magical without one having primacy over the other is the most central aspect of the magic realist text.

Magic in African American literature, thus, has origins in beliefs and superstitions that inform black folklore and is, therefore, distinct from other literary traditions that merge the real and the magical. In an interview with Gail Caldwell, "Morrison nods at the comparison between black American folklore and magic realism, though she says that she was well into *Song of Solomon* before she discovered Gabriel Garcia Marquez. 'Their stuff was so readily available to them—that mixture of Indian and Spanish. Whereas I felt the preachers, the storytelling, the folklore, the music was very accessible to me, but I felt almost alone. It wasn't only mine, but I didn't have any literary precedent for what I was trying to do with the magic.'"[8]

Morrison clearly roots her use of the supernatural in distinct African American cultural traditions ranging from storytelling to folklore and music. This allows her to create her works around distinctive African American narrative modes, while reworking, as I hope to demonstrate, the use of folklore in black American literature.

Edward P. Jones reiterates Morrison's ideas about the role of magic in black writing. In the plot of his first novel, *The Known World* (2003), the magical emerges occasionally in an otherwise realistic narrative. These supernatural incidents, which are left unexplained, point toward a view of the world in which the real and the magic share the same space. In an interview the author explains how this sense of magic has its roots in African American folklore:

> I was raised among a people who believe that if a person is killed on a city street, the blood of that person will show on that spot every time it rains . . . I was raised to believe that one's hair should be taken from combs and brushes and burned . . . because the hair could somehow get out into the world where birds could find it, make a nest of the hair, and give the person headaches . . .
>
> Given all that, it's easy to create a situation where lightning runs away from a man because the lightning doesn't think it's time for the man to die . . . So the supernatural events are just another way of telling the story by someone who grew up thinking that the universe did weird things all the time.[9]

Jones describes a system of beliefs, which seeks to explain the inexplicable. Lines are drawn between certain events so that an ordering principle emerges. This allows a disenfranchised people to make sense of the world outside officially sanctioned organizations and discourses. Hence, the supernatural as "another way of telling the story" is a vehicle of empowerment in the construction of narratives that challenge and resist hegemonic forms of representation.

In the same way that in *Corregidora*, Jones removes the hierarchic relationship between standard and black English in order to validate orality as an authoritative means of recording history, magical realist writers dismantle the hierarchy between Western and African American ways of representing the world. The direct result of this type of narrative, thus, is the questioning of hegemonic forms of discourse. In this sense, it is not only the dynamics of power between the oral and the written word that authors like Morrison address, but they also promote valid means of representing personal and collective history and those links that intrinsically connect the two. The removal of the hierarchy between the real and the magical enlarges the narrative space so that a distinct record of the African American experience can emerge. The rejection of a binary polarization between the dominant traditions and other African American "way[s] of knowing things" is evident in the lack of explanation, or justification for the use of the supernatural in *The Known World* and *Beloved*.

Morrison's use of folklore revises that of Walker's in *Jubilee*. While the latter structured her narrative around those cultural, religious, and musical practices, which illustrated the distinctness of African American traditions, Morrison conveys a world conceived and represented according to those traditions. In other words, in *Jubilee* the allegory and myth are part of storytelling and have didactic and entertaining roles in a realist narrative. The tales of the "silly cat and the wise spider"[10] told by Vyry to her children transport the young to a world of fantasy, while teaching them essential survival skills about the real world. Nevertheless, in the harsh everyday experiences presented in *Jubilee*, reality and fantasy are not to be confused. In *Beloved*, the folk beliefs in the supernatural transgress the realm of storytelling and permeate the *real* world of the novel, shaping both its representation and the presented version of history.

Magical realist texts, as Lois Parkinson Zamora suggests, "share (and extend) the tradition of narrative realism"[11] in their attempt to recreate experienced realities. "The crucial difference is that," as Zamora goes on to say, "magical realist texts amplify the very conception of 'experienced reality' by presenting fictional worlds that are multiple, permeable, transformative, animistic."[12] Thus, if empirical notions of reality become somewhat ambiguous and unreliable in the magical realist text, the act of reading necessarily has to be renegotiated. "This repositioning of the reader with respect to truth-claims of the narrative," Zamora states, "further obliges us to recognize our responsibility for the constitution of *all* meanings in the world, to recall our fundamental and necessary implication in the definition of reality as such."[13] This is particularly relevant in literary works, such as *Beloved*, which point toward a revision of cultural constructs of race and history as established in the hegemonic discourse.

In her article "Unspeakable Things Unspoken: The Afro-American Presence in American Literature," Morrison explains the *in media res* opening of *Beloved*:

> Because the *in media res* opening that I am so committed to is here excessively demanding [*sic*]. It is abrupt and should appear so. No native informant here. The reader is snatched, yanked, thrown into an environment completely foreign, and I want it as the first stroke of the shared experience that might be possible between the reader and the novel's population. Snatched just as the slaves were from one place to another, from any place to another, without preparation and without defense. No lobby, no door, no entrance—a gangplank, perhaps (but a very short one).[14]

The demanding entrance into the world of 124 Bluestone Road is Morrison's first step toward removing those elements of predictability, which the reader of more conventional narratives might expect. Beyond the doorway, in the presence of "a baby's venom,"[15] the reader is not only "thrown into an environment completely foreign" but is also thrown into one that challenges the notion that the boundaries of reality are somewhat determined and knowable. The text does not simply present a historical context, which the reader might not be acquainted with, but *snatches* her or him into a realm that unsettles the very notion of what can be perceived as *real*.

In contrast, the realist text presents an imaginary universe that is subjected to the rules of physical phenomena. The world is apprehended and portrayed in accordance with the belief that time-space reality is governed by permanent and immutable principles. Hence, realism in literature aims to create the illusion that there is a correspondence between actual physical interactions and the world imagined by the writer. This gives the reader the reassuring feeling that physical phenomena can be explained and the world can be, ultimately, known. In this way, conventional realist narratives engage the reader in ways that assure them with a comfortable verisimilitude between the familiar world and the imaginary one. However, as we enter a world where specters gain bodily form and display insatiable appetites, it becomes increasingly difficult to name and describe what is disclosed to us. In *Beloved*, Morrison interrogates both the nature of reality and its representation, introducing an innovative narrative form that reflects a cosmology where the boundaries between the earthly and the ghostly become blurred. In this context, as Wendy B. Faris observes, "The magic grows almost imperceptibly out of the real, and the narrator registers no surprise, with the result that the element of surprise is redirected onto the history we are about to witness, which constitutes the nasty shock."[16] In this scheme, the magical resides alongside the real, psychological time competes with chronological time, and narrative linearity and progression are challenged by circularity as memory becomes the main narrative framework. Hence, the reader experiences a double sense of dislocation, working through a narrative that poses ontological questions while revising the means of accessing and representing the past.

This sense of dislocation experienced by the reader, or what Faris calls "unsettling doubts,"[17] constitutes one of the primary elements of the magical realist text.[18] In the magical realist text's attempt to challenge preconceived notions of what is veritable, the reader is confronted with conflicting interpretations of events, or characters. Beloved is who Sethe thinks she is, her daughter returned from the dead; the motherless child, a victim of sexual abuse as Stamp Paid suggests; and the survivor of the Middle Passage as it is implied in the traumatized language of her monologue. The author's construction of this sense of doubt does not aim to confuse or distance the readers but to increase their participation in the creation of the text. Thus Morrison's text can be seen as what Roland Barthes describes as the "text of bliss." A text that "imposes a state of loss, the text that discomforts . . . , unsettles the reader's historical, cultural, psychological assumptions, the consistency of his [or her] tastes, values, memories, brings to a crisis his [or her] relation to language."[19] Realistic literature provides the reader with the pleasure that has its origin in the familial world that it presents. The magical realist narrative, on the other hand, defies, unsettles, and challenges the reader's perceptions of reality. However, it is important to notice that the supernatural in magical realist texts, as Faris observes, "refuses to be entirely assimilated into their realism; it does not brutally shock but neither does it melt away . . . And because it disrupts reading habits, that irreducible grain increases the participation of the readers, contributing . . . to texts co-created by their readers."[20] In an interview with Claudia Tate, Morrison corroborates this, "My writing expects," the novelist states, "demands participatory reading, and I think that is what literature is supposed to do."[21]

The supernatural presence in Morrison's text is, thus, distinct from that of traditional African American ghost stories. "The ghost tale as it evolved during and after slavery," as Geraldine Smith-Wright observes, "described, often metaphorically, creative ways that Blacks coped with white oppression and also suggested codes of conduct to strengthen the Black community."[22] The specter in *Beloved* functions as a means of translating the absences of African American history into tangible presences, revising the tradition of the ghost tale in search of "new representations . . . in order to impart a stronger sense of the unpresentable,"[23] as Jean-François Lyotard puts it. "[T]he purpose of making [Beloved] real," as Morrison states, "is making history possible, making memory real—somebody walks in the door and sits down at the table so you have to think about it, whatever they may be."[24] In this sense, the postmodern quality of Morrison's work in its innovative narrative strategies reworks African American folk tradition. Her version of magic realism provides the necessary narrative strategy through which the marginal history can be reclaimed and reimagined.

Morrison's text, hence, poses questions about the recovery of the ancestors' undocumented and fundamentally "unpresentable" past. There is no record of those who died en route aboard slave ships. "[T]hey never survived in the lore; there are no songs or dances or tales of these people,"[25] as Morrison explains. On the other hand, the novel also explores the difficulties in recreating a past lost in the caverns of memory. Morrison's characters, as the novelist herself states, "don't want to talk, they don't want to remember, they don't want to say it, because they're afraid of it."[26] The use of the magical in *Beloved*, then, corresponds with a desire to ground the text in a historical reality for which there is no record and that strikes a dissonant cord with officially sanctioned forms of discourse. This "desire for narrative freedom from realism, and from univocal narrative stance," as Faris states, also "implicitly correspond[s] textually in a new way to a critique of totalitarian discourses of all kinds."[27] According to Theo L. D'haen, magical realism enables writers to displace hegemonic ideologies by "first appropriating the techniques of the 'centr-al' line and then . . . create an alternative world *correcting* so-called existing reality, and thus to right the wrongs this 'reality' depends upon. Magical realism thus reveals itself as a *ruse* to invade and take over dominant discourse(s)."[28] Thus magical realism facilitates the displacement of the hegemonic control over discourse and recovers the silenced voices of those who remained outside history and who were, therefore, obliterated from *realistic* modes of representation. In *Beloved*, as Morrison explains, "[t]he fully realized presence of the haunting is both a major incumbent of the narrative and sleight of hand. One of its purposes is to keep the reader preoccupied with the nature of the incredible spirit world while being supplied a controlled diet of the incredible political world."[29]

Beloved: Rememory and Selfhood

In *Beloved*, Morrison continues the tradition of Margaret Walker by reclaiming the past and constructing a narrative out of a fragmented history while assuming the role of the novelist who seeks to correct the historical record. However, Morrison's departure from realism and her construction of a multifaceted character who is better characterized by her "in-between" nature—between real and magic, earthly and ghostly, and between being Sethe's dead child and the survivor of the Middle Passage—the representative of the first

Africans in America, broadens the narrative space of the historical novel, revising that which it is possible to depict and the means by which it can be depicted. Hence, the character of Beloved reworks the representation of nineteenth-century African American history as a time period (i.e., slavery, Civil War, and Reconstruction), opting for a mythical sense of time where the unveiling of one layer of history reveals another. In this mythical notion of time, "[t]he gap between Africa and Afro-America and the gap between the living and the dead and the gap between the past and the present does not exist,"[30] as Morrison puts it. In Beloved, the history of people of African descent from its origins in the New World finds an epicenter.

In this way, Morrison's revision of the African American historical novel entails, as Faris observes in relation to other magical realist texts, "that historical events and myths are both essential aspects of our collective memory."[31] In this context, Morrison's concept of "rememory" is a central aspect of a narrative that aims to smudge time linearity and broaden the limits of representation of historical events. The prefix "re" suggests repetition, the never-ending resurfacing of the same memories, and untold or unclaimed recollections, which remain ghostly presences in the present. Morrison reworks Jones's notion that a past of slavery can hold a powerful grip on the present. However, while the latter's protagonist has to deal with the compulsive narration of her ancestors' slavery and a history, which is passed on to her in minute detail, Morrison presents characters whose unwillingness to remember transforms their daily existence in "the day's serious work of beating back the past."[32] It is this reluctance to remember and the inability to articulate the past ("How can I say things that are pictures?"[33] Beloved asks) that ultimately keeps Morrison's characters "loaded with the past and hungry for more, it left [them] no room to imagine, let alone plan for, the next day."[34]

The concept of "rememory" is central to the interpretation of *Beloved* as a magical realist text precisely because it is not contained in the boundaries of personal experience but it inhabits the shared place of the collective memory:

> "I used to think it was my rememory. You know. Some things you forget. Other things you never do. But it's not. Places, places are still there. If a house burns down, it's gone, but the place—the picture of it—stays, and not just in my rememory, but out there, in the world. What I remember is a picture floating around out there outside my head. I mean, even if I don't think it, even if I die, the picture of what I did, or knew, or saw is still out there. Right in the place where it happened."
>
> "Can other people see it"? asked Denver
>
> "Oh, yes. Oh, yes, yes, yes."[35]

In *Beloved*, Morrison relies on the parallel between the concept of "rememory" (i.e., the never-ending resurfacing of past recollections) and, to paraphrase Zamora, the construction of a transhistorical context for self[36] in the character of Beloved in order to represent the traumatic history of slavery. Spectral presences in the magical realist text, as Zamora puts it, "unsettle modernity's (and the novel's) basis in progressive, linear history: they float free in time, not just here and now but then and there, eternal and everywhere."[37] Thus, in the same way that Sethe's notion of rememory transcends the realm of the individual psyche, the presence of Beloved suggests "a model of the self that is collective: subjectivity is not singular but several, not merely individual or existential but mythic, cumulative, participatory"[38] to return to Zamora. This is exemplified not only in the several ways different characters interpret the presence of Beloved in Sethe's house but also in the merging of the voices and the characters of mother, daughter, and sisters in the text.

The interior dialogues of Beloved, Denver, and Sethe that follow the latter's recognition that the peculiar young woman, staying in her house is in fact her daughter who had returned from "the other side,"[39] illustrate the sharing of their psychological realms. Sethe's interior dialogue acquires the form of an explanatory note to her daughter, interrupted by the thought that ultimately the need to explain is made redundant by the nature of their relationship: "When I explain it she'll understand, because she understands everything already,"[40] or "But you know all that because your are smart."[41] Morrison's construction of a collective self is also signaled by the blurring of the individual physical contours of mother and daughter. Once again the body emerges in Morrison's text as a central signifier. Here it can be interpreted as a point of intersection for mother and daughter, individual and collective histories, past and present, earthly and ghostly, and the real and the magical. In this way, Morrison revises the representative voice present of the slave narrative discussed in first chapter. For the former slave as Gates Jr., states, "The act of writing . . . constituted the act of creating a public, historical self of the individual author, but also the 'self,' as it were, of the race" [42] and from the written individual story evolves the unwritten collective history. In *Beloved*, the merging of the characters' memories and the fractured language of their interior speeches become a way of representing both individual and collective histories from the Middle Passage to Cincinnati of the 1870s. In this context it is interesting to note that when Sethe thinks of ways of explaining what she did to her daughter Beloved, she evokes the collective history of the community: Sethe feared that Beloved might leave before she could understand that worse than what happened to her "was what Baby Suggs died of, what Ella knew, what Stamp saw and what made Paul D tremble."[43] Even in the context of Beloved's story, slavery remains the ultimate horror.

The meaning of Sethe's pronouncement that "when I tell you you mine, I also mean I'm yours"[44] echoes Beloved's words: "I am looking for the join . . . she knows I want to join . . . I am gone now I am her face . . . now we can join,"[45] or "I am not separate from her there is no place where I stop her face is my own and I want to be there in the place where her face is and to be looking at it."[46] For Mieke Bal, "The mixture of fusion with the mother and the fragmentation of the self . . . speaks of the early infant's lack of formed ego."[47] For Bal, "The fragmentation and fusion that inhibit the formation of subjectivity are here used to represent the difficulty of remembering a traumatic past . . . and in turn represent the most painful of its experiences, the impossibility of mother-child relationships."[48] In *Beloved*, the effects of slavery in the formation of family bonds, especially that of mother and child, is a central issue. However, what I would like to emphasize less is the lack of the formation of an independent sense of self but rather Morrison's revision of the very notion of selfhood. The novelist clearly creates an ambiguous notion of subjectivity, smudging both the physical and the psychological outlines of the individual self. This ambiguity, constructed around the paradoxes such as the negation of separation between mother and daughter, their sharing of the same face, while Beloved wants to be "in the place where [Sethe's] face is and to be looking at it," unsettles both the reader's notion of self and creates an instability around univocal forms of discourse.

These interior dialogues represent Morrison's articulation of the "unspeakable thoughts, unspoken"[49] of the women of 124. In *Beloved*, the representation of the traumatic past is rarely verbalized and the interior dialogue allows Morrison to represent the "unpresentable." Denver's descent into silence, which follows her discovery or recollection of her mother's deed, suggests the difficulty in verbalizing the horrific past. However, it is this retreat from the verbalized world that allows her to become aware of the spectral presence: "So quiet. Made me want to read faces and learn how to figure out what people were thinking, so I didn't need to hear what they said. That's how come me and Beloved could play together. Not talking."[50] This reluctance to verbalize the past corresponds to a calcification of traumatic memories, which not shared, or transformed into storytelling, or song, as in the case of Jones's *Corregidora*, hold in their grip those who become their vessels. The relationship between a solitary child and the ghost of her sister is marked by a false sense of companionship and a profound sense of loss signaled by Denver's descent into muteness. Thus the past needs to be shared and actualized in the context of a community formed by *real* people.

When the polyphonic dialogue between Sethe, Denver, and Beloved takes place Morrison's notion of subjectivity is once more complicated. These characters share a psychological realm where "unspeakable thoughts unspoken" can be articulated, but the call-and-response structure of their silent dialogue evokes individual impulses. In the uniformity of their chorus resides a claim for individuality: "You are mine."[51] For Sethe these words represent an opportunity to break the vicious cycle of her memories and look forward to a future, a move from *kairos* into *chronos*, to use Frank Kermode's terminology[52]: "I'm here. I lasted . . . Now I can look at things again because she's here to see them too."[53] For Denver the words of the refrain constitute a quest for companionship, a desire to share both the burden of the knowledge about a mother who loves her enough to kill them, and the waiting for their father, "an angel man . . . who could look at you and tell where you hurt and he could fix it too."[54] For Beloved the chorus denotes a yearning for her lost mother, an acknowledgment of her past, her history both as Sethe's daughter and the survivor of the Middle Passage. This merging of individual and collective history in the character of Beloved is illustrated in her memory of Sethe "tak[ing] flowers away from leaves she puts them in a round basket,"[55] which reflects the song sung by the man with white teeth aboard the slave ship: "I love him because he has a song when he turned around to die I see the teeth he sang through his singing was soft his singing is of the place where a woman takes flowers away from their leaves and puts them in a round basket."[56] The song sung by Sethe and by the man aboard the slave ship echo each other. In establishing this connection between these two fragmented memories, Morrison points to Beloved's multiple subjectivity. In the same way that the songs echo each other, Beloved's multiple self as Sethe's daughter, the survivor of the Middle Passage, the motherless child, and victim of sexual abuse reflect each other, like a sequence of mirrors, to encompass the complexity of African American experience.

Beloved: Community

In the magic realist text, as Zamora illustrates, "[t]his slippage from the individual to the collective to the cosmic is often signaled by spectral presences."[57] In other words, the character of Beloved creates a "magical instability"[58] in the narrative, allowing characters and narrative voices to form a magnetic center that challenges ideas of individuality in realistic modes of representation. Thus Beloved constitutes an epicenter, as already suggested, from which several threads of African American history can be unraveled. These are not only the storylines of the women of 124 Bluestone Road, or of Paul D, but those of the entire black community. Beloved's character, therefore, also functions as a magnetic center for individual and collective histories, whose mythical overtones reverberate in the closing of the novel.

It is important to emphasize that the role of the mythical in Morrison's representation of history depends on the acceptance of the magical or the supernatural in the black community of Cincinnati. When Ellen tells Stamp Paid that "'people who die bad don't stay in the ground.' He couldn't deny it. Jesus Christ himself didn't."[59] Thus when the women of the community gather around Sethe's house to pray and exorcise the ghost, they do not look for an explanation outside the realm of the magical. Even those, like Lady Jones, "who didn't believe the story and hated the ignorance of those who did"[60] do not offer a realistic explanation of the story circulated by the Bodwin's servant. It is the community's firm belief in the magical and its manifestation in the cultural and religious practice of the exorcism that ultimately frees Sethe from the haunting.

Morrison's representation of the community's conviction in the magical recalls that of Zora Neale Hurston in short stories such as "Uncle Monday" and "Black Death," simultaneously complicating Morrison's assertions that when she began experimenting with narrative modes, which included magical elements, she felt "almost alone." Morrison goes on to say, "It wasn't only mine, but I didn't have any literary precedent for what I was trying to do with magic." This is not to say that Morrison's use of the magical is purely mimetic when compared to Hurston's work, but we can say that in the latter Morrison had the literary precedent she was apparently seeking.[61] In Hurston's "Black Death," for example, the faith of the black community in Morgan, the witch doctor, is conveyed by the repetition of phrases such as "they know,"[62] "but the villagers knew,"[63] or "but the Negroes knew instantly,"[64] which function as a chorus in the text. The recurrence of these phrases is central in representing the community's firm belief in the magical. The magical functions in the text as a means of illustrating how the disenfranchised people of Eatonville deal with their grievances without the interference of the white community who appeared in the text only to write erroneous death certificates and was wholly unaware of the supernatural and rather sinister occurrences that took place in the black community. Both Hurston's emphasis on how the magical depends on the belief of the group and how the supernatural functions in the community divorced from hegemonic means of political, social, and religious organization is reflected in Morrison's novel, as illustrated by the way the women react to the news about the haunting of 124 and the fact that Mr. Bodwin cannot decode what he witnessed on a sweltering day outside the house where he was born.

The magical realist text, as Foreman puts it, "unlike the fantastic or the surreal, presumes that the individual requires a bond with the traditions and the faith of the community, that s/he is historically constructed and connected."[65] This link between individual and community, individual and the religious and cultural practices of the group functions in the narrative as a means of connecting personal and collective history, revealing the central role of the supernatural in the novel as an element of connection. In the ritual of exorcism the individual and collective histories of the community come together once again. If the women gather around 124, to rescue Sethe, it is their personal past that urges them to come forward. In the women's murmur ("Yes, yes, yes, oh yes."[66]) that follows the lead prayer, there is an implicit articulation of the belief in Christian and African American faiths. On the other hand, this response to the prayer's call encapsulates the women's personal and collective experience of enslavement that led them to Sethe's house. The community is here largely symbolized by Ella, for whom "[t]here was . . . something very personal in her fury"[67] when she heard about the haunting. Standing in front of Sethe's house, Ella recalls the white baby she delivered but whom she refused to nurse: "It lived five days never making a sound. The idea of that pup coming back to whip her too set her jaw working and then Ella hollered."[68] It is the scarred tissue of the memory of slavery that brings these women together to exorcise a past, which ultimately, could come to haunt any of them. It is interesting to note that the repetition of the adverb "yes," this monosyllabic articulation of faith, memory, and history, ends with Ella's howl, evoking Granny Ticey's "bloodcurdling yell"[69] and Jake's "terrible groan"[70] in *Jubilee*: "Instantly the kneelers and the standers joined her. They stopped praying and took a step back to the beginning. In the beginning there were no words. In the beginning was the sound, and they all knew what that sound sounded like."[71] Thus, for Morrison, the unspeakable memory of slavery is in many ways, as Valerie Smith puts it, "prelinguistic."[72] In the group's wail, Morrison yet again fuses personal and collective, the present and the past—not only the historical past but also the mythical past, the beginning of time before the word, before memory, before history, while reaffirming the difficulty in constructing a coherent narrative out of the chaotic experience of slavery. In this shared wail, there is healing for both individual and community that comes from the realization that the personal past finds an echo in the group's collective history.

In *Beloved*, the bond between individual and community is critical to their mutual survival. The community is capable of harboring jealousies and resentments, but its primary role in the novel is that of rescuer and healer, suggesting the importance of recovering communal values. However, Morrison also portrays the individual's struggle with the principles and ethics established by the community. Sethe strived to be independent;

pilfering from her employer was only another way to avoid joining the other black people waiting their turn in the back of the store for the last white person to be served, but the world that Morrison creates is far from white notions of individualism and self-reliance. A white girl helped Sethe to give birth to Denver, Stamp Paid and Ella helped her cross the river, Baby Suggs housed her and healed her deformed feet and the "tree" on her back, the Bodwins saved her from the gallows, the women freed her from the haunting, and, at the end of the novel, Paul D returns to care for her. "Nobody in the novel, no adult Black person," as Morrison explains, "survives by self-regard, narcissism, selfishness. They took the sense of community for granted. It never occurred to them that they could live outside it. There was no life out there, and they wouldn't have chosen it anyway."[73] The occasional gesture of white philanthropism is not without importance in the novel, but it is the bond between a people who shared the horrific experience of slavery that Morrison emphasizes that is central to the interpretation of the novel as a magical realist text.

Stigmata: From the Fantastic to the Magical Real

In *Stigmata*, the relationship between individual and community is also critical to the representation of history in the novel and to the introduction of the supernatural as its central narrative device. Perry addresses the perils of the divorce between individual and community. However, her treatment of this theme is different from other works that equate the detachment between individual and community with the geographical and cultural distance between the rural South and the urban North, revising a prevailing image of the South as a somewhat unchanged society immune to capitalism and the politics of class and consumption. The South in contemporary black women's writing, as Susan Willis states, "is never portrayed as even a partial wage-labor economy, even though many Southerners have worked for a wage . . . and a percentage of these have been black. What black women are documenting in the writing is the essential characteristic of the system as a whole as it arose out of slavery . . . As a non-wage economy, the South is very often depicted as a nonmoney economy."[74]

The South is seen, therefore, as a site where there is still a strong sense of community and responsibility toward the elements of the group, contrasting with the unbridled individualism attributed to the North. In *Praisesong for the Widow* and *Song of Solomon*, Paule Marshall and Morrison, respectively, present characters that are divorced from their history and ancestry and are trapped in an obsessive materialism in the urban industrialized North. These novelists attempt to retrieve those traditions gradually lost in time and in the migration from the rural South to the industrialized North. For Morrison, one of the roles of the African American novel is to revive those cultural practices lost in the Great Migration: "Now my people. We 'peasants,' have come to the city, that is to say, we live with its values. There is a confrontation between old and new values. It's confusing. There has to be a mode to do what the music did for blacks, what we used to be able to do for each other in private and in that civilization that existed underneath the white civilization."[75]

The distinction that Morrison makes between old and new values is often seen in the separation between the South and the North in African American history. In 1940, 77 percent of the African American population lived in the South. Between that time and 1970 more than five million African Americans, most of them unemployed owing to the introduction of mechanical cotton pickers, migrated to the North.[76] This change constitutes the largest internal migration in the history of the United States and had given origin to a profound change in black American culture. The journey from South to the North in the work of contemporary female writers soon became synonymous with two diverse, if not antithetical, modes of living: one in the North characterized mainly by industrialization, a politics of consumption, and individualism; and the other in the South dominated by the agrarian mode of living, and a strong sense of community.

In the 1960s the prohibition of discrimination on the basis of race, national origin, religion, and gender introduced by the Civil Rights Act produced unforeseen effects in the African American community, among which the most significant was the emergence of a politics of class. Middle-class professional blacks separated themselves from the black working class by living in separate areas, and attending different schools and churches as illustrated in Dawn Turner Trice's first novel, *Only Twice I've Wished for Heaven* (1997). Trice portrays this social change by creating a black middle-class estate inhabited by black professionals: "Within the confines of that ivy-lined wrought-iron fence lived this elite group of people who had been allowed to purge their minds of all those things that reminded them of what it meant to be poor and downtrodden. Once here, Lakelandites didn't look back . . . And they vowed to put their bodies and their beliefs into this great blender and leave it there until the whitewashed folk who came out no longer resembled the pageant of folk who had entered."[77] Trice's descriptions of this gated community depict the cultural differences, which accompanied the changes in the African American social landscape in Chicago during the 1970s. In *Linden Hills* (1985), Gloria Naylor also creates a private residential estate inhabited by African Americans who exchanged their identity, past, or ties with family and community to obtain a lease in the exclusive neighborhood. Here "they could forget that the world spelled black with capital nothing . . .

Linden Hills wasn't black; it was successful. The shining surface of their careers . . . only reflected the bright nothing that was inside of them."[78] Social mobility and the establishment of middle-class ghettos are represented in terms of loss of identity, community, and history.

One of the consequences of these divisions within black society was that by the 1970s the South gained an almost mythical dimension for African American writers. It became the symbol of "the values of the tribes," of a mode of living free from the capitalist and consumer malaise, and the only place from which they could reconstruct African American cultural identity as separate and distinct from the dominant white culture. In conclusion, the South became, as Willis puts it, "the reservoir of [African American] culture."[79]

In *Stigmata*, Perry also represents the South as the place of the ancestors, the cradle of African American culture and history, but in her work it is not a landscape frozen in time and divorced from the forces that affected African American society at large. The portrayal of social change and adoption of white middle-class values are critical aspects for the interpretation of this novel and its use of the magical since the supernatural is not promptly accepted by every individual of the community created in the novel. In this narrative Perry explores the tensions between the fantastic and the magical real in order to represent not only individual attitudes toward the supernatural but also the implications inherent in the detachment between the individual and the beliefs of the community. Thus Perry reworks Morrison's representation of the supernatural as part of the community's shared and accepted system of beliefs.

In *The Fantastic: A Structural Approach to a Literary Genre*, Tzvetan Todorov states that

> the fantastic . . . lasts only as long as a certain hesitation: a hesitation common to the reader and character, who must decide whether or not what they perceive derives from "reality" as it exists in the common opinion . . . If he [or she] decides that the laws of reality remain intact and permit an explanation of the phenomena described, we say that the work belongs to another genre: the uncanny. If, on the contrary, he [or she] decides that new laws of nature must be entertained to account for the phenomena, we enter the genre of the marvellous.
>
> The fantastic therefore leads a life full of dangers, and may evaporate at any moment.[80]

In *Stigmata*, Perry plays with these conventions of the fantastic, which, as Todorov defines it, depends on the reader's and the character's hesitation "between a natural and a supernatural explanation of the events described"[81] and the supernatural accepted, or the marvelous, what we have been calling magical realism. In this novel the protagonist's journey is one from the fantastic, the estrangement from her family and society at large, to magical realism, signaled by the acceptance of the supernatural and her return to the community.

Upon receiving a trunk containing among other things the diary of her great-great-grandmother and a quilt sewn by her grandmother, Lizzie begins to journey through these women's past. The trunk functions in the narrative as kind of Pandora's box. The contents of which need to be interpreted and understood so that the released sorrowful past can become a force of regeneration. In *Stigmata*, the device of time traveling does not simply imply that a character becomes a mere observer or participant in the events of another era. Lizzie does not witness her foremothers' lives from a distance, but rather she becomes Ayo and Grace: "When I open [my eyes] again, Grace is with me—or I am with her . . . I sit on the old bed with Grace, marveling that I can move her fingers and toes."[82] Thus Lizzie's experiences of the supernatural suggest a sense of "fluid identities and interconnectedness,"[83] as Faris puts it in relation to another magical realist work. Nonetheless, the manner in which Lizzie represents these first journeys to the past suggests that the character is still in the realm of the fantastic. In this way, allowing for Todorov's scheme, *Stigmata* is a fantastic-marvelous narrative, part of "[a] class of narratives that are presented as fantastic and that end with an acceptance of the supernatural. These are the narratives closest to the pure fantastic, for the latter, by the very fact that it remains unexplained, unrationalized, suggests the existence of the supernatural. The frontier between the two will therefore be uncertain."[84]

I will argue that once we enter the realm of the magic accepted, our perception of the world according to permanent time-space reality principles is changed in order to accommodate phenomena that are not subject to physical laws. In this context, we leave the fantastic and enter the magical real. Nonetheless, what is important to emphasize here is the fickleness of the fantastic text, a genre that "leads a life full of dangers, and may evaporate at any moment." This is a critical aspect in Perry's narrative since this transition from the fantastic to the magical real will mark the central character's shift from a place of isolation to one where history can be shared and actualized.

However, while the boundary between the real and the magical is not seamless, Lizzie struggles to make sense out of her experiences: "A sound startles me . . . My eyes fly open and I look down. At my feet a hairbrush lay on the wood floor, and as I bend to pick it up I absently consider the fact that my mother's new carpet, the carpet just installed three months ago, seems to have disappeared . . . For a moment I can't think, can't feel my body in this place. I can only see the scene before me."[85]

The narration of this episode contains elements that express the character's hesitation between the real and the magical. The expression that "seems to have disappeared" illustrates this vacillation between a more *natural* explanation of the event and the experience of the supernatural. This is reinforced by the fact that Lizzie cannot "for a moment" feel her body in this other supernatural realm. This expression of her inability to think and "feel [her] body" is significant since it directs the reader's interpretation of the narrated occurrence toward the world of the dreams. An interpretation corroborated by the character who articulates it in contradictory terms: "I get up slowly, painfully. The whole episode didn't feel like a dream, but I must have slept, and in an awkward position."[86] Without these elements, which denote doubt, "we should be plunged into the world of the marvellous,with no reference to everyday reality,"[87] as Todorov observes. The language used to communicate the experience of the supernatural is, thus, at the crossroads between the real and the magical and constitutes one of the central aspects of the discourse of the fantastic.

For Todorov, "The supernatural is born of language, it is both its consequence and its proof: not only do the devil and vampires exist only in words, but language alone enables us to conceive what is always absent: the supernatural. The supernatural thereby becomes a symbol of language, just as the figures of rhetoric do."[88] This is particularly relevant in texts that attempt to represent the absences in the African American historical record. When the first-person narrator declares that the tangible and familiar world of her parents' house "seems to have disappeared" or "[it] didn't feel like a dream, but I must have slept," she creates with language this other space, which does not correspond to the perceived reality, or to an unquestioned magical realm, but to a space of hesitation between the two; she conceives a place for the fantastic. This hesitation between the real and the fantastic becomes a prevailing pattern in the novel until Lizzie begins to make sense of her experiences: "I don't know who to tell. Not them, the parents, who'll say how I was dreaming. No, I was there. I was Grace . . . Gotta be a dream. I was sitting here daydreaming,"[89] or "When I woke up, or came to, or whatever, it didn't feel like a dream . . . But I had to be asleep."[90] It is worth noting that the substantive "dream" functions as a symbol for the unexplained, for Lizzie's "fantastic out-of-body story."[91] Unable to make sense of her experience, Lizzie resorts to everyday language in an attempt to normalize her experience of the supernatural. In this sense, language becomes the essential connection between the magical and the real and the missing link to the magical real is faith, as already discussed in relation to *Beloved*. "To begin with," as Alejo Carpenter puts it, "the phenomenon of the marvellous [magical realism] presupposes faith."[92]

Lizzie's experiences expressed in a language of hesitation to skeptical interlocutors contribute to her gradual alienation from social structures in which there is no place for the magical: her middle-class family, educational system, and later, Western medicine. "Unlike magical realism," as Foreman states, "the fantastic and the uncanny posit an individual who experiences a world beyond the community's parameters."[93] The opening of *Stigmata* is meaningfully set in a psychiatric hospital. This "padded cell"[94] functions in the narrative as a literal and symbolic space of rupture between the protagonist and her community. This is signaled most significantly by Lizzie's relationship with her parents and the orderly middle-class world they create in which the magical is interpreted as mental disorder. Perry uses constructs of class and consumption in order to represent this alienation from the rituals and beliefs of the ancestors: "There used to be a woman who came in once a week to 'do' for Mother and she got her feelings hurt a lot until she understood her place and our place and the way things were supposed to be. Our house was a shrine to middle-class order. Not just neat, not just clean, but true to the standards demanded by our position in this little belch of a town."[95] In Perry's work, the South of the 1970s to the mid-1990s is clearly not represented as the "nonmoney economy," which Willis identifies as prevailing in contemporary African American women's writing. In *Stigmata*, Southern black society is not free from the politics of class that emerged in the North during the same period. In this context, it is worth noting how notions of consumption interfere with the way characters interpret the world. Years of Western education and a self-conscious adoption of white middle-class values obscure the vision of Lizzie's father. When he sees the trunk with the family relics passed on to Lizzie, he misinterprets it as mere property missing its magical significance: "'It's all really interesting. But no reason to hide it away, is there? All that mystery, all that talk about giving it at the right time to the right person.' He rolls his eyes. 'That trunk should be your property, shouldn't it, Sarah?'"[96] In a milieu where objects are interpreted according to their monetary value, they also become a means of emotional expression. The red Mustang given to Lizzie by her father as a reward "from being on the right side of normal"[97] takes the place of the words he cannot articulate: "More where that came from, his weary eyes promise as he hands me the keys."[98] This inability to express emotion verbally contrasts visibly with the world Morrison created in *Beloved*, where the community finds ways of sharing an experience for which there are hardly any words, even when they resort to the "prelinguistic" howl that delivers Sethe.

Lizzie's mother, "speaking her college-bred English,"[99] also lost the essential connection with her ancestors, which would allow her to interpret the world in a way distinct from that of the hegemonic white culture. Looking at her mother's quilt, a composition in which she narrates the history of her ancestors, Mrs. Dr. DuBose cannot read the text before her. Educated in a history that follows chronology, and is therefore linear, she cannot decode the circular narrative before her: "'What kind of quilt is that anyway? Just some pictures stuck to a background. No rhyme or reason.' She [her mother] wrote about it like it was supposed to mean something."[100] In this way, the newly found quilt is in the danger of being lost as a source of meaning. In her well-known essay "In Search of Our Mother's Gardens," Alice Walker points to the importance of quilts as textual evidence of black women's imagination, which flourished in a creatively adverse soil: "In fanciful, inspired, and yet simple and identifiable figures, it portrays the story of the Crucifixion. [The quilt] is made with bits and pieces of worthless rags, it is obviously the work of powerful imagination and deep spiritual feeling."[101] For the meaning to be recovered, Sarah has to recognize the quilt as a text that can be read and interpreted and a medium through which her mother expressed her creativity and historical legacy.

Stigmata: Secret Self

The separation between Lizzie and her parents is also signaled by Perry's usage of a first-person narrator. Morrison's omniscient narrator works in the narrative as an element of connection, interlacing the necessarily individual experiences of slavery in order to represent the collective African American history. Hence, in the magical realist text, the belief in the supernatural is reinforced by nondramatized omniscient narrators. If magic incidents are narrated by such narrators, as Todorov states, "we should immediately be in the marvellous; there would be no occasion, in fact, to doubt his [or her] words . . . It is no accident that tales of the marvellous rarely employ the first person."[102] Hence, the belief in the magical is closely related to the reliability of an omniscient narrator who takes the magical for granted and, therefore, as a continuum of the real. The dramatized narrator in the first-person narrative, in turn, is particularly suitable and more common in fantastic narratives because, as Todorov puts it, "[t]his narrator discourse has an ambiguous status, . . . emphasizing one or another of its aspects: as the narrator's, the discourse lies outside the test of truth; as the character's it must pass the test."[103] In other words, the "character can lie, while the narrator must not."[104] In the description of the same episode by the narrator and the character, the gaps between the first and the latter's discourse are obvious: "The ground slowly rolls under my feet. I smell—taste—sweat and blood and months of misery. The scent knocks me dizzy for a moment and I stumble forward. Then I am pulled, jerked . . . I see the deck, the water beyond and the line of dark bodies going jerkily forward into the ghost-land."[105] The narrator's depiction of a slave ship in such sensorial terms illustrates the authenticity of Lizzie's experience. However, when the character attempts to reconstruct that same episode her fragmented account reconstructs the necessary hesitation in the fantastic narrative: "I was on a ship. . . . A slave ship, Daddy. . . . Maybe I was just sleepwalking. . . . I keep . . . winking out. . . . I said *sometimes* it's like I get drowsy. Other times I'm just doing something else and I have a flash back of some moment or some place. I remember something that I know can't be true."[106]

This tension between the narrator's and the character's discourse keeps the essential doubt (to believe or disbelieve) characteristic of the fantastic narrative. This is critical in a work that explores the tension between the fantastic and the magical real between the character's alienation from the community and the necessity to understand individual experience in the context of the group's history.

In her attempt to bridge the gap between African American culture and the Western way of life adopted by her parents, which ultimately resulted in her 14-year sojourn in several psychiatric hospitals, Lizzie "gather[s] up the lies necessary for [her] escape."[107] These lies, which she calls her "story of redemption,"[108] as we will later understand, are less an act of deceit than a counter narrative that allows her to function in a social structure in which the supernatural is interpreted as a mental disorder.

In *Stigmata*, the first-person account, which emphasizes the isolation of the main character, is reinforced by the usage of a journal, with its connotations of secrecy, as the main narrative structure. The text is shaped around the nonchronological entries of Lizzie's diary. The lack of chronological sequence serves a double purpose: on one hand it functions as a way to defer information to the reader; on the other hand, it emphasizes the difficulty in articulating the traumatic past. Thus Perry breaks down the sequence of the diary in order follow distinct African American narrative modes shaped around gradually enlarging circles. This reflects the narrative of life stories constructed from memory, the circular form of narrative quilts or the circular form of call and response of blues stanzas. I will return to this at a later stage to explore the relationship between written and oral or folk forms of recording African American history. What is important to consider here, however, is the fact that despite the circular shape of the narrative, the dates that open each chapter serve as a constant reminder that what we are reading is, in fact, a journal. This significant choice of form allows Perry to create a tension between the essential need to connect with others, implied in the circular structure of the narrative, and the isolation of a character who constructs a narrative in a medium that is supposed to conceal rather than reveal the narrated experience.

It is worth noting that the journal becomes a way of organizing, articulating, and reconciling with the traumatic past, reflecting a process similar to that of the slave narratives. "The diary," as Lizzie's great-grandmother tells her in relation to the memoir she inherited, "is the key, baby. The diary. The quilt. Just the keys that unlock the door to what you call the past."[109] However, the healing process is but partial when the knowledge of the past gained by Lizzie cannot be shared: "I close the journal loudly. The world is a circle of light made by my bedside lamp and I'm lonely inside it. The silence outside the circle presses against the hospital walls. The journal eases my mental pain and illuminates it, makes everything swimming through my head touchable."[110]

Closing her "journal loudly," Lizzie expresses her frustration, while drawing attention to her solitude. With no one to hear the loud noise of her logbook closing, Lizzie's gesture is one of defeat. The circle imagery in African American historical fiction, as we have seen, usually suggests an acknowledgment of the past, a sense of history that will resurface until it is recognized, shared, and transformed into storytelling (or song) and into meaningful ways of passing it on without crippling the listener with its unbearable burden. However, here the circle evokes what was formed in *Corregidora* by Great Gram's arms around the young Ursa, a circumference of entrapment and profound isolation. The use of the vocable "touchable" is significant. While the journal allows Lizzie to organize her experience and make it "touchable" in her mental landscape, the world around her remains silent and, therefore, confines her experience to the realm of vague dreams and mental illness, rather than the tangible reality Lizzie experiences.

The journal also highlights the importance of recording history and passing it on, while calling the reader's attention to the ideologies underlying the production of historical records. Dr. Brun, the white female psychiatrist, suggests a journal as a form of therapy for Lizzie: "It'll be completely private,"[111] the doctor says, while paradoxically asking her patient to share it with her. If the doctor struggles with issues of privacy, she cannot help being prescriptive in relation to what Lizzie should write: "This journal is supposed to be a dream journal, not a critique of me."[112] If the categorization of Lizzie's supernatural experiences as dreams is convenient to maintain the orderly world of Western medicine, the doctor's directions about what her African American female patient should write call attention to the difficulty in accepting the authority of the black self over the written text. This emphasizes a chasm in the relationship between blacks and whites in America and, as Williams puts it, "too many white people are unable to disabuse themselves of the notion that a black person . . . cannot have true self-agency, that enablement must always come under the auspices of some white person."[113] Nevertheless, it is interesting to note that the portrayal the relationship between blacks and whites is dramatically different from novels discussed in previous chapters. In late twentieth-century Birmingham, Lizzie's response is very distinct from the vacant smiles and humming with which Dessa resisted the white amanuensis: "'I'm not finished,' I snap back. 'And it's my fucking journal. I don't even have to read it to you if I don't want to.' I slam the book shut."[114] The doctor apologizes but proceeds to question Lizzie about her "dreams." Thus, in *Stigmata*, race relations in the first decades after the civil rights movement are characterized not by issues of superiority or dominance but by misconceptions mainly based on hegemonic cultural constructs, which are articulated in the text in terms of divisions between mental sanity and insanity, the real and the magical. It is worth noting that characters such as Lizzie's parents and Dr. Harper (the black psychiatrist), immersed in white middle-class values, are also guilty of transforming the magical, accepted, and shared in *Beloved* into mental disorder.

As in novels previously discussed, in *Stigmata* the scarred body is a central signifier in the reconstruction African American history. From Vyry's marked back, "[t]he scars were webbed and . . . had ridges like a washboard"[115]; to the disfigurement of Dessa's "loins [which] looked like a mutilated cat face. Scar tissue plowed through her pubic region so that no hair would ever grow there again"[116]; the tree engraved on Sethe's back described by Paul D in a moment of (com)passion as "the decorative work of an ironsmith too passionate for display"[117] and instants later as "a revolting clump of scars" [118]; and Beloved's "smile under her chin,"[119] the scarred body functions as a textual record of slavery. The metaphorical descriptions of these texts suggest the lack of ordinary language to express the horrific marks of slavery. In Perry's work, stigmata also embody the tangible nature of historical memory—a historical memory, which is as fragmented and webbed as the scars it left.

Stigmata: Multiple Subjects

In the magical realist text, the disfigurement of the body and physical pain, as Faris states, constitutes "a form of historical knowledge, . . . [which] causes us to 'know' history in a horrifying new and different way."[120] In Perry's novel, the scarred body functions as conductor of history. On one level, the stigmata work as a physical manifestation of Morrison's concept of rememory, the never-ending resurfacing of a traumatic and partially lost history. On another level, it functions as a powerful means to transform abstract history into a tangible reality. At this level it works as an element of connection between the ancestors and Lizzie, the past and present, and the real and the magical: "[Y]ou're marked so you won't forget this time, so you will remember."[121] In this context, it is worth noting that when Lizzie makes reference to her marked body, she evokes her bond with the foremothers: "A spasm of pain sears my back. I gasp, trying to keep my focus, and in that moment Grace steps forward and takes the blow. We stand together in her battered body, bent double with pain.[122] In this passage grandmother and granddaughter stand together in a magical realm receiving the blow which marked the back of the first woman of the family, Ayo, the African. Lizzie's 'maze of scars, from neck to waist and beyond, permanent remembrance of the power of time folded back upon itself'"[123] are the evidences of a forgotten history. Like Morrison's rememory, Perry's stigmata constitute the urgent call of history pressing against the forgetfulness of time.

However, the ancestral apparition in Perry's novel is quite different from Morrison's unforgiving ghost. It is worth noting that when "Grace steps forward to take the blow," she emerges as a protective figure. In this sense, the name "Grace" becomes highly significant. According to Christian beliefs only the grace of God can free humanity from its original sin, which in the context of Perry's work can be equated with the loss of African American history. On another level, it is worth noting the distinction made by St. Thomas Aquinas between nature and the supernatural. According to Aquinas, the former can be known by reason while the latter can only be understood through the *grace* of God. Thus Lizzie's grandmother functions in the text as a bridge to the magical and the knowledge of the past it holds.

The acquisition of that knowledge is a painful process, and the "[p]roof of lives intersecting from past to present" is the imprint of slavery in Lizzie's body.[124] The use of the vocable "intersection" highlights the novel's attempt to represent the effects of slavery in contemporary America. In this way, like Beloved, Perry's protagonist functions in the text as an epicenter for African American history. Lizzie's experience of the supernatural allowed her to learn the ancestors' names and their history by becoming like them in a fusion of minds and bodies, literally moving inside them, "mov[ing] [their] fingers and toes," and returning home "with dirty feet"[125] from old African dust: "I can see her [Grace] and I can see through her. I remember what her body feels like. And both of us, me and her, are sort of superimposed on another person [Ayo]."[126] This points toward a sense of subjectivity, which is multiple rather than individual, a narrative strategy central to the representation of a sense of forgotten history in the magical realist text. The merging of individual subjectivity with that of ancestral others embodies a collective memory that needs to be honored and remembered. This notion of subjectivity evokes Morrison's representation of a transhistorical self in *Beloved.* In this way, the apparitions in both Perry's and Morrison's works "refuse to remain locked into modern categories of individual psychology, insisting instead that the self is actualized by participation in communal and cosmic categories,"[127] as Zamora puts it.

The notion of self in *Stigmata* is, therefore, not only multiple but also mythical: "I come from a long line of forever people. We are forever. Here at the bottom of heaven we live in the circle. We back and gone and back again . . . This is for those whose bones lay sleepin in the heart of mother ocean for those who tomorrows I never knew who groaned and died in that dark damp aside me. You rite this daughter for me and for them."[128] This correlation between the notion of multiple subjectivity and a mythical sense of self is essential, as we have seen in relation to *Beloved*, to enlarge the narrative space in order to contain more distant layers of the past, intersecting both personal, familial, and collective history: "*You rite this daughter for me and for them.*" Here there is a clear evocation of the slave narrative as a personal and collective record. However, the historical record constructed by Ayo and her descendants, unlike traditional slave narratives, does not bear witness solely to the lives these women lived and those of their immediate communities. Perry's construction of a mythical notion of self as an authoritative narrating agent of a history that intersects broader notions of identity, time, and reality allows her to include the history of those who did not leave a trace in realistic modes of representation. In this context, the usage of the adverb "forever" to describe the lineage of women who are made to remember their historical past emphasizes the centrality of the supernatural element in the magical realist text. Without the supernatural as an essential narrative device in the resurfacing of history, the line of "*Forever people*" would have been disrupted and with it the connection to the Middle Passage, the beginning of African American history. This is a beginning that has been extended in the works of African American women writers. Walker, Jones, Butler, and Williams clearly locate it in slavery, while Morrison reaches back in order to represent the Middle Passage.[129] Ayo's narrative also suggests the imperative to remember the history of those buried in the Atlantic Ocean, evoking the "Sixty Million and more"[130] to whom Morrison's novel is dedicated, but her memories of the homeland, of her mother, and of a way of life that was whole constitute a more innovative strategy in Perry's work. The narrative of Ayo's kidnapping is significantly preceded by the description of an ordinary day in which daughter and mother rose early to walk the dusty road, which led to the market where they sold the cloth that the latter wove and dyed, highlighting the child's sense of loss: "*I los my family that day I los my home that day*."[131] Perry's reference to Ayo's home as "Afraca"[132] and her intonation as the "strange voice of hers from Afraca"[133] on one hand emphasizes Ayo's loss of a sense of geographical and cultural identity. The distinctiveness of her home place is lost in a substantive that describes a whole continent, stressing the memories vanished in the transatlantic crossing. On the other hand, the usage of the continent's name to indicate a person's homeland also calls attention to standardized and uniform Western representations of what, ultimately, is a vast and culturally and linguistically varied region. The concept of hegemonic discourse is, thus, a fluid one.

With Lizzie's acknowledgment of her multiple subjectivity, the fact that she is "[o]ld and young at the same time,"[134] there is a narrative departure from the fantastic, the "soft opening and closing of a door between adjacent worlds"[135] to an acceptance of "the forces that have brought [her] to stand here with a clear view of the past and the present and the marriage of both."[136] It is worth noting that the "adjacent" worlds—close but separate, on the frontier of which resided the place for hesitation between the real and the magical—become married and one when the hesitation dissipates and Lizzie understands that past and present and the magical and the real are part of the same realm. In this way, according to Todorov's theoretical approach to the fantastic, *Stigmata* can be included among "works that sustain the hesitation characteristic of the true fantastic for a long period, but that ultimately end in the marvellous or in the uncanny."[137] When the sense of hesitation dissipates, the frontier between the real and the magical, which Todorov describes as "a frontier between two adjacent realms"[138] is also dissolved and both character and reader enter in the magical real.

Stigmata: The Quilt of Memory

When Lizzie finally leaves the psychiatric hospital and returns to her parents' house, she knows that the past needs to be remembered and actualized in the context of the community. The actualization of the historical past by cultural practice is an essential means of recovering African American history. In this context, folk traditions such as religious rituals, song and storytelling, food and quilt making constitute an important means of bearing witness to the past, as discussed in relation to *Jubilee*. Thus it is interesting to note that among Beloved's fractured memories of the Middle Passage, there is a record of a song, a cultural scrap, a testimony of the humanity of the person who sang it and of those who listened to it. In Perry's novel that fragment of cultural memory is a piece of blue cloth that Ayo brought from Africa, creased in a ball enclosed in her fist as a tangible memory of home. The scrap of fabric functions in the narrative as a link to Africa, but it also symbolizes the passing on of the historical testimony along the generational line. Ayo's mother, the master dyer, made and tinted the fabric, Ayo brought it from Africa, Grace uses a piece in her quilt and puts another fragment in the trunk as a family relic destined for her granddaughter and "a very old bit of blue cloth"[139] reaches Lizzie, which she uses in her own quilt to be passed on the next generation. The "bit of blue cloth" recalls the "teeny faded blue piece from Great Grandpa Ezra's uniform that he wore in the Civil War"[140] pieced in a quilt in Walker's short story "Everyday Use" where quilting is also represented as a means of passing on African America tradition and history.

"Quilts," as Floris Barnett Cash states, "can be used as resources in reconstructing the experiences of African-American women. They provide a record of their cultural and political past . . . The voices of black women are stitched within their quilts."[141] In this sense, the quilt constitutes another form of oral history: "I'm telling Grace's story with this quilt—just as she told Ayo's story with hers—and the fabric has to hold up at least until the next story teller comes along."[142] The use of vocables such as "telling" and "story teller" highlight the function of the quilt as a significant narrative form. "The narrative quilts," as Cash observes, "are a distinct American form."[143] However, as this critic goes on to say, the "use of appliqued [*sic*] techniques is rooted in African culture."[144] In this way, Lizzie's appliquéd quilt, "[l]ike Grandmamma Grace's,"[145] reflects the hybrid nature of African American tradition. The technique Lizzie uses in the making of the quilt is similar to that used in the tapestries of West Africa, while the narrative structure roots it in an American tradition, evoking the geographical and cultural journey of black people from the African continent to the New World.

In this way, Lizzie's sense of design points to a distinct African American aesthetic. For example, it is worth noting Lizzie's reference to the African American artist Romare Bearden.[146] Bearden's modernist aesthetic combines traditional black American techniques such as the patterns of quilt making and jazz with photography in order to represent a tableau of past and present and personal and collective experience of the people of African descent in America. "Through his work," as Sharon F. Patton observes, "Bearden attempted to create . . . an autobiography, and a historical narrative of black life,"[147] recalling the personal and historical record, which Lizzie attempts to design. In his collages, Bearden "effectively captured both contemporary urban black life and the quickly disappearing rural southern black life . . . Quickly he developed an iconography of black culture and life."[148] The pictorial representation of history in Bearden's photomontages is particularly relevant to Lizzie for whom the quilt is a means of "reclaiming [her] sixty-one-year-old daughter,"[149] Sarah, by revealing to her a lost history via a sequence of images.

Sarah is Lizzie's mother, weakened by the years her daughter spent in psychiatric institutions, but she is also Grace/Lizzie's daughter, the child abandoned by her mother at the age of seven when the weight of the past drove her away from the present, her family, and her community. Thus, in *Stigmata*, like the texts previously discussed, the mother-daughter relationship is the focal point of history. Lizzie engages her mother/daughter in the making of the quilt as an attempt to reveal her multiple subjectivities. However, when Sarah lost her connection to the ancestors, she also lost those distinct African American ways of passing on the testimony and is, therefore, confused by Lizzie's choice of form for her quilt: "'You could tell better what was going on if the pictures were in a row,' Mother grumbles . . . 'This is hopelessly jumbled.'"[150] Sarah finds "the design unsettling"[151] because her Western education taught her to read history as a chronological and, therefore, linear narrative.

Hence, the quilt functions in the narrative as vehicle of cultural recovery. Quilt making, as a group activity, is an important aspect of what Perry attempts to achieve with this specific usage of African American folklore. In this context, the process of sewing the blanket is as important as the end product. According to Pat Ferrero, quilting bees were "invaluable agents of cultural cohesion and group identity."[152] Thus in order to recognize in the quilt the story of her own mother and Lizzie's multiple identities as Lizzie, Ayo, and Grace, Sarah has to engage in African American traditional cultural practice. In other words, the quilt serves an instrument for Sarah's reintegration in the community's traditions and history, establishing a common ground for the reunion between mother and daughter and past and present. Quilts, as Olga Idriss Davis puts it, reveal "the choice of symbols Black women used within their community to create a shared, common meaning of self and the world. Thus the quilt serves as a vehicle for re-inventing the symbolic expression of identity and freedom."[153] The symbolic or pictorial nature of quilts is critical in the representation of African American history. In *Stigmata*, images are a crucial means of depicting a traumatic history. The symbolic quality of the images used both in the quilt and in John Paul's paintings not only emphasize distinct African American narrative modes, which do not use the written word as a mode of representation, but also highlight the difficulty in using verbal language to express the experience of slavery, evoking Beloved's words: "[H]ow can I say things that are pictures?"

In this way, as Davis observes in relation to African American children's literature, quilt making in the works of black women writers functions as a means of "conceptualiz[ing] identity and redefin[ing] history, setting in place a dialectical tension between traditional learning and critical literacy. While traditional learning encourages the dominant discourse of cultural hegemony, critical literacy redefines the parameters of knowledge and power by making space for oppressed voices to name their experience, reclaim their history, and transform their future."[154]

Thus Perry's use of the quilt as a means of challenging hegemonic forms of discourse continues and expands the tradition established in the works of Walker, Jones, Williams, and Morrison in which folk traditions, song, and storytelling emerge as central vehicles for the recreation of African American identity.

In the African American novel, oral traditions emerge as an effective means of imparting a sense of identity, community, history, and the valuable life skills essential for the survival of an oppressed group. In her novel, Perry also recovers this didactic role of folk traditions. Thus Perry establishes a link between quilting and storytelling as means of recovering history and actualizing the past via cultural practice. Cuesta Benberry writes, "Quilts are narrative rather than abstract. They flow directly out of the oral tradition which used storytelling as a way to impart the culture and preserve the history of the people. Storytelling and the story quilt impart moral and spiritual lessons as well as personal family genealogy for future generations. To view a story quilt is to learn about the quilters, their families, values and life experiences."[155]

It is precisely this cultural and spiritual lesson, which Lizzie hopes Sarah will gain. With each stitch the women sew a continuous female lineage connecting the present to the African past. The quilt, however, is also about the future not only in the sense that it allows the testimony to be passed to the next generation but also as a means of healing and overcoming the traumatic past: "That's what this quilt is about. The past. And putting the past aside when we're through."[156] Hence, there is a sense that if the past must be acknowledged, it also needs to be transformed. "*Everything said in the beginning must be said better than in the beginning*,"[157] as Ursa Corregidora says, pointing to the necessity of representing history so that it can be acknowledged without crippling those who journey back to the ancestral past. Cultural practices such as storytelling, song, and quilting enable the representation of a traumatic history while facilitating the necessary establishment of a frontier between personal history and familial and collective experience so that the past does not become a trap for those who engage with it, a place where the horror offers little possibility of healing and reconciliation. In *Stigmata*, functioning in conjunction with the recovery of traditional cultural practices as a means of reimagining the past in ways that are meaningful and useful in the present is the characters' acceptance of the magical. This acceptance of the supernatural makes the journey back to the past a cathartic passage, allowing the transcendence of a ghostly past and the communion with the ancestors.

In this context, memory and the conscious act of remembering are key issues in the construction of a context in which past and present can be reconciled: "I am free, I remember. These things can't hurt me anymore. The story on those diary pages belongs to me, but they don't own me. My memories live somewhere spacious now; the airless chamber of horrors has melted into the ground."[158] Lizzie's initial experience of the supernatural trapped her in a painful cycle of repetition in which she acted out a ghostly past for which there seemed to be no room or purpose in the present. Moreover, like Ursa, she struggled to find "somewhere spacious" where she could reconcile her life with the ancestral past. The "airless chamber of horrors" evokes the oppressive atmosphere of the hold of slave ship, but it also suggests Lizzie's entrapment in a web of old and dusty memories. The engagement with a traumatic past is a painful journey and it constitutes a simultaneous process of discovery of the ancestral other and of one's self. Thus it is significant that just before Sarah recognizes in Lizzie her long lost mother, she carries the quilt, "the keys that unlock the door to what you call the past," "like a gushing wound that she cradles close to her chest."[159] The red cloth draped in Sarah's arms evokes both the bloody history of the foremothers and the pain of its memory for their descendants. Once Lizzie, and later Sarah, understands that the magical is a means of reviving a lost and forgotten past, history becomes a regenerative force. Hence, Lizzie's link between remembrance and liberty is central to Perry's concept of history. The reconstruction of the past via the foremothers' memories enables Lizzie to attain a freedom that comes from an understanding of her personal experience in the context of the collective history. This sense of freedom is not equated with the physical liberty sought by the slaves; it corresponds to a spiritual freedom or, in other words, the ability to claim control over a free inner self, since, as Morrison's Sethe states, "[f]reeing yourself [is] one thing; claiming ownership of that freed self [is] another."[160] Memory, therefore, offers cathartic possibilities when transformed into narrative modes that allow the individual to share it and honor it in the context of the community.

This recognition of the past expressed in the faith of the community is central to the interpretation of *Stigmata* as a text that begins in the fantastic and ends in the magically real, signaling the recovery of a lost history. Lizzie and Sarah reclaim the foremothers' story, acknowledging the importance of the past in their lives in twentieth-century America. The present is, therefore, imbedded in the past, and history is spatial rather than temporal. In this context, it is important to emphasize the significance of Lizzie's quilt where past and present merge in a graphic space. This evokes the techniques used in Bearden's collages where African American history is represented, as Patton states, in "an overall shallow pictorial space . . . There is a similar jazz-rhythm created for the eye in the juxtaposition of different-sized figures in one spatial plane."[161] The concept of juxtaposition of different figures and their projection in a "pictorial space" is useful in articulating Perry's representation of identity, the supernatural, and history. Lizzie's experience of the supernatural juxtaposes past and present in a space shared by her and her foremothers. In this space in which past and present come together, their identities are also juxtaposed in order to represent a sense of self that is multiple, mythical, and therefore representative of the African American experience. In this sense, chronological history gives way to a spatial sense of history characterized by the converging of times and identities in the shared space of memory. Thus quilt making becomes a canvas of synthesis in which seemingly contradictory forces such as past and present, personal and collective can be contained, evoking Houston Baker Jr.'s view of the blues as a "a robust matrix, where endless antinomies are mediated and understanding and explanation finds conditions of possibility."[162] Bearden's collages also contain these paradoxical elements. His technique, as Ralph Ellison states, reflects "leaps in consciousness, distortions, paradoxes, reversals, telescoping of time and surreal blending of styles, values, hopes and dreams which characterize much of the Negro history."[163] In this context, quilt making as a form of synthesis, mirrors the magical realist text in its attempt to present real and the magical as part of the same continuum, while revising the hegemonic historical record.[164]

Stigmata: Recovering the Lost History

Linear history allowed Sarah to live in a straight line, with her back turned to her past, the process of making the quilt allows her to acknowledge history as a force present in the shared space of memory—a space inhabited by the living and the dead. It is Sarah's revision of a sense of history based on white Western modes of representation that allows her to acknowledge the ancestors and their sorrowful history, realizing that "the slaves who were our selves had so much to say,"[165] as Ntozake Shange puts it. This clearly contrasts with other works in which black history remains irretrievable. In *Kindred*, Butler's protagonist finds herself being repeatedly taken back from 1976 California to an 1813 plantation to answer a cry for help from her slave ancestor Rufus. Although Dana saves his life several times, being black and female in nineteenth-century Southern America, she is made into his slave. In this way, in similar ways to Lizzie, Dana is initiated into her ancestors' past by having firsthand experience of what they endured in slavery. Dana soon learns that a "slave was a slave" and "[a]nything could be done to her."[166] After being struck by Rufus,[167] Dana resists his rape attempt and kills him, at the cost of her left arm. Similar to other times, when her life is at risk, she returns to the present. This time her return is final since, with Rufus dead, there is nobody to call her to the past.

Back in the twentieth-century, Dana and her white husband Kevin, who was also transported to the past, travel South to "[t]ouch solid evidence that those people existed,"[168] and what they had experienced. They "found the court-house an old church, [and] a few other buildings that time had not worn away"[169] and in an old newspaper article, they read that "Mr. Rufus Weylin had been killed when his house caught fire and was partially destroyed"[170]; however, the only information they found about the other slaves with whom Dana lived in bondage was a "notice of [their] sale,"[171] and nothing could be unearthed of Dana's ancestors.

In *Kindred*, black people's history is marked by its invisibility and discontinuity. Once the intersection between past and present was more real for Dana than their distinction; however, back in her time, she realizes that her history, like her body, is fragmented. Dana's physical loss functions as a metaphor for a history that cannot be recovered. Although Dana learned the names of the ancestors and heard their stories, she cannot reclaim the ancient tradition of storytelling, like Lizzie reclaimed that of quilt making, and communicate the learned history: "If I told anyone else about this, anyone at all, they wouldn't think we were so sane."[172] In this way, without a language to organize and communicate her experience, "Dana's physical fracturing," as Karla F. C. Holloway points out, "takes both a physical and a spiritual form, it is doubly disabling."[173] In *Kindred*, "[h]istory . . . is a nightmare from which [one] is trying to awake."[174] Neither Dana nor Kevin knows how to convey their experiences, and for them past and present are irremediably separated. Butler spends considerable time describing life in slavery, narrating in detail the work of slaves, their living conditions, and the relationships they establish with each other. However, in the end of the novel, her characters fail to communicate the importance of this knowledge of the past to their contemporary experiences.

Baby of the Family (1989) by Tina McElroy Ansa is another example of a novel that represents the past as irrevocably lost. Seven-year-old Lena, who from the moment of birth is recognized as having the power to see and communicate with ghosts, is initiated into her past by the ghost of the slave Rachel. The specter sets a spell on the child, immobilizing her so that she cannot run away and so the past can be passed on: "'Child,' she said softly. 'Do you know how long I been waiting for somebody like you to come along so I can tell them all of this, so I can share some of this?'"[175]

With Rachel, Lena learns that slavery is not something "[she] read about in school."[176] However, when the child recovers her mobility and she moves away from the ghost, her only reaction comes in the form of unnerved cry: "Seeing Rachel, hearing the ghost's story, knowing that she was the only one who saw her and that she better not tell anyone or she could get sick . . . It was all too much."[177] Lena's hysterical fit expresses the despair that emanates from the fact that she, like Dana, has no means to organize and communicate her experience. Lena's inability to mirror Rachel's gesture and tell the story of the slave and the story of that afternoon on the beach where they both met makes the link between the past and the present irretrievably lost.

History is for Lena and Dana an experience of profound isolation and displacement, since what they witness cannot be articulated in the context of their lives. Hence, the fissure between past and present cannot be bridged. The magical realist text offers that link between the present and a lost history, between the individual and forgotten ancestors, translating absence into tangible presence. Thus the supernatural, as Zamora states, "embod[ies] the fundamental magical realist sense that reality always exceeds our capacity to describe or understand or prove and that the function of literature is to engage this excessive reality, to honor that which we may grasp intuitively but never fully or finally define."[178] As evident in *Beloved* and *Stigmata*, magical realism becomes an essential form of expression to address such incomplete definitions, such traumatic pasts.

In *Stigmata*, the ancestral presence escapes the defining principles that govern realist narratives, but Perry's novel does not aim to explain the unexplainable. Rather, it seeks to enlarge a narrative space constricted by realist principles of time, space, and identity in order to represent the silenced voices of history. In order to achieve this, the novelist uses a series of narrative techniques, producing a written patchwork of Lizzie's and her foremothers' histories, creating a narrative space for the contemporary narrator and the voices of the ancestors. The supernatural represents the central vehicle for the representation of history, but Perry uses others, constructing an intricate narrative pattern. A primary characteristic of this narrative is a call-and-response structure,, which facilitates the dialogue between Lizzie and her foremothers. Her memory of the day Ayo was kidnapped in an African market encapsulates the call-and-response structure that informs the novel. Ayo's mother puts "her hand on [Ayo's/Lizzie's] head"[179] and wakes her up: "We have a long way. We must start."[180] This call from the ancestor initiates the critical journey from home to the market. For Ayo, this is a trip without return that symbolizes other journeys, the Middle Passage and Lizzie's return to the ancestral past. The ancestors' call from the past is the primary medium of historical reconstruction. In "*old memor[ies] comin to visit,*"[181] Ayo and Grace summon Lizzie to the past. Ayo's call is urgent, "*all pain,*" but Grace, as already mentioned, acts as a protective figure. Her scope to shield Lizzie from the unrelenting force of the past is very limited but she intervenes to share Lizzie's pain and, more importantly, to help her granddaughter to make sense out of her experiences. Lizzie cannot resist her foremothers' call and, in turn, Grace responds to her granddaughter's pain and confusion:

> *Well,* says Grace, in an almost mocking tone. *We was back there. There in that ole house back up in them woods. That there was the night, baby chile, that almost did me in.*
>
> "Yeah," I think, trying to focus through the pill-induced haze.
>
> . . . *Yeah,* she continues, *that Ayo, she rushed in without warning and there I am flat on my back, wiping up blood from some old wound from some dead time.*
>
> . . . "On the ship?" I ask . . .
>
> *On the ship. Couldn't get off . . . So they drug me off and everywhere that iron chain touched me blood run like a river, down my arms and ankles and . . .*
>
> "Onto the deck of the ship," I whispered, sitting up in bed . . . It's dark for a moment and then, miraculously, there's sunlight and cool salty air and—raw, unapologetic pain.
>
> *You see?* Grace says matter-of-factly as I give up and let loose a stabbing scream.[182]

Grace's words cannot prepare Lizzie for the pain she is about to experience—the pain of Ayo aboard the slave ship—but her presence functions as a means of representing the bond between the three women and dramatizes the need for dialogue between past and present. The repetition of vocables and phrases such as "Yeah" and "On the ship" reflects the repetition characteristic of blues stanzas and mirrors their call-and-response structure. Perry's construction of this call-and-response structure goes beyond the dialogue established between individual characters and articulates the necessary dialogue between the dead and the living, magical and the real, and the past and the present.

The figure of the ancestor as a mediator between past and present who will show the path of historical and cultural recovery also appears in Marshall's *Praisesong for the Widow*. Avey's engagement with the past is initiated by a call from her great-aunt Cuney who appears to her in dreams, a disruptive force in her orderly middle-class life: "A hand raise . . . she was motioning for her to come on the walk that had been a ritual with them during the Augusts she had spent as a girl on Tatem Island."[183] Later in the narrative, the hand of another ancestral figure functions in the text as an extension of Aunt Cuney's hands, replicating the call to the past: Lebert "was holding her firmly by the elbow," dragging her to the boat that will take them to the island of Carriacou, and to Avey's personal and ancestral past. In Morrison's *Song of Solomon*, Milkman also responds to the forebear's call to the past: "[T]here was no way for him to resist climbing up toward her outstretched hands, her fingers spread wide for him."[184] Circe's call incites Milkman to enter the past, and, embracing him, she transforms the abstract past into a concrete, tangible experience. It is important to stress that in Perry's narrative and in those of Morrison and Marshall, the call of the ancestor is represented as an overpowering force, which demands a response. It is also worth noting how both Marshall and Morrison create figures, which defy the boundaries of realistic characterization, belonging to a realm where there are no fixed frontiers between life and death, past and present, the real and the magical. These are characters who like Ayo and Grace create a space of ambiguity, which facilitates the portrayal of a history lost in realistic modes of representation.

Stigmata is also structured around Lizzie's journal entries interwoven with Joy's diary (signaled in italics), which in turn contains Ayo's dictated narrative. Joy's journal is a narrative of dialogical intimacy clearly lost with the disintegration of family units when several generations no longer live in close proximity. This facilitates not only the necessary trust to relate the experience of slavery but also the record of the mundane tasks that bond families and communities: "*Frank got Mama garden turned over. She say she gon wait another week though cause she say more frost comin. Meantime she makin a little dress . . . for the girl baby she say is comin. Aint no baby comin Mama I say . . . She cant get here cause Im in the way she say.*"[185] The use of "I say," "she say" is a clear mark of the continuous dialogue between mother and daughter, but the representation of the ordinary in this passage reveals Ayo's sixth sense, the one that allowed her to predict weather and the arrival of her granddaughter, and foresee her own death. Joy's silent wait for a child after being "*married a long time*"[186] is also subtly revealed. In the call-and-response strategy, repetition is a key issue in passing on history. It is by repetition that history is shared and memorized. For example Ayo's dedication of her narrative is repeated with variations. These variations are quite minor, but they signal the reappearance of certain passages in Joy's diary, emphasizing their importance in Ayo's story.[187]

Quilt making, the form that both Grace and Lizzie choose to recount the ancestral past, is another narrative technique used by Perry to represent a fragmented and layered history. Quilting functions in the novel as a parallel narrative of these women's past, illustrating possible and meaningful ways of bearing witness to the past outside the boundaries of the written word. In *Stigmata*, quilt making is a form of validating oral history as a legitimate way of recording history. However, it is important to emphasize that Perry makes a concerted attempt to reconcile the "dialectical tension," to return to Davis's phraseology, between literacy and orality by establishing a parallel written and oral record of African American history in the use of journals and quilts. This is a significant attempt to reconcile the tensions inherent in the works of African American historical fiction that reclaim and emphasize oral traditions in the confinements of the written text. Hence, it is worth noting that Ayo's "strange voice of hers from Afraca" is recorded in Joy's journal, making the written record a central vehicle for the retrieval of the ancestor's voice.

Perry's representation of the written record as a valid way to record African American history and the introduction of Joy's journal both as a narrative device and as evidence that former slaves recorded their stories and passed them on to the subsequent generations in contexts completely outside the abolitionist circuit constitute an innovative aspect of Perry's novel. In addition, she continues and reworks the tradition of the African American novel. Williams's Dessa, like Ayo, also entrusts her life story to her descendant, rejecting the figure of a white abolitionist as amanuensis. *Dessa Rose* ends with the protagonist entrusting her life story to her grandchild, who in turn will "say it back,"[188] producing a written record of the foremother's history. In *Stigmata*, the reader witnesses the importance of that written record in the lives of the women of Ayo's lineage, stressing how the written word can be populated with a distinct African American cadence, intention, and imagination, to paraphrase Mikhail Bakhtin. This clearly contrasts with the distrust of the written word in *Corregidora* and Morrison's assertion that Beloved's story is not one "to pass on."[189] In fact, the only written record of *Beloved*, besides the news clip of her mother's deviant deed, are seven letters engraved in her tombstone given in exchange for a few minutes of sex.

In the refrain of the final chapter of *Beloved*, "It was not a story to pass on,"[190] there is an obvious inherent paradox. The story has already been passed on to the reader and history, which in the closing of the novel emerges as the occasional "knuckles brushing a cheek in sleep seeming to belong to the sleeper,"[191] has already been presented "as muscle and flesh for the real and living bones of history," [192] as Walker puts it, and resurrected by the author's imagination. In this way, in the ending of *Beloved*, Morrison plays with preconceived notions of reality in order to demonstrate how realistic modes of representation limit the unexplained and, more importantly, do not recreate a history for which there are no records. Thus the closing of *Beloved* serves as a metafictional commentary on illusion, an illusion that does not emanate from the magical but from realistic modes of representation. Magical realist authors, as Zamora puts it, "write *against* the illusionism of narrative realism by heightening their own narrative investment in illusion. They undermine the credibility of narrative realism by flaunting the relative *in*credibility of their own texts. In short, they point to literary devices by which "realistic" literary worlds are constructed and constrained, and they dramatize by counterrealistic narrative strategies the ways in which those literary worlds (and their inhabitants) may be liberated."[193]

In this way, the magical realist text is essentially a text of counter narrative that aims at critiquing, revising, and transforming the world as perceived in hegemonic forms of representation. In the African American text this exercise of transformation aims at recreating stereotypical views of identity and history. The supernatural emerges both in *Beloved* and *Stigmata* as the central agent for this transformation of the world. This necessity to transform linear history and narratives comes from practices of institutional abuse and a need to fill in the gaps of a lost history, unsettling forms of univocal discourse. According to Salman Rushdie, "[T]he fiction of the Victorian age, which was realist, has . . . been inadequate as a description of the world for some time now . . . For realism to convince, there must be a fairly broad agreement between the author and the reader about the nature of the world that is being described." However, as Rushdie goes on to say, "now we don't have this kind of consensus about the world."[194] In this sense, the magical realist text emerges as text of polyphony. In the African American context, the ancestral apparition emerges as a voice that needs to be rescued from the caverns of time and memory. However, for the past to be recovered, the ancestors' voices have to find an echo in those of the descendants so that the historical record can be revised and actualized; history becomes a space in which time is freed from simple linearity, a world that is "multiple, permeable, transformative, animistic."

Conclusion

Having as their point of departure the idea that "the past," as James Baldwin notes, "is all that makes the present coherent, and further, that the past will remain horrible as long as we refuse to assess it honestly,"[1] African American women writers embark upon representations of history that aim to connect past and present and individual and community. In this context, history emerges as the central vehicle of cultural reconstruction, of community renewal, and self-discovery.

The texts selected for the present study represent African American history written from a female perspective. Each work offers new narrative strategies in order to represent slavery, and works within a literary tradition that is reimagined and revised. In this sense, Margaret Walker's *Jubilee*, Gayl Jones's *Corregidora*, Sherley Anne Williams's *Dessa Rose*, Toni Morrison's *Beloved*, and Phyllis Perry's *Stigmata* constitute a literary corpus, which sets and reflects the narrative and thematic trends of contemporary African American fiction written by women, signaling the establishment of a poetics that gives shape and cohesion to a literary tradition, which has often been disrupted. The critical center of these novels is the recreation of the ancestral past. In their representations of the past, black women writers recover the oral traditions developed and tested in an experience of slavery, and history of oppression and adversity. In this exercise of recovering and recreating the oral tradition, they also reclaim their literary foremothers—women whose works have largely remained outside the literary canon. People, as Walker states in a 1979 interview,

> don't know about Zora Neale Hurston or Nella Larson. They don't know that Georgia Douglass Johnson . . . was a bestseller in her day. Frances Ellen Watkins Harper was selling her poetry successfully before the Civil War, in the 1850s . . . Nobody remembers these women. Jessie Fauset. Or a woman who published much later than the Renaissance, but who was there at the time—Dorothy West. A woman who was the wife of Paul Laurence Dunbar—Alice Dunbar Nelson. There are a baker's dozen of these women in the Twenties, and then, in the last thirty years to forty years, you could name another dozen.[2]

Phillis Wheatley, Harriet Jacobs, Harriet Wilson, Pauline Hopkins, among others are names that could be added to Walker's list. African American women writers have been at the forefront of creating a literary tradition. In 1773, Wheatley became the first African American to publish a book of poetry, while in 1841, Ann Plato was the first African American to publish a book of essays, and in 1859 Wilson was the first person of African descent to publish a novel. The scenario outlined by Walker began to change in the 1970s and 1980s with the emergence of Black Studies departments and the publication of anthologies such as *The Norton Anthology of African American Literature* (1997) edited by Henry Louis Gates Jr. and Nellie Y. McKay and the series by nineteenth-century black women writers published by the Schomburg Center, which made available to the wider public texts that had long been out of print. In spite of such developments, there are authors who remain poorly studied and outside the mainstream American canon. In his foreword to the *Schomburg Library of Nineteenth-Century Women Writers*, Henry Louis Gates Jr. discusses the disruption and fragmentation of this literary tradition: "[T]he writings of nineteenth-century Afro-Americans in general have remained buried in obscurity, accessible only in research libraries or in overpriced and poorly edited reprints. Many of these books have never been reprinted at all."[3] However, despite the discontinuities that mark the African American literary tradition, eighteenth- and nineteenth-century black female writers, as Gates states, "founded and nurtured the black women's literary tradition, which must be revived, explicated, analyzed, and debated before we can understand more completely the formal shaping of this tradition."[4]

In this context, it is important to acknowledge the role of Walker, Jones, Williams, and Morrison as academics involved in the study of black American literature and culture. Walker dedicated her life to the study and promotion of African American culture. She founded the Institute for the Study of History, Life, and Culture of Black People at Jackson State University (now renamed the Margaret Walker Alexander National Research Center) and a few years later, in 1973, she organized the Phillis Wheatley Festival. Jones was an assistant professor of English and African American and African studies at the University of Michigan from 1976 until the early 1980s. In 1973 Williams became the first African American literature professor at the University of California at San Diego, La Jolla, and began a distinguished teaching career. She was also an advisory editor of *Callaloo* and the *Langston Hughes Review*. By the time of her premature death in 1999, she was head of the writing section of the University of California–San Diego Department of Literature. Morrison has also lectured in English and African American literature at several universities since 1955. During her years as a senior editor for Random House, she edited the works of women writers such as Toni Cade Bambara and Angela Davis and two of Jones's novels, *Corregidora* and *Eva's Man* (1976). Moreover, these writers "revived, explicated, analyzed, and debated" African American literature in theoretical studies such as Walker's *Richard Wright, Daemonic Genius, A Portrait of the Man, A Critical Look* (1988), *How I Wrote Jubilee and Other Essays on Life and Literature* (1990), and *On Being Female, Black, and Free: Essays by Margaret Walker, 1932–1992* (1997), Williams's *Give Birth to Brightness: A Thematic Study in Neo-Black Literature* (1972), Jones's *Liberating Voices: Oral Tradition in African American Literature* (1991), and Morrison's *Playing in the Dark: Whiteness and the Literary Imagination* (1992). In their roles as artists, lecturers, critics, biographers, and editors, these writers rediscover and address the African American literary tradition while shaping its new directions.

In tracing the development of the representation of slavery from Walker's *Jubilee* (1966) to Perry's *Stigmata* (1998), it became evident how the novels discussed establish an intertextual dialogue with other works in the African American literary tradition that focus on a female perspective of black history and experience, illustrating the importance of the legacy of nineteenth-century black women writers. In this context, Jacobs's *Incidents in the Life of a Slave Girl: Written by Herself* is benchmarking work since it establishes important concerns and themes in the work of contemporary female authors. Jacobs's preoccupation with the representation of slavery from the viewpoint of the female slave, her recognition of the importance of her narrative in the correction and establishment of the American historical record, and her quest for literacy, voice, and authority over her experience set important trends, which contemporary writers revisit and rework. Another important text is Harriet Wilson's novel, which signals the necessary gaps left in nineteenth-century writings by women. These omissions that "would most provoke shame in our good anti-slavery friends"[5] constitute a critical focus of the contemporary novels here discussed. Wilson's work also emphasizes the complexities of the African American experience, addressing issues of miscegenation and racism in the North.

In the second half of the nineteenth-century, Harper's work marks an important departure from the autobiographical genre and identifies the novel as a central form to target mass readership and construct positive images of African Americans. Both Harper and Hopkins were too concerned with devising a black, middle-class elite that could be a role model for, and a leader of, the masses to create protagonists that could be considered a representative. However, their legacy in the establishment of the didactic novel is of major significance. The desire to enlighten their readers about African American history and to revise and add to its record is a central element in the works of Walker, Jones, Williams, Morrison, and Perry.

This desire to inform their readership about a lost past is intrinsically linked to a sense of social responsibility that informs African American literature. Toni Cade Bambara sees the role of literature as an instrument of social change: "My responsibility to myself, my neighbors, my family and the human family is to try to tell the truth . . . I do not think that literature is *the* primary instrument of social transformation, but I think it has potency."[6] Similarly, for Audre Lorde, "the question of social protest and art is inseparable . . . I loved words. But what was beautiful had to serve the purpose of changing my life . . . That's the beginning of social protest."[7] This is a view shared by authors discussed throughout this study, which Williams summarizes by stating, "The imaginative work . . . [is about] showing people something about themselves and their relationship to the world. I really believe that my writing has a purpose: to teach and delight."[8] In the exploration of the past, thus, lies a concern with the present and the direction of American society as a whole. Writers such as Jacobs, Harper, and Hopkins, as discussed in Chapter 1, wrote to effect social change, a trend in which I have argued is developed by these contemporary novelists.

The intertextual dialogue established in the works of African American women writers is established not only with nineteenth-century works but also with contemporary texts. For example, in *The Living Is Easy*, Dorothy West expresses how "[s]lavery was too hard a thing to tell a child,"[9] a theme that Jones dramatizes in *Corregidora*. Central to Jones's work is also the recreation of the mother figure. Jacobs's *Incidents* and Zora Neale Hurston's *Their Eyes Were Watching God* create mother figures that will do anything within their power to shield their children from a particularly antagonistic society. This is a notion of motherhood that predominates female African American literature and that greatly differs from the mothers created by Jones. However, an examination of the mother figure in contemporary works such as Maya's grandmother in Maya Angelou's *I Know Why the Caged Bird Sings*; Eva Peace, the matriarch in Morrison's *Sula*; and Mama Day in the eponymous novel (1988) by Gloria Naylor continue to recreate the figure of the mother in ways that reflect those established by Jacobs and Hurston, creating a critical context in which to evaluate the originality of Jones's voice. Perhaps the most memorable recreation of Jones's egotistical and manipulative mothers is Tina McElroy Ansa's Mudear, the domineering mother figure in *Ugly Ways* (1993), who, like Great Gram and Gram, challenges the archetype of African American motherhood characterized by boundless selflessness and compassion toward her offspring.

Issues of name and naming constitute an important subject not only in Jones's *Corregidora* but also in *Jubilee*, *Dessa Rose*, *Beloved*, and *Stigmata*. These are also addressed in the work of other African American writers, illustrating both the intertextual dynamics established by their works and the cohesion of their poetics. Marsha Hunt, for example, addresses issues related with the complexity of African American names in both her second novel, *Free*, and in *Repossessing Ernestine: The Search for a Lost Soul*, her autobiographical account of her reunion with her grandmother.

In discussing the dialogic relationship established between the works of Walker, Jones, Williams, Morrison, Perry, and other contemporary novels it is important to emphasize the significance of the former in setting major trends in the African American fiction. For example, Walker's narrative, with its focus on the daily experience of slavery, influenced recently published novels such as Connie Briscoe's *A Long Way from Home* and Lalita Tademy's *Cane River*. The story of the genesis of *Jubilee* related in "How I Wrote *Jubilee*" creates a significant link between the creative act of writing, historical research, and familial lore. This patchwork made up of historical fact and fiction is the primary framework of the contemporary African American historical novel. In this context, it is interesting to consider Tademy's "Author's Note" to her novel in which she explains the genesis of the book, the years she spent researching her familial past in order to "write a book of fiction deeply rooted in years of research, historical fact, and family lore,"[10] clearly reflecting Walker's artistic project. Another interesting aspect of Tademy's work is her use of images and photographs, which appear mainly at the beginning and end of the novel. These create a visual context that links the fictional world of the novel to the real world of the people it seeks to represent. This recalls Walker's foreword to *Jubilee*. Walker does not include images of her ancestors but does provide a description of a photograph of her great-grandmother, who is the Vyry of the novel, creating an association between the fictional character and the real person: "In [the photograph] she is wearing a dress of black maline and her shawl is of yellow and red challis. From spinning the thread to weaving the cloth, the garments are entirely her handiwork."[11] This image of Walker's maternal great-grandmother could have easily been used to describe the self-reliant, talented, and hardworking Vyry. Thus Walker's influence in the African American historical novel lies in the construction of a genealogical narrative, her innovative use of folklore as the main framework of her narrative, her attention to verisimilitude and historical accuracy, and also in the details, such as the description of her maternal great-grandmother's photograph, which are recreated in subsequent novels, illustrating the critical place that her work occupies in the African American literary tradition.

One of the most significant contributions of Jones's *Corregidora* to the poetics of the African American novel is her approach to voice. In order to solve the tension between the third-person narrator's standard English and the characters' speech in vernacular, Jones breaks out of the framed narrative model. This is a critical moment in the representation of the female self. Removing the hierarchical relationship between standard English and black vernacular, Jones authenticates African American oral tradition and confers her character authority over the narration of her experience. This is a narrative model followed by J. California Cooper in *Family*. *Corregidora* is also influential in representing how the dynamics of slavery continue beyond emancipation and condition the lives of generations of African Americans. Ursa's quest is to honor and transform her foremothers' past so that she can make a present for herself in which the memories of her foremothers and her own life story can be reconciled and translated in her songs. In *Sassafrass, Cypress and Indigo* (1983), Ntozake Shange's character, Indigo, learns from an early age to acknowledge and reconcile her present circumstances with her slave past. This is a legacy, which helps Indigo to find ways of expressing herself, playing the fiddle until "the slaves who were ourselves made a chorus round the fire, till [she] was satisfied she wasn't silenced. She had many tongues, many spirits who loved her."[12]

The most prevailing trend in African American literature is not the presentation of characters who feel comfortable with their ancestral past, but rather it is of those who have difficulty in reconciling with that history. For Avey Johnson in *Praisesong for the Widow* and Milkman Dead in *Song of Solomon*, the ancestral past belongs in the realm of abstract history. However, the past, as Barbara Christian notes, "intrudes itself upon their consciousness through a dream and/or a song especially the sense of dis-ease [the characters] feel in the present."[13] In both *Praisesong for the Widow* and *Song of Solomon*, the journey back to the past and the communion with the ancestors is fundamental in achieving a sense of wholeness in the present. It is interesting to note that in both Morrison's and Paule Marshall's novels the absolute truth-telling form of Jones's Great Gram and Gram is relocated in the myths of Solomon, the flying African, and the Ibos people, who were able to walk on water as if it were solid ground. Myth constitutes, for these novelists, an effective means of transforming the harrowing experience of slavery into stories that can be recounted and shared in the context of the community. In *Linden Hills*, Naylor presents a rather less hopeful scenario and Laurel's suicide and the death of both Priscilla and Luther Nedeed in the climactic scene of the house fire represent the malaise of a neighborhood whose residents are divorced from their roots and the wider African American community. Jones's exploration of the past as a ghostly presence in the present thus remains a significant influence in the novels published in the 1980s and 1990s.

In the novels discussed, the female body emerges as a central signifier. In the historical novel, the scarred female body bears the history of the slave experience. In the works set in more recent times, the female characters might not feel the jagged texture of their scarred skin, but the dynamics of slavery influence the way they relate to their bodies. In *I Know Why the Caged Bird Sings* (1969) and *The Bluest Eye* (1970), Maya Angelou and Morrison, respectively, explore the ways African American girls' self-image are shaped by white models of beauty, dramatizing a profound sense of inadequateness felt by their characters. In *Praisesong for the Widow*, Marshall represents Avey's surrender to consumerism and her loss of identity through her chemically straightened hair, while in Naylor's *Linden Hills*, Willa Prescott Nedeed's nightly application of the bleach cream rubs off her color and identity, making her a quasi-invisible figure in her community. Hence, there is a significant dialogic relationship between the historical representation of the female experience and the works that create contemporary characters burdened by the dynamics established by slavery.

In this context, it is important to emphasize the originality of *Dessa Rose*. In Williams's novel the black body represents more as a site of healing than awkwardness and it is the white body that is redefined for the reader. Looking at the white woman through Dessa's eyes, the white body becomes the locus of strangeness and unattractiveness conventionally identified with the black skin and physiognomy, dislocating whiteness as an archetype for the familiar and appealing. The white body is, thus, racialized.

Morrison's *Beloved* marks a critical departure from realism. In this novel, magical realism provides the necessary narrative strategy through which a lost history can be recreated. Her use of the magical is rooted in African American beliefs and superstitions that inform black folklore, and, thus, develops a tradition established by Hurston in texts such as "Uncle Monday" and "Black Death." However, Morrison's use of the spectral presence in order to transform the gaps, or absences of the African American historical record into a concrete reality marks a major development in the representation of the slave experience. Cooper's *Family*, Perry's *Stigmata*, and Bertice Berry's *Redemption Song* (2000) are examples of novels that respond to Morrison's narrative model. Since the publication of *Beloved*, other phantoms haunt the fiction of black women writers. The ghost of the slave Rachel, as discussed in Chapter 5, appears to Lena in Ansa's *Baby of the Family* to teach the child an important lesson about history. In the sequel to that novel, *The Hand I Fan With* (1996), another ghost of a slave, Herman, returns to the town of Mulberry in Georgia to help the now 45-year-old Lena to regain a lost sense of identity and purpose in her life. In this way, Morrison's magical realist narrative opens the path for other female writers to explore and reimagine the supernatural, a central element of the African American folk tradition.

In her latest slavery novel, *A Mercy* (2008), Morrison reworks some of the magical elements employed in *Beloved* in a novel that clearly resonates with its literary antecedents. In a seventeenth-century homestead, four women find themselves "unmastered"[14] upon the death of Jacob Vaark. Reminiscent of *Dessa Rose*, these women are isolated and united by their struggle for survival and motherhood. *A Mercy* is ultimately, similar to the other novels previously discussed, a tale about gaining authority over one's life story. Florens's narrative, carved with a nail into the walls of the dead master's unfinished mansion, is her only means of dealing with the loss of her mother, lover, and freedom and her sole vehicle for self expression. Although engraved in the form of a written text, Florens's narrative is perhaps one of Morrison's more innovative representations of the slave's voice and African American orality. Florens's mother also narrates her capture in Africa and the Middle Passage. Hers is a disembodied voice reminding us of the resurfacing of the traumatic history of African Americans, the rememories that do not to sink in the black Atlantic.

In their quest to represent the female African American experience, the writers discussed here seek and develop distinct African American narrative modes. In these novels memory is a critical element not only because it is crucial to the reconstruction of an unwritten past but also because the way one remembers shapes the structure of the narrative. In this way, with the exception of Walker's *Jubilee*, these are novels in which chronological sequence is disrupted in order to unfold a narrative line structured around memory, emphasizing the difficulty in verbalizing a traumatic past. Thus the linear narrative gives place to a spiral one and the act of reading becomes one navigating gradually larger circles until a more complete picture emerges. This reflects the circular form of narrative quilts and the form of call and response of blues stanzas. The oral tradition, as Jones states, "offers [black women writers] continuity of voice as well as its liberation."[15] Thus these novelists engage in the double exercise of acknowledging black oral traditions, while reinventing them in order to pursue new modes of representing the African American experience.

Notes

Introduction

1. Thomas C. Holt, *African-American History* (Washington, DC: American Historical Association, 1997), 1.
2. Gunnar Myrdal as quoted by Ralph Ellison, "*An American Dilemma*: A Review," in *Shadow and Act* (New York: Vintage Books, 1972), 315.
3. Ibid., 317.
4. Ibid.
5. See James Joyce, *Portrait of the Artist* (London: Wordsworth Classics, 1992), 253.
6. Ellison, "*American Dilemma*," 316.
7. Holt, *African-American History*, 2.
8. Ellison, "Some Questions and Some Answers," in *Shadow and Act* (New York: Vintage Books, 1972), 263.
9. Elizabeth Clark-Lewis, *Living In, Living Out: African American Domestics and the Great Migration* (New York: Kodansha, 1995), 4.
10. Ibid., viii.
11. Ibid., 198.
12. Ibid., 23.
13. Ibid., 178.
14. Ibid.
15. Holt, *African-American History*, 2
16. Deborah E. McDowell, *"The Changing Same": Black Women's Literature, Criticism and Theory* (Bloomington: Indiana University Press, 1995), 21.
17. Claudia Tate, ed. *Black Women Writers at Work* (New York: Continuum, 1983), 105.
18. Houston A. Baker Jr., *The Journey Back: Issues in Black Literature and Criticism* (Chicago: University of Chicago Press, 1980), 53.
19. Maryemma Graham and Deborah Whaley, "Introduction: The Most Famous Person Nobody Knows," in *Fields Watered with Blood: Critical Essays on Margaret Walker*, ed. Maryemma Graham (Athens: University of Georgia Press, 2001), 1.

20. Ashraf H. A. Rushdy, "Neo-Slave Narrative," in *The Oxford Companion to African American Literature*, ed. William L. Andrews et al. (New York: Oxford University Press, 1997), 534.
21. Joyce Pettis, "Margaret Walker: Black Woman Writer of the South," in *Southern Women Writers: The New Generation*, ed. Tonette Bond Inge (Tuscaloosa: University of Alabama Press, 1990), 11–12.
22. Graham and Whaley, "Introduction," 8.
23. Charlotte Goodman, "From Uncle Tom's Cabin to Vyry's Kitchen: The Black Female Folk Tradition in Margaret Walker's *Jubilee*," in *Tradition and the Talents of Women*, ed. Florence Howe (Urbana: University of Illinois Press, 1991), 336.
24. Barbara Christian, "'Somebody Forgot to Tell Somebody Something': African-American Women's Historical Novels," in *Wild Women in the Whirlwind: Afra-American Culture and the Contemporary Literary Renaissance*, ed. Joanne M. Braxton and Andrée Nicola McLaughlin (London: Serpent's Tail, 1990), 334.
25. Minrose C. Gwin, "Jubilee: The Black Woman's Celebration of Human Community," in *Conjuring: Black Women, Fiction, and Literary Tradition*, ed. Marjorie Pryse and Hortense J Spillers (Bloomington: Indiana University Press, 1985), 138.
26. Elizabeth Ann Beaulieu, *Black Women Writers and the American Neo-Slave Narrative: Femininity Unfettered* (London: Greenwood Press, 1999), 17.

Chapter 1

1. John Hope Franklin and Alfred A. Moss, *From Slavery to Freedom: A History of African Americans* (New York: McGraw Hill, 1994), 250.
2. Ibid., 254.
3. W. E. B. Du Bois, as quoted by Herbert Aptheker in *A Documentary History of the Negro People in the United States: From the Reconstruction Era to 1910* (New York: Citadel, 1951), 753
4. Ibid., 759, Paul Laurence Dunbar, as quoted by Herbert Aptheker.
5. Frances Smith Foster, introduction to *Iola Leroy, or, Shadows Uplifted*, by Frances E. W. Harper (New York: Oxford University Press, 1988), xxx–xxxi.
6. Frances E. W. Harper, as quoted by Melba Joyce Boyd in *Discarded Legacy: Politics and Poetics in the Life of E. W. Harper, 1825–1911* (Detroit, MI: Wayne State University Press, 1994), 40.
7. Hazel V. Carby, *Reconstructing Womanhood: The Emergence of the Afro-American Woman Novelist* (New York: Oxford University Press, 1987), 66.
8. Frances E. W. Harper, *Minnie's Sacrifice, Sowing and Reaping, Trial and Triumph: Three Rediscovered Novels* (Boston: Beacon, 1994), 91.
9. Ibid., 16.
10. Ibid., 51.
11. Ibid., 72.
12. Ibid., 62.
13. Ibid., 64.

14. Ibid., 36.
15. Ibid., 65.
16. Ibid.
17. Ibid., 35.
18. Ibid., 73.
19. Jacqueline K. Bryant, *The Foremother Figure in Early Black Women's Literature: Clothed in My Right Hand* (New York: Garland, 1999), 73.
20. Harper, *Minnie's Sacrifice*, 75.
21. See Frances E. W. Harper, *Iola Leroy, or, Shadows Uplifted* (New York: Oxford University Press, 1988), 97–98.
22. Ibid., 97.
23. Ibid., 101.
24. Mary Prince, *The History of Mary Prince, A West Indian Slave: Related by Herself*, in *Six Women's Slave Narratives* (New York: Oxford University Press, 1988), 11.
25. Harper, *Iola Leroy*, 39.
26. Ibid., 38.
27. Ibid., 149.
28. Harriet Jacobs, *Incidents in the Life of a Slave Girl*, ed. Henry Louis Gates Jr. (New York: Oxford University Press, 1988), 6.
29. Harper, *Iola Leroy*, 262.
30. Jacobs, *Incidents*, 302.
31. Harper, *Iola Leroy*, 275–76.
32. Ibid., 269.
33. Ibid., 169.
34. Ibid., 199.
35. Ibid., 274.
36. Ibid., 279.
37. Ibid.
38. Ibid.
39. Ibid.
40. M. Giulia Fabi, "Reconstructing Literary Genealogies: Frances E. W. Harper's and William Dean Howells's Race Novels," in *Soft Canons: American Women Writers and Masculine Tradition*, ed. Karen L. Kilcup (Iowa City: University of Iowa Press, 1999), 60.
41. Ibid., 61.
42. Harper, *Iola Leroy*, 130.
43. Harper, *Minnie's Sacrifice*, 71.
44. Harper, *Iola Leroy*, 129.
45. Ibid., 154.
46. Ibid., 205–10.
47. Ibid., 250–51.
48. Harper, *Minnie's Sacrifice*, 91.
49. Harper, *Iola Leroy*, 263.

50. Benjamin F. Lee, introduction to *The Work of Afro-American Women* by Gertrude N. F. Mossell (Philadelphia: George S. Ferguson, 1908), 4.
51. Carby, *Reconstructing Womanhood*, 96.
52. Frances E. W. Harper, “Woman’s Political Future,” address in *The World’s Congress of Representative Women*, ed. May Wright Sewall (Chicago: Rand McNally, 1894), 433–37. Accessed December 17, 2010, http://babel.hathitrust.org/cgi/pt?id=uc1.b3713658.
53. Ibid.
54. Fannie Barrier Williams, “The Intellectual Progress of the Colored Women of the United States since the Emancipation Proclamation,” address in *The World’s Congress of Representative Women*, ed. May Wright Sewall (Chicago: Rand McNally, 1894), 696–711. Accessed December 17, 2010, http://babel.hathitrust.org/cgi/pt?id=uc1.b3713659.
55. Ibid.
56. Williams, “Intellectual Progress.”
57. Harper, “Woman’s Political Future.”

[1] Williams, “Intellectual Progress.”

58. Ibid.
59. A. J. Cooper, “Discussion of the Same Subject [The Intellectual Progress of the Colored Women of the United States Since the Emancipation Proclamation],” address in *The World’s Congress of Representative Women*, ed. May Wright Sewall (Chicago: Rand McNally, 1894), 711–15. Accessed December 17, 2010, http://babel.hathitrust.org/cgi/pt?id=uc1.b3713659.
60. Ibid.
61. Ibid.
62. Ibid.
63. Ibid.
64. Ibid.

Chapter 2

1. See Maryemma Graham, introduction to *How I Wrote Jubilee and Other Essays on Life and Literature*, by Margaret Walker (New York: Feminist Press, 1990), xv.
2. Ibid.
3. Ibid., xvi.
4. Margaret Walker, “Growing Out of Shadow,” in *How I Wrote Jubilee and Other Essays on Life and Literature*, ed. Maryemma Graham (New York: Feminist Press, 1990), 3.
5. Ibid., 5.
6. See Walker, “A Literary Legacy from Dunbar to Bakara,” in *How I Wrote Jubilee*, 69.
7. Maryemma Graham and Deborah Whaley, “Introduction: The Most Famous Person Nobody Knows,” in *Fields Watered with Blood: Critical Essays on Margaret Walker*, ed. Maryemma Graham (Athens: University of Georgia Press,

2001), 18. See also Graham, introduction to *How I Wrote Jubilee*, xiii; Walker, "Richard Wright," *How I Wrote Jubilee*, 35.

8. Walker, "Growing Out of Shadow," 3–4.
9. John Hope Franklin and Alfred A. Moss, *From Slavery to Freedom: A History of African Americans* (New York: McGraw-Hill, 1994), 384.
10. Walker, "New Poets of the Forties and the Optimism of the Age," in *How I Wrote Jubilee*, 104.
11. Ibid.
12. Ibid., 103.
13. Richard Wright, "Blueprint for Negro Writing," in *The Norton Anthology of African American Literature*, ed. Henry Louis Gates Jr. and Nellie Y. McKay (New York: Norton, 1997), 1381.
14. Ibid., 1382.
15. Ibid., 1384.
16. Walker, "Willing to Pay the Price," in *How I Wrote Jubilee*, 23.
17. Joyce Pettis, "Margaret Walker: Black Woman Writer of the South," in *Southern Women Writers: The New Generation*, ed. Tonette Bond Inge (Tuscaloosa: University of Alabama Press, 1990), 16.
18. Kay Bonetti, "Margaret Walker," in *Conversations with American Novelists: The Best Interviews from the Missouri Review and the American Audio Prose*, ed. Kay Bonetti et al. (Columbia: University of Missouri Press, 1997), 173.
19. Walker, "The Humanistic Tradition of Afro-American literature," in *How I Wrote Jubilee*, 128.
20. Walker, *Richard Wright, Daemonic Genius: A Portrait of the Man, A Critical Look at His Work* (New York: Warner Books, 1988), 7.
21. Walker, "Humanistic Tradition," 130.
22. Pauline Hopkins, *Contending Forces: A Romance Illustrative of Negro Life North and South* (New York: Oxford University Press, 1988), 13.
23. Harriet Jacobs, *Incidents in the Life of a Slave Girl*, ed. Henry Louis Gates Jr. (New York: Oxford University Press, 1988), 285.
24. Frances Ellen Watkins Harper, *Iola Leroy, or, Shadows Uplifted* (New York: Oxford University Press, 1988), 261.
25. Walker, "Humanistic Tradition," 130.
26. Graham, introduction to *How I Wrote Jubilee*, x.
27. Walker, "How I Wrote *Jubilee*," in *How I Wrote Jubilee*, 53.
28. Ibid., 52–53.
29. Henry Louis Gates Jr., "Frederick Douglass and the Language of the Self," *The Yale Review* 70 (July 1981): 593.
30. Frederick Douglass, *Narrative of the Life of Frederick Douglass: An American Slave* (New York: Signet, 1968), 22.
31. Barbara Christian, "'Somebody Forgot to Tell Somebody Something': African-American Women's Historical Novels," in *Wild Women in the Whirlwind: Afra-American Culture and the Contemporary Literary Renaissance*, ed. Joanne M. Braxton and Andrée Nicola McLaughlin (London: Serpent's Tail, 1990), 333.

32. Toni Morrison, "Site of Memory," in *Memoir*, ed. William Zinsser (Boston: Houghton-Mifflin, 1987), 109–10.
33. Harriet E. Wilson, *Our Nig; or, Sketches from the Life of a Free Black, In a Two Story House, North. Showing that Slavery's Shadows Fall Even There* (New York: Random House, 1983), 3.
34. Wilson, preface to *Our Nig*, 3.
35. See Henry Louis Gates Jr., introduction to *Our Nig*, by Harriet E. Wilson (New York: Vintage Books, 1983), xiii.
36. See Wilson, *Our Nig*, 14–15.
37. Gates, introduction to *Our Nig*, xxix.
38. Walker, "How I Wrote *Jubilee*," 64.
39. Ibid., 51.
40. Ibid.
41. Ibid., 56.
42. Ibid., 58.
43. Ibid., 56.
44. Patricia A. Turner, "African Americans," in *American Folklore: An Encyclopaedia*, ed. Jan Harold Brunvand (New York: Garland, 1996), 9.
45. Friederike Hajek, "Margaret Walker's *Jubilee:* Oral History, the Fiction of Literacy and the Language of a Black Text," in *Rewriting the South: History and Fiction*, ed. Lothar Hönnighausen and Valeria Gennaro Lerda (Tübingen, Germany: Francke, 1993), 392.
46. Wright, "Blueprint," 1382.
47. H. Nigel Thomas, *From Folklore to Fiction: A Study of Folk Heroes and Rituals in the Black American Novel* (Westport, CT: Greenwood, 1988), 137–38.
48. Jacqueline Miller Carmichael, *Trumpeting a Fiery Sound: History and Folklore in Margaret Walker's Jubilee* (Athens: University of Georgia Press, 1998), 9.
49. James E. Spears, "Black Folk Elements in Margaret Walker's *Jubilee*," *Mississippi Folklore Register* 14, no. 1 (Spring 1980): 15.
50. Walker, *Jubilee* (New York: Bantam Books, 1967), 3.
51. Walker, "How I Wrote *Jubilee*," 60.
52. Spears, "Black Folk Elements," 15.
53. Walker, "How I Wrote *Jubilee*," 60.
54. Ibid., 54.
55. In "How I Wrote *Jubilee*," Margaret Walker states that in 1948 she sketched the development of the plot using the folk sayings verbatim as an outline. See "How I Wrote *Jubilee*," 54.
56. Kimberly Rae Connor, "Spirituals," in *The Oxford Companion to African American Literature*, ed. William L. Andrews et al. (New York: Oxford University Press, 1997), 693.
57. "Swing Low, Sweet Chariot," in *The Norton Anthology of African American Literature*, ed. Henry Louis Gates Jr. and Nellie Y. McKay (New York: Norton, 1997), 13n1.
58. Walker, *Jubilee*, 3–4.
59. Ibid., 5.

60. Ibid.
61. Ibid., 3.
62. Ibid.
63. Ibid., 6.
64. Ibid.
65. Ibid., 5.
66. Ibid., 14.
67. Ibid., 12.
68. Ibid.
69. Ibid.
70. Ibid., 10.
71. Walker, *Jubilee*, 10.
72. Deborah Gray White, *Ar'n't I a Woman? Female Slaves in the Plantation South* (New York: Norton, 1985), 149.
73. Ibid., 148.
74. Franklin and Moss, *From Slavery to Freedom*, 117.
75. Walker, *Jubilee*, 4.
76. Ibid.
77. Ibid., 5.
78. White, *Ar'n't I a Woman?* 69.
79. Martha Harrison, as quoted by Maryse Condé in "Some African-American Fictional Responses to Gone with the Wind," *Yearbook of English Studies* 26 (1996): 215.
80. White, *Ar'n't I a Woman?*, 31.
81. Ibid.
82. Franklin and Moss, *From Slavery to Freedom*, 139.
83. William Harper, as quoted by White in *Ar'n't I a Woman?*, 39.
84. Franklin and Moss, *From Slavery to Freedom*, 139.
85. Minrose C. Gwin, "Jubilee: The Black Woman's Celebration of Human Community," in *Conjuring: Black Women, Fiction, and Literary Tradition*, ed. Marjorie Pryse and Hortense J. Spillers (Bloomington: Indiana University Press, 1985), 137.
86. Walker, *Jubilee*, 7–8.
87. Ibid., 9.
88. Ibid., 7–8.
89. Ibid., 13.
90. Charlotte Goodman, "From Uncle Tom's Cabin to Vyry's Kitchen: The Black Female Folk Tradition in Margaret Walker's *Jubilee*," in *Tradition and the Talents of Women*, ed. Florence Howe (Urbana: University of Illinois Press, 1991), 331.
91. Walker, *Jubilee*, 14.
92. Ibid., 11.
93. Ibid., 3–4.
94. See Walker, "How I Wrote *Jubilee*," 62.
95. Walker, *Jubilee*,15.

96. Ibid., 16.
97. Ibid., 17.
98. Ibid., 20.
99. Ibid., 110.
100. Ibid., 111.
101. Ibid., 94.
102. Ibid., 22.
103. White, *Ar'n't I a Woman?*, 47–49.
104. Walker, *Jubilee*, 8.
105. Harriet Martineau, as quoted by White in *Ar'n't I a Woman?*, 51.
106. See Elizabeth Fox-Genovese, *Within the Plantation Household: Black and White Women of the Old South* (Chapel Hill: University of North Carolina Press, 1988), 34.
107. Ibid., 110.
108. Walker, *Jubilee*, 34.
109. Fox-Genovese, *Within the Plantation Household*, 315.
110. Ibid., 35.
111. Walker, *Jubilee*, 15.
112. Ibid., 25.
113. Ibid.
114. Ibid., 36.
115. Ibid., 35–36.
116. Ibid., 36.
117. Ibid., 138.
118. Ibid., 141.
119. John Hope Franklin and Loren Schweninger, *Runaway Slaves: Rebels on the Plantation* (New York: Oxford University Press, 2000), 210.
120. Ibid.
121. White, *Ar'n't I a Woman?* 70.
122. Ibid., 71.
123. This does not mean that slave mothers did not runaway, or that they did not do so successfully with their children, but they were very reluctant to abscond without them. White points out that of the "hundred fifty-one fugitive women advertised for in the 1850 New Orleans newspapers, none was listed as having run away without her children" (*Ar'n't I a Woman?*, 71).
124. Walker, in *How I Wrote Jubilee*, 58. See also *Jubilee*, 58, 157, 212, 213, 226, 227.
125. Leon F. Litwack, *Been in the Storm So Long: The Aftermath of Slavery* (New York: Vintage, 1979), 162.
126. Walker, *Jubilee*, 184.
127. Ibid.
128. Ibid., 252.
129. Ibid., 254.
130. Felix Haywood, "The Death of Slavery," in *Sources of the African-American Past: Primary Sources in American History*, ed. Roy E. Finkenbine (New York: Longman, 1997), 81.

131. Walker, *Jubilee*, 396.
132. W. E. B. Du Bois, *The Souls of Black Folk*, in *Norton Anthology of African American Literature*, ed. Henry Louis Gates Jr. and Nellie Y. McKay (New York: Norton, 1997), 617–18.
133. Walker, *Jubilee*, 266.
134. Ibid., 280.
135. Ibid., 290.
136. Ibid., 299–300.
137. Gates, "Frederick Douglass," 593.
138. Fred D'Aguiar, *The Longest Memory* (London: Vintage, 1995), 2.
139. Walker, *Jubilee*, 377.
140. D'Aguiar, *Longest Memory*, 138.
141. Walker, *Jubilee*, 307.
142. Bayley Wyatt, "A Right to the Land," in *Sources of the African-American Past*, 88.
143. Ida B. Wells, *A Red Record*, in *Norton Anthology: African American Literature*, 596.
144. Ibid., 597.
145. "Individual Testimony," in *A Documentary History of the Negro People in the United States: From the Reconstruction Era to 1910*, ed. Herbert Aptheker (New York: Citadel Press, 1951), 582.
146. Ibid., 586.
147. Walker, *Jubilee*, 299.
148. Ibid.
149. Elizabeth Ann Beaulieu, *Black Women Writers and the American Neo-Slave Narrative: Femininity Unfettered* (London: Greenwood Press, 1999), 21.
150. Walker, *Jubilee*, 360.
151. Ibid., 363.
152. See Walker, *Jubilee*, 291 ("But when Vyry dished up the steaming hot stew she fed everyone of the white family as well as her own and made the poor white family and her husband feel they were doing her a favor").
153. Ibid., 360.
154. Walker, "Humanistic Tradition," 132.
155. Walker, *Jubilee*, 370.
156. Ibid., 366.
157. Walker, "How I Wrote *Jubilee*," 65.
158. Ibid., 54.
159. Melissa Walker, *Down from the Mountain Top: Black Women's Novels in the Wake of the Civil Rights Movement, 1966–1989* (New Haven, CT: Yale University Press, 1991), 21.
160. Ibid.
161. Walker, *Jubilee*, 396.
162. Walker, "How I Wrote *Jubilee*," 63.
163. Walker, *Jubilee*, 397.
164. Ibid., 402.

165. Ibid., 406.
166. Ibid., 407.
167. Gwin, "Black Woman's Celebration," 136.
168. Phanuel Egejuru and Robert Elliot Fox, "An Interview with Margaret Walker," *Callaloo: A Journal of African American and African Arts and Letters* 2, no. 2 (1979): 29.
169. William J. Harris, "Black Aesthetic," in *The Oxford Companion to African American Literature*, 69.
170. Hoyt Fuller, "Towards a Black Aesthetic," in *Norton Anthology: African American Literature*, 1856.
171. Larry Neal, "The Blacks Arts Movement," in *Norton Anthology: African American Literature*, 2040.
172. Hajek, "Margaret Walker's *Jubilee*," 391.
173. Margaret Walker, interview by Kay Bonetti. "Margaret Walker," in *Conversations with American Novelists*, 182.
174. Phyllis Rauch Klotman, "'Oh Freedom': Women and History in Margaret Walker's *Jubilee*," *Black American Literature Forum* 11 (1977): 140.
175. Pettis, "Margaret Walker," 12.

Chapter 3

1. Larry Neal, "The Black Arts Movement," in *Within the Circle: An Anthology of African American Literary Criticism from the Harlem Renaissance to the Present*, ed. Angelyn Mitchell (London: Duke University Press, 1994), 184.
2. Etheridge Knight, as quoted by Neal, "The Black Arts Movement," 185.
3. Addison Gayle Jr., "The Black Aesthetic," in *The Norton Anthology of African American Literature*, ed. Henry Louis Gates Jr. and Nellie Y. McKay (New York: Norton, 1997), 1876.
4. Hoyt Fuller, "Towards a Black Aesthetic," in *The Norton Anthology of African American Literature*, ed. Henry Louis Gates Jr. and Nellie Y. McKay (New York: Norton, 1997), 1813.
5. Maulana Karenga, "Black Art: Mute Matter Given Force and Function," in *The Norton Anthology of African American Literature*, ed. Henry Louis Gates Jr. and Nellie Y. McKay (New York: Norton, 1997), 1976.
6. Octavia Butler, interviewed by Frances M. Beal, "Black Women and the Science Fiction Genre: Interview with Octavia Butler," *Black Scholar* 17, no. 2 (April 1986): 15.
7. Octavia Butler, interviewed by Randall Kenan, "An Interview with Octavia E. Butler," *Callaloo: A Journal of African American and African Arts and Letters* 14, no. 2 (Spring 1991): 496.
8. See Charles H. Rowell, "An Interview with Octavia E. Butler," *Callaloo: A Journal of African American and African Arts and Letters* 20, no. 1 (Winter 1997): 51.

9. Gayl Jones, interviewed by Rowell, "An Interview with Gayl Jones," *Callaloo: A Journal of African American Arts and Letters* 5:3, no. 16 (October 1982), 32–53, 45.
10. Ibid., 42.
11. Gayl Jones, interviewed by Claudia Tate, ed., *Black Women Writers at Work* (New York: Continuum, 1983), 93.
12. Ibid., 95.
13. Gayl Jones, interviewed by Michael Harper, "Gayl Jones: An Interview," in *Chant of Saints: A Gathering of Afro-American Literature, Art, and Scholarship* (London: University of Illinois Press, 1979), 352.
14. Gayl Jones, interviewed by Rowell, "Interview with Gayl Jones," 53.
15. Gayl Jones, interviewed by Harper, "Gayl Jones: An Interview," 356.
16. Ibid., 362.
17. Gayl Jones, *Liberating Voices: Oral Tradition in African American Literature* (London: Harvard University Press, 1991), 199.
18. See Rowell, "Interview with Gayl Jones," 32–37.
19. Ibid., 33.
20. Ashraf H. A. Rushdy, *Remembering Generations: Race and Family in Contemporary African American Fiction* (Chapel Hill: University of North Carolina Press, 2001), 4.
21. Gayl Jones, *Corregidora* (London: Camden Press, 1988), 3.
22. Ibid., 8–9.
23. Marsha Hunt, *Free* (London: Penguin Books, 1993), 9–10.
24. Marsha Hunt, *Repossessing Ernestine: The Search for a Lost Soul* (London: Flamingo, 1997), 154.
25. Ralph Ellison, "Hidden Name and Complex Fate," in *Shadow and Act* (New York: Vintage Books, 1972), 148.
26. Ibid., 154.
27. Jones, *Corregidora*, 54.
28. Ibid., 11.
29. Frank Kermode, *The Sense of an Ending: Studies in the Theory of Fiction* (New York: Oxford University Press, 1967), 47.
30. Ibid.
31. Jones, *Corregidora*, 14.
32. Ibid., 11, 13, 23.
33. Dorothy West, *The Living Is Easy* (New York: Feminist Press, 1982), 90–91.
34. Joanne M. Braxton, "Ancestral Presence: The Outraged Mother Figure in Contemporary Afra-American Writing," in *Wild Women in the Whirlwind: Afra-American Culture and the Contemporary Literary Renaissance* ed. Joanne M. Braxton and Andrée Nicola McLaughlin (London: Serpent's Tail, 1990), 300–301.
35. Harriet Jacobs, *Incidents in the Life of a Slave Girl*, ed. Henry Louis Gates Jr. (New York: Oxford University Press, 1988), 175, 177.
36. Ibid., 175.
37. Ibid., 177.

38. Ibid., 175.
39. Zora Neale Hurston, *Their Eyes Were Watching God* (London: Virago Press, 1995), 34–35.
40. Ibid., 31.
41. Ibid., 37.
42. Maya Angelou, *I Know Why the Caged Bird Sings* (New York: Bantam Books, 1980), 39.
43. Ibid., 160.
44. Ibid., 162.
45. Ibid., 161.
46. Ibid., 162.
47. Ibid., 161.
48. Toni Morrison, *Sula* (London: Picador, 1991), 30.
49. Ibid., 31.
50. Ibid., 72.
51. Ibid., 71.
52. Ibid., 47.
53. Ibid., 76.
54. Braxton, "Ancestral Presence," 314.
55. Alice Walker, *Meridian* (London: Women's Press, 1997), 87.
56. Jones, *Corregidora*, 79.
57. Ibid., 78.
58. Ibid., 22.
59. Ibid.
60. Karl Marx, as quoted by Adam McKible, "'These Are the Facts of the Darky's History': Thinking History and Reading Names in Four African American Texts," *African American Review* 28, no. 2 (Summer 1994): 224.
61. Sally Robinson, *Engendering the Subject: Gender and Self-Representation in Contemporary's Women Fiction* (Albany: State University of New York Press, 1991), 151.
62. Ibid., 151–52.
63. Jones, *Corregidora*, 11.
64. Ibid.
65. Ibid., 23; italics mine.
66. Ibid.
67. Amy S. Gottfried, "Angry Arts: Silence, Speech, and Song in Gayl Jones's *Corregidora*," *African American Review* 28, no. 4 (Winter 1994): 560–61.
68. Jones, *Corregidora*, 114.
69. Ibid., 116.
70. Janice Harris, "Gayl Jones's *Corregidora*," *Frontiers: Journal of Women Studies* 5, no. 3 (Fall 1980): 2.
71. Jones, *Corregidora*, 118.
72. Ibid., 122.
73. Ibid., 116.
74. Ibid., 121.

75. Ibid., 131.
76. Ibid., 121.
77. Melvin Dixon, *Ride Out the Wilderness: Geography and Identity in Afro-American Literature* (Urbana: University of Illinois Press, 1987), 115.
78. Jones, *Corregidora*, 124.
79. Ibid., 104.
80. Ibid., 111.
81. Ibid., 121.
82. Ibid., 147.
83. Ibid., 45.
84. Ibid., 148.
85. Harris, "Gayl Jones's *Corregidora*," 3.
86. Jones, *Corregidora*, 154.
87. Ibid., 152.
88. Ibid., 66.
89. Ibid., 154–55.
90. Ibid., 151.
91. Ibid.
92. Ibid., 154.
93. Ibid., 89.
94. Ibid., 45.
95. Ibid.
96. Ibid., 154.
97. Ibid., 159.
98. Ibid., 151.
99. Ibid.
100. Ibid., 167.
101. Ibid., 4.
102. Ibid.
103. Ibid., 167.
104. Ibid., 89.
105. Ibid., 26.
106. Ibid., 6.
107. Ibid., 26.
108. Ibid., 45.
109. Ibid.
110. Ibid., 46.
111. Ibid., 60.
112. Ibid., 6.
113. Ibid., 46.
114. Ibid.
115. Ibid., 59.
116. Ibid., 54.
117. Ibid., 96–97; italics mine.
118. Ibid., 103.

119. Sherley A. Williams, "The Blues Roots of Contemporary Afro-American Poetry," in *Chant of Saints: A Gathering of Afro-American Literature, Art, and Scholarship* (London: University of Illinois Press, 1979), 125.
120. Houston A. Baker Jr., *Blues, Ideology, and Afro-American Literature: A Vernacular Theory* (Chicago: University of Chicago Press, 1984), 5.
121. Williams, "Blues Roots," 127.
122. Baker, *Blues*, 7.
123. Jones, *Corregidora*, 66.
124. Marilee Lindemann, "'This Woman Can Cross Any Line': Power and Authority in Contemporary Women's Fiction," in *Engendering the Word: Feminist Essays in Psychosexual Poetics*, ed. Temma F. Berg et al. (Chicago: University of Illinois Press, 1989), 115.
125. Baker, *Blues*, 7.
126. Ellison, "Richard Wright's Blues," in *Shadow and Act* (New York: Vintage Books, 1972), 78–79.
127. Lindemann, "'This Woman,'" 115–16.
128. Hélène Cixous, "The Laugh of Medusa," in *New French Feminism: An Anthology*, ed. Elaine Marks and Isabelle de Courtivon (Amherst: University of Massachusetts Press, 1980), 257.
129. Mikhail Bakhtin as quoted by Henry Louis Gates Jr., *The Signifying Monkey: A Theory of African American Literary Criticism* (New York: Oxford University Press, 1988), 2.
130. Jones, *Corregidora*, 85.
131. Ibid., 77.
132. Ibid., 183.
133. Ibid., 184.
134. Ibid.
135. Ibid.
136. Ibid.
137. Ibid.
138. Ibid., 185

Chapter 4

1. Thomas C. Holt, *African-American History* (Washington, DC: American Historical Association, 1997), 6.
2. Robert Penn Warren, "The Uses of History in Fiction," *Southern Literary Journal* 1, no. 2 (Spring 1969): 61.
3. Sherley Anne Williams, "The Lion's History: The Ghetto Writes Back," *Soundings: An Interdisciplinary Journal* 76, no. 2–3 (Summer–Fall 1993): 248.
4. Warren, "Uses of History," 61.
5. Williams, "Lion's History," 251.
6. Ibid., 251–52.
7. Ibid., 252.
8. Ibid., 253.

9. Sherley Anne Williams, "author's note" to *Dessa Rose* (London: Virago, 1998), 5.
10. Ruth Ronen, *Possible Worlds in Literary Theory* (Cambridge: Cambridge University Press, 1994), 179.
11. Ibid., 179.
12. Williams, "Lion's History," 256.
13. Williams, *Dessa Rose*, 39.
14. Ibid., 52, 56.
15. Ibid., 47.
16. Mieke Bal, *Narratology: Introduction to the Theory of Narrative* (Toronto: University of Toronto Press, 2002), 50.
17. Williams, *Dessa Rose*, 18.
18. Ibid., 37.
19. Ibid., 44–45.
20. Ibid., 44.
21. Ibid., 50.
22. Williams, "I Sing This Song for Our Mothers," in *Peacock Poems* (Hanover, NH: Wesleyan University Press, 1975), 79–83. In fact, in the poem, the writer already traces the story line that she will later develop in her novel.
23. Stephanie Sievers, "Escaping the Master('s) Narrative? Sherley Anne Williams's Rethinking of Historical Representation in 'Meditations on History,'" in *Re-Visioning the Past: Historical Self-Reflexivity in American Short Fiction*, ed. Bernd Engler and Oliver Scheiding (Trier, Germany: Wissenschaftlicher, 1998), 366.
24. Williams, *Dessa Rose*, 39.
25. Williams, "Lion's History," 256.
26. Williams, *Dessa Rose*, 58.
27. Ibid., 24.
28. Ibid., 38.
29. Ibid., 42.
30. Ibid.
31. Ibid., 43.
32. Deborah Gray White, *Ar'n't I a Woman?: Female Slaves in the Plantations of the South* (New York: Norton, 1985), 27.
33. Barbara Johnson, as quoted by Sidonie Smith in "Resisting the Gaze of Embodiment: Women's Autobiography in the Nineteenth Century," in *American Women's Autobiography: Fea(s)ts of Memory*, ed. Mango Culley (Madison: University Press of Wisconsin, 1992), 34.
34. Williams, *Dessa Rose*, 23.
35. Toni Morrison, *Playing in the Dark: Whiteness and Literary Imagination* (London: Harvard University Press, 1992), 52.
36. Ibid., 63.
37. Judith Butler, as quoted by Smith in "Resisting the Gaze," 80.
38. Williams, *Dessa Rose*, 44.
39. White, *Ar'n't I a Woman*, 29.

40. Farah Jasmine Griffin, "Textual Healing: Claiming Black Women's Bodies, the Erotic and Resistance in Contemporary Novels of Slavery," in *Callaloo: A Journal of African American and African Arts and Letters* 19, no. 2 (Spring 1996): 591.
41. Williams, *Dessa Rose*, 21.
42. John Hope Franklin and Loren Schweninger, *Runaway Slaves: Rebels on the Plantation* (New York: Oxford University Press, 2000), 6.
43. Franklin and Schweninger, *Runaway Slaves*, 13.
44. Nehemiah observes that in Georgia "[n]ews of this uprising, despite the efforts of some civil boosters to keep it quiet, was rippling through the state, spreading consternation and fear in its wake." Williams, *Dessa Rose*, 31; see also 26, 27, 28, 29.
45. Williams, *Dessa Rose*, 29.
46. Franklin and Schweninger, *Runaway Slaves*, 8.
47. Williams, *Dessa Rose*, 36.
48. Ibid., 32.
49. Ibid., 21.
50. Ibid., 37.
51. Ibid., 41.
52. Ibid., 23.
53. Mary Kemp Davis, "Everybody Knows Her Name: The Recovery of the Past in Sherley Anne Williams's *Dessa Rose*," *Callaloo: A Journal of African American and African Arts and Letters* 12, no. 3 (Summer 1989): 547
54. Williams, *Dessa Rose*, 23.
55. Ibid., 30.
56. Jane Mathison-Fife, "*Dessa Rose*: A Critique of Received History of Slavery," *Kentucky Philological Review* 8 (1993): 30.
57. Jacquelyn A. Fox-Good, "Singing the Unsayable: Theorizing Music in *Dessa Rose*," in *Black Orpheus: Music in African American Fiction from the Harlem Renaissance to Toni Morrison*, ed. Saadi A. Simawe (New York: Garland, 2000), 24.
58. Williams, *Dessa Rose*, 29.
59. Ibid., 30–31.
60. Ibid., 29.
61. Ibid., 29–30.
62. Ibid., 35.
63. Ibid., 51.
64. Fox-Good, "Singing the Unsayable," 16.
65. See Williams, *Dessa Rose*, 51.
66. Ibid., 68.
67. Houston A. Baker Jr., *Long Black Song: Essays in Black American Literature and Culture* (Charlottesville: University Press of Virginia, 1972), 13.
68. Williams, *Dessa Rose*, 36.
69. Ibid., 64.
70. Ibid., 65.

71. Ibid., 67.
72. Angela Y. Davis, "Black Women and Music: A Historical Legacy of Struggle," in *Wild Women in the Whirlwind: Afra-American Culture and the Contemporary Literary Renaissance*, ed. Joanne M. Braxton and Andrée Nicola McLaughlin (London: Serpent's Tail, 1990), 10.
73. Harriet Jacobs, *Incidents in the Life of a Slave Girl*, ed. Henry Louis Gates Jr. (New York: Oxford University Press, 1988), 109.
74. Davis, "Black Women and Music," 10.
75. Williams, *Dessa Rose*, 55.
76. Ibid.
77. Ibid., 54–55.
78. This was discussed in detail in Chapter 3 of the present study.
79. Williams, *Dessa Rose*, 55.
80. Joanne M. Braxton, "Ancestral Presence: The Outraged Mother Figure in Contemporary Afra-American Writing," in *Wild Women in the Whirlwind: Afra-American Culture and the Contemporary Literary Renaissance*, ed. Joanne M. Braxton and Andrée Nicola McLaughlin (London: Serpent's Tail, 1990), 300.
81. Ann E. Trapasso, "Returning to the Site of Violence: The Restructuring of Slavery's Legacy in Sherley Anne Williams's *Dessa Rose*," in *Violence, Silence, and Anger: Women's Writing as Transgression*, ed. Deirdre Lashgari (Charlottesville: University Press of Virginia, 1995), 223.
82. Shelli B. Fowler, "Marking the Body, Demarcating the Body Politic: Issues of Agency and Identity in *Louisa Picquet* and *Dessa Rose*," *College Language Association Journal* 40, no. 4 (June 1997): 474.
83. Ibid., 477.
84. Maya Angelou, *I Know Why the Caged Bird Sings* (New York: Bantam Books, 1980), 4.
85. Toni Morrison, *The Bluest Eye* (London: Virago, 1994), 13.
86. Ibid., 14.
87. Williams, *Dessa Rose*, 86.
88. Ibid., 81.
89. bell hooks, "Representing Whiteness in the Black Imagination," in *Cultural Studies*, ed. Lawrence Grossberg et al. (London: Routledge, 1992), 338–42.
90. Williams, *Dessa Rose*, 83. "Mammy would have a time trying to explain this dream. A white woman—Is that your enemies?"
91. Ibid., 117.
92. Ibid., 101–2.
93. See Elizabeth Fox-Genovese, *Within the Plantation Household: Black and White Women of the Old South* (Chapel Hill: University of North Carolina Press, 1988), 315.
94. Williams, *Dessa Rose*, 101. The contrast between Rufel's paleness and the infant's dark skin is emphasized several times in the text: "She herself liked to watch the baby as he nursed . . . the contrast between his mulberry-colored mouth and the pink areola surrounding her nipple, between his caramel-colored fist and the rosy cream of her breast" (102).

95. Ibid., 101.
96. Ibid., 128.
97. Ibid., 127.
98. Ibid., 130.
99. Ibid.
100. Ibid.
101. Elizabeth Ann Beaulieu, *Black Women Writers and the American Neo-Slave Narrative: Femininity Unfettered* (London: Greenwood Press, 1999), 37.
102. Williams, *Dessa Rose*, 150.
103. Ibid.
104. Ibid., 117.
105. Keith Byerman, as quoted by Ashraf H. A. Rushdy in "Reading Mammy: The Subject of Relation in Sherley Anne Williams' *Dessa Rose*," *African American Review* 27, no. 3 (Fall 1993): 366.
106. See Williams, *Dessa Rose*, 99.
107. Rushdy, "Reading Mammy," 370.
108. Williams, *Dessa Rose*, 92.
109. Ibid., 93.
110. Rushdy, "Reading Mammy," 370.
111. Ibid., 375.
112. Williams, *Dessa Rose*, 118–19.
113. Ibid., 121.
114. Ibid., 120.
115. Ibid., 83–85.
116. Ibid., 90.
117. Ibid., 123.
118. Ibid.
119. Ibid., 117.
120. Ibid., 123.
121. Rushdy, "Reading Mammy," 376.
122. Williams, *Dessa Rose*, 129.
123. Ibid., 125.
124. Ibid., 128.
125. Ibid., 134–35.
126. Ibid., 136.
127. Ibid., 137.
128. Ibid.
129. Ibid., 139.
130. Ibid., 175.
131. Ibid., 148.
132. Nicole R. King, "Meditations and Mediations: Issues of History and Fiction in *Dessa Rose*," *Soundings: An Interdisciplinary Journal* 76, no. 2–3 (Summer–Fall 1993): 365.
133. Williams, *Dessa Rose*, 138.

134. Valerie Martin, "The Means of Evil," *The Guardian: Guardian Review* (July 31, 2004): 18.
135. Williams, *Dessa Rose*, 138.
136. Deborah E. McDowell, "Negotiating Between Tenses: Witnessing Slavery After Freedom—*Dessa Rose*," in *Slavery and the Literary Imagination: Selected Papers from the English Institute, 1987*, ed. Deborah E. McDowell and Arnold Rampersad (Baltimore, MD: Johns Hopkins University Press, 1989), 151.
137. Williams, *Dessa Rose*, 136.
138. Ibid., 97.
139. Ibid., 140.
140. Ibid., 154.
141. Ibid.
142. Ibid., 138. See also 128, 129.
143. Ibid., 169.
144. Ibid., 172–73.
145. Ibid., 184.
146. Ibid., 171.
147. Ibid., 173.
148. Ibid., 189.
149. Ibid., 201–2.
150. John D'Emilio and Estelle B. Freedman, *Intimate Matters: A History of Sexuality in America* (New York: Harper & Row, 1988), 94.
151. Ibid.
152. Ibid., 94–100.
153. Ibid., 96.
154. Williams, *Dessa Rose*, 185.
155. Ibid., 124–25.
156. Ibid., 125.
157. Ibid., 213.
158. Ibid., 230.
159. Ibid., 222.
160. Ibid.
161. Ibid., 221.
162. Ibid., 227.
163. Ibid., 225.
164. Ibid., 228.
165. Ibid., 226.
166. Ibid., 223.
167. Ibid.
168. Ibid., 231.
169. Ibid., 231–32.
170. Ibid., 224.
171. Ibid., 220, "He"—[Rufel] looked over her shoulder at Nemi—"just mistook my girl for somebody else," 227.
172. Ibid., 227.

173. Ibid., 232.
174. Ibid., 236.
175. Robert Stepto, *From Behind the Veil: A Study of Afro-American Narrative* (Urbana: University of Illinois Press, 1979), 166.
176. See Gayl Jones, interviewed by Charles H. Rowell, "An Interview with Gayl Jones," *Callaloo: A Journal of African American Arts and Letters* 5:3, no.16 (October 1982): 33.
177. Williams, *Dessa Rose*, 174.
178. Ibid., 197.
179. Ibid., 234.
180. Ibid., 182.
181. Ibid., 192.
182. Ibid., 227.
183. Mikhail Bakhtin, as quoted by Henry Louis Gates Jr. in *The Signifying Monkey: A Theory of African American Literary Criticism* (New York: Oxford University Press, 1988), 2.
184. Gayl Jones, *Liberating Voices: Oral Tradition in African American Literature* (London: Harvard University Press, 1991), 166.
185. See Williams, *Dessa Rose*, 168, 206, 209.
186. Ibid., 173, 177, 178, 193.
187. Ibid., 199, 225.
188. Ibid., 236.
189. Gayl Jones, *Corregidora* (London: Camden Press, 1988), 22.
190. Williams, *Dessa Rose*, 236.

Chapter 5

1. Gayl Jones, interviewed by Charles H. Rowell, "An Interview with Gayl Jones," *Callaloo: A Journal of African American Arts and Letters* 5:3, no. 16 (October 1982): 42.
2. Gayl Jones, interviewed by Rowell, "Interview with Gayl Jones," 42.
3. Henry Louis Gates Jr., "Criticism in the Jungle," in *Black Literature and Literary Theory*, ed. Henry Louis Gates Jr. (New York: Methuen, 1984), 4.
4. See Toni Morrison, "Rootedness: The Ancestor as Foundation," in *Black Women Writers (1950–1980): A Critical Evaluation*, ed. Mari Evans (Garden City, NY: Anchor-Doubleday, 1984), 343.
5. Ibid.
6. P. Gabrielle Foreman, "Past-On Stories: History and the Magically Real, Morrison and Allende on Call," in *Magical Realism: Theory, History, Community*, ed. Lois Parkinson Zamora and Wendy B. Faris (Durham, NC: Duke University Press, 1995), 300.
7. Morrison, "Rootedness," 343.
8. Toni Morrison, interviewed by Gail Caldwell, "Author Toni Morrison Discusses Her Latest Novel *Beloved*," in *Conversations with Toni Morrison*, ed.

Danille Taylor-Guthrie (Jackson: University Press of Mississippi, 1994), 242–43.

9. Edward P. Jones, "An Interview with Edward P. Jones," in *The Known World* (New York: Amistad, 2004), 5.
10. Margaret Walker, *Jubilee* (New York: Bantam Books, 1967), 285.
11. Lois Parkinson Zamora, "Magical Romance/Magical Realism: Ghosts in U. S. and Latin American Fiction," in *Magical Realism: Theory, History, Community*, ed. Lois Parkinson Zamora and Wendy B. Faris (Durham, NC: Duke University Press, 1995), 500.
12. Ibid.
13. Ibid.
14. Toni Morrison, "Unspeakable Things Unspoken: The Afro-American Presence in American Literature," in *Within the Circle: An Anthology of African American Literary Criticism from the Harlem Renaissance to the Present*, ed. Angelyn Mitchell (London: Duke University Press, 1994), 396.
15. Morrison, *Beloved*, 3.
16. Wendy B. Faris, *Ordinary Enchantments: Magical Realism and the Remystification of Narrative* (Nashville, TN: Vanderbilt Press, 2004), 14. In relation to the fact that the narrator or characters do not register surprise in relation to the narrated events, notice, for example, the matter of fact way in which Morrison opens the novel, or how Paul D perceives a ghostly presence as soon as he enters Sethe's house and simply asks, "You got company?" To this question Sethe simply replies, "Off and on" (8) as if they were talking about real people.
17. Ibid., 17.
18. Ibid., 7. In *Ordinary Enchantments,* Faris suggests five primary characteristics of the magical realistic text: "First, the text contains an 'irreducible element' of magic; second, the descriptions in magical realism detail a strong presence of the phenomenal world; third the reader may experience some unsettling doubts in the effort to reconcile two contradictory understandings of events; fourth, the narrative merges different realms; and, finally, magical realism disturbs received ideas about time, space, and identity." See also Faris's "Sheherazade's Children: Magical Realism and Postmodern Fiction," in *Magical Realism: Theory, History, Community*, ed. Lois Parkinson Zamora and Wendy B. Faris (Durham, NC: Duke University Press, 1995).
19. Roland Barthes, *The Pleasure of the Text*, trans. Richard Miller (Oxford: Blackwell, 1992), 207.
20. Faris, *Ordinary Enchantments*, 8–9.
21. Claudia Tate, ed., *Black Women Writers at Work* (New York: Continuum, 1983), 125.
22. Geraldine Smith-Wright, "In Spite of the Klan: Ghosts in the Fiction of Black Women Writers," in *Haunting the House of Fiction: Feminist Perspectives on Ghosts Stories by American Women*, ed. Lynette Carpenter and Wendy K. Kolmar (Knoxville: University of Tennessee Press, 1991), 145.
23. Jean-François Lyotard, *The Postmodern Condition: A Report on Knowledge* (Minneapolis: University of Minnesota Press, 1984), 81.

24. Toni Morrison, interviewed by Marsha Darling, "In the Realm of Responsibility: A Conversation with Toni Morrison," *Conversations with Toni Morrison*, ed. Danielle Taylor-Guthrie (Jackson: University Press Mississippi, 1994), 249.
25. Toni Morrison, interviewed by Darling, "Realm of Responsibility," 247.
26. Darling, "Realm of Responsibility," 248.
27. Faris, "Sheherazade's Children," 180.
28. Theo L. D'haen, "Magical Realism and Postmodernism: Decentering Privileged Centers," in *Magical Realism: Theory, History, Community*, ed. Lois Parkinson Zamora and Wendy B. Faris (Durham, NC: Duke University Press, 1995), 195.
29. Morrison, "Unspeakable Things," 396.
30. Darling, "Realm of Responsibility," 247.
31. Faris, *Ordinary Enchantments*, 16.
32. Morrison, *Beloved*, 73.
33. Ibid., 210.
34. Ibid., 70.
35. Ibid., 35–36.
36. See Zamora, "Magical Romance/Magical Realism," 504.
37. Ibid., 498.
38. Ibid.
39. Morrison, *Beloved*, 200.
40. Ibid.
41. Ibid., 204.
42. Henry Louis Gates Jr., "Frederick Douglass and the Language of the Self," *The Yale Review* 70 (July 1981): 599.
43. Morrison, *Beloved*, 251.
44. Ibid., 203.
45. Ibid., 213.
46. Ibid., 210.
47. Mieke Bal, *Narratology: Introduction to the Theory of Narrative* (Toronto: University of Toronto Press, 2002), 25.
48. Ibid.
49. Morrison, *Beloved*, 199.
50. Ibid., 206.
51. Ibid., 216.
52. See Frank Kermode, *The Sense of an Ending: Studies in the Theory of Fiction* (New York: Oxford University Press, 1967), 47.
53. Morrison, *Beloved*, 201.
54. Ibid., 208.
55. Ibid., 210.
56. Ibid., 211.
57. Zamora, "Magical Romance/Magical Realism," 501.
58. Ibid.
59. Morrison, *Beloved*, 188.
60. Ibid., 257.

61. See Gail Caldwell, "Morrison Discusses *Beloved*," 242–43.
62. Zora Neale Hurston, "Black Death," in *The Complete Short Stories* (New York: Harper Perennial, 1996), 202.
63. Ibid., 203.
64. Ibid., 208.
65. Foreman, "Past-On Stories," 286.
66. Morrison, *Beloved*, 258.
67. Ibid., 256.
68. Ibid., 259.
69. Walker, *Jubilee*, 14.
70. Ibid., 11.
71. Morrison, *Beloved*, 259.
72. Valerie Smith, "'Circling the Subject': History and Narrative in *Beloved*," in *Toni Morrison: Critical Perspectives Past and Present*, ed. Henry Louis Gates Jr. and K. A. Appiah (New York: Amistad, 1993), 349.
73. Toni Morrison, interviewed by Elsie B. Washington, "Talk with Toni Morrison," in. *Conversations with Toni Morrison,* ed. Danille Taylor-Guthrie (Jackson: University Press of Mississippi, 1994), 235.
74. Susan Willis, *Specifying: Black Women Writing the American Experience* (London: Routledge, 1990), 10–11.
75. Morrison, "Rootedness," 344.
76. See John Hope Franklin and Alfred A. Moss, *From Slavery to Freedom: A History of African Americans* (New York: McGraw-Hill, 1994), 470–76.
77. Dawn Turner Trice, *Only Twice I've Wished for Heaven* (New York: Anchor Books, 1997), 20.
78. Gloria Naylor, *Linden Hills* (London: Minerva, 1992), 16–17.
79. Willis, *Specifying*, 94.
80. Tzvetan Todorov, *The Fantastic: A Structural Approach to a Literary Genre*, trans. Richard Howard (New York: Cornell University Press, 1975), 41.
81. Ibid., 33.
82. Phyllis Perry, *Stigmata*, 1998 (London: Piatkus, 1999), 57.
83. Faris, *Ordinary Enchantments*, 25.
84. Todorov, *The Fantastic*, 52.
85. Perry, *Stigmata*, 53–54.
86. Ibid., 56.
87. Todorov, *The Fantastic*, 38.
88. Ibid., 82.
89. Perry, *Stigmata*, 74.
90. Ibid., 83.
91. Ibid., 82.
92. Alejo Carpenter, "On the Marvelous Real in America," in *Magical Realism: Theory, History, Community*, ed. Lois Parkinson Zamora and Wendy B. Faris (Durham, NC: Duke University Press, 1995), 86.
93. Foreman, "Past-On Stories," 286.
94. Perry, *Stigmata*, 1.

95. Ibid., 30.
96. Ibid., 22.
97. Ibid., 26.
98. Ibid.
99. Ibid., 25.
100. Ibid., 23.
101. Alice Walker, "In Search of Our Mothers' Gardens," in *In Search of Our Mothers' Gardens: Womanist Prose* (London: Women's Press, 1984), 239.
102. Todorov, *The Fantastic*, 83.
103. Ibid., 86.
104. Ibid., 85.
105. Perry, *Stigmata*, 86.
106. Ibid., 101.
107. Ibid., 4.
108. Ibid., 5.
109. Ibid., 120.
110. Ibid., 219.
111. Perry, *Stigmata*, 206.
112. Ibid., 209–10.
113. Sherley Anne Williams, "Telling the Teller: Memoir and Story," in *The Seductions of Biography*, ed. Mary Rhiel and David Suchoff (New York: Routledge, 1996), 183.
114. Perry, *Stigmata*, 210.
115. Walker, *Jubilee*, 406.
116. Williams, *Dessa Rose* (London: Women's Press, 1998), 154.
117. Morrison, *Beloved*, 17.
118. Ibid., 21.
119. Ibid., 275.
120. Faris, *Ordinary Enchantments*, 192.
121. Perry, *Stigmata*, 214.
122. Ibid., 125.
123. Ibid., 205.
124. Ibid.
125. Ibid., 106.
126. Ibid., 140.
127. Zamora, "Magical Romance/Magical Realism," 544.
128. Perry, *Stigmata*, 7.
129. Examples of accounts of the Atlantic crossing of kidnapped slaves from Africa to the New World occur in Paule Marshall's *Praisesong for the Widow* (London: Plume, 1983); Charles Johnson's *Middle Passage* (London: Picador, 1991); Barbara Chase-Riboud's *Echo of Lions* (New York: William Morrow, 1989); and Sandra Jackson-Opoku's *The River Where Blood is Born* (New York: Ballantine, 1997).
130. Toni Morrison, *Beloved*, dedication.
131. Perry, *Stigmata*, 51.
132. Ibid., 50.

133. Ibid., 51.
134. Ibid., 45.
135. Ibid., 55.
136. Ibid., 155.
137. Todorov, *The Fantastic*, 44.
138. Ibid.
139. Perry, *Stigmata*, 17.
140. Alice Walker, "Everyday Use," in *The Complete Stories* (London: Women's Press, 1994), 53.
141. Floris Barnett Cash, "Kinship and Quilting: An Examination of an African-American Tradition," *Journal of Negro History* 80, no. 1 (Winter 1995): 30.
142. Perry, *Stigmata*, 64.
143. Cash, "Kinship and Quilting," 34.
144. Ibid.
145. Perry, *Stigmata*, 60.
146. Ibid., 52.
147. Sharon F. Patton, *African-American Art* (New York: Oxford University Press, 1998), 189.
148. Ibid., 187–88.
149. Perry, *Stigmata*, 94.
150. Ibid.
151. Ibid.
152. Pat Ferrero, as quoted by Cash in "Kinship and Quilting," 32.
153. Olga Idriss Davis, "The Rhetoric of Quilts: Creating Identity in African-American Children's Literature," *African American Review* 32, no. 1 (Spring 1988): 68.
154. Ibid.
155. Cuesta Benberry, *Always There: The African-American Presence in American Quilts* (Louisville: Kentucky Quilt Project, 1992), 114.
156. Perry, *Stigmata*, 229.
157. Gayl Jones, *Corregidora* (London: Camden Press, 1988), 54.
158. Perry, *Stigmata*, 46–47.
159. Ibid., 225.
160. Morrison, *Beloved*, 95.
161. Patton, *African-American Art*, 189.
162. Houston Baker Jr., *Blues, Ideology, and Afro-American Literature: A Vernacular Theory* (Chicago: University of Chicago Press, 1987), 7.
163. Ralph Ellison, as quoted by Patton, *African-American Art*, 189.
164. Ibid., 191. It is interesting to note that the technique of collage, which borrows images from a variety of sources varying from paintings and photographs to the media also attempts to blur the distinctions between the real and the unreal, transforming the way the world is perceived. Hence, the collage, like the magical realist text, aims to enlarge the narrative space so that established representations of the world are challenged.
165. Ntozake Shange, *Sassafrass, Cypress and Indigo* (London: Minerva, 1996), 27.
166. Octavia E. Butler, *Kindred* (London: Women's Press, 1995), 260.

167. Ibid., 259–61.
168. Ibid., 264.
169. Ibid., 262.
170. Ibid.
171. Ibid.
172. Ibid., 264.
173. Karla F. C. Holloway, *Moorings & Metaphors: Figures of Culture and Gender in Black Women's Literature* (New Brunswick, NJ: Rutgers University Press, 1992), 113.
174. James Joyce, *Ulysses* (London: Penguin Books, 1992), 42.
175. Tina McElroy Ansa, *Baby of the Family* (London: Spectre, 1996), 183.
176. Ibid., 177.
177. Ibid., 188.
178. Zamora, "Magical Romance/Magical Realism," 498.
179. Perry, *Stigmata,* 24. It is worth noticing that Ayo's mother's hand calling her daughter and encouraging her to begin the journey recalls the hands of other ancestral figures who, with their hands, call on their descendants to engage with the past. See Marshall's *Praisesong for the Widow* and Morrison's *Song of Solomon.*
180. Perry, *Stigmata*, 24.
181. Ibid., 73.
182. Ibid., 146–47.
183. Marshall, *Praisesong*, 32.
184. Toni Morrison, *Song of Solomon* (London: Picador, 1989), 239.
185. Perry, *Stigmata*, 33–34.
186. Ibid., 34.
187. Perry, *Stigmata*. See, for example, pages 7 and 17. "I remember" (7) is later presented as "I choose to remember" (17); "This is for whose bones lay sleepin in the heart of the ocean" (7) is subsequently recorded as "This is for whose bones lay in the heart of the ocean"; "the aside" (7) is replaced by "beside."
188. Williams, *Dessa Rose*, 236.
189. Morrison, *Beloved*, 274.
190. Ibid., 274, 275.
191. Ibid., 275.
192. "How I Wrote *Jubilee*," in *How I Wrote Jubilee and Other Essays on Life and Literature*, ed. Maryemma Graham (New York: Feminist Press, 1990), 58.
193. Zamora, "Magical Romance/Magical Realism," 501.
194. Salman Rushdie as quoted by Faris, *Ordinary Enchantments*, 144.

Conclusion

1. James Baldwin, *Notes of a Native Son* (London: Michael Joseph, 1964), 14.
2. Margaret Walker interviewed by Phanuel Egejuru and Robert Elliot Fox, "An Interview with Margaret Walker," *Callaloo: A Journal of African American and African Arts and Letters* 2, no. 2 (1979): 34–35.

3. Henry Louis Gates Jr., foreword to *Incidents in the Life of a Slave Girl*, by Harriet Jacobs (New York: Oxford University Press, 1988), xvi.
4. Ibid., xvii–xviii.
5. Harriet E. Wilson, preface to *Our Nig; or, Sketches from the Life of a Free Black, In a Two Story House, North. Showing that Slavery's Shadows Fall Even There* (Random House, 1983), 3.
6. Toni Cade Bambara interviewed by Claudia Tate, ed., *Black Women Writers at Work* (New York: Continuum, 1983), 17–18.
7. Audre Lorde interviewed by Tate, *Black Women Writers*, 108.
8. Sherley Anne Williams interviewed by Tate, *Black Women Writers*, 210.
9. Dorothy West, *The Living Is Easy* (New York: Feminist Press, 1982), 90–91.
10. Lalita Tademy, *Cane River* (London: Headline, 2001), v.
11. Margaret Walker, *Jubilee* (New York: Bantam Books, 1967), x.
12. Ntozake Shange, *Sassafrass, Cypress and Indigo* (London: Minerva, 1996), 28.
13. Barbara Christian, "'Somebody Forgot to Tell Somebody Something': African-American Women's Historical Novels," in *Wild Women in the Whirlwind: Afra-American Culture and the Contemporary Literary Renaissance*, ed. Joanne M. Braxton and Andrée Nicola McLaughlin (London: Serpent's Tail, 1990), 328.
14. Toni Morrison, *A Mercy* (New York: Vintage Books, 2008), 8.
15. Gayl Jones, *Liberating Voices: Oral Tradition in African American Literature* (London: Harvard University Press, 1991), 179.

Bibliography

Primary Sources

Angelou, Maya. *I Know Why the Caged Bird Sings*. 1969. New York: Bantam Books, 1980.

Ansa, Tina McElroy. *Baby the Family*. 1989. London: Spectre, 1996.

———. *Ugly Ways*. New York: Harvest American Writing, 1993.

———. *The Hand I Fan With*. New York: Anchor Books, 1996.

Baraka, Amiri. "Black Art." In *The Norton Anthology of African American Literature*, edited by Henry Louis Gates Jr. and Nellie Y. McKay. New York: Norton, 1997.

Berry, Bertice. *Redemption Song: A Novel*. New York: Doubleday, 2000.

Briscoe, Connie. *A Long Way from Home*. New York: Harper Collins, 1999.

Butler, Octavia E. *Kindred*. 1979. London: Women's Press, 1995.

Chase-Riboud, Barbara. *The Echo of Lions*. New York: William Morrow, 1989.

Cooper, J. California. *Family*. New York: Doubleday, 1991.

———. *In Search of Satisfaction*. New York: Anchor Books, 1994.

———. *The Wake of the Wind*. New York: Anchor Books, 1998.

Crafts, Hannah. *The Bondswoman's Narrative*. Edited by Henry Louis Gates Jr. London: Virago, 2002.

D'Aguiar, Fred. *The Longest Memory*. 1994. London: Vintage, 1995.

Douglass, Frederick. *Narrative of the Life of Frederick Douglass: An American Slave*. New York: Signet, 1968.

Gaines, Ernest J. *The Autobiography of Miss Jane Pittman*. 1971. New York: Bantam Books, 1972.

Harper, Frances Ellen Watkins. *Minnie's Sacrifice, Sowing and Reaping, Trial and Triumph: Three Rediscovered Novels*. Edited by Frances Smith Foster. Boston: Beacon, 1994.

———. *Iola Leroy, or, Shadows Uplifted*. 1892. New York: Oxford University Press, 1988.

Hopkins, Pauline. *Contending Forces: A Romance Illustrative of Negro Life North and South*. 1900. Edited by Henry Louis Gates Jr. New York: Oxford University Press, 1988.

Hunt, Marsha. *Free*. London: Penguin Books, 1992.

———. *Repossessing Ernestine: The Search for a Lost Soul*. 1996. London: Flamingo, 1997.

Hurston, Zora Neale. *Their Eyes Were Watching God*. 1937. London: Virago Press, 1995.

———. "Uncle Monday." In *The Complete Short Stories*. 1995. New York: Harper Perennial, 1996.

———. "Black Death." In *The Complete Short Stories*. 1995. New York: Harper Perennial, 1996.

Jackson-Opoku, Sandra. *The River Where Blood Is Born*. New York: Ballantine, 1997.

Jacobs, Harriet. *Incidents in the Life of a Slave Girl*. 1861. Edited by Henry Louis Gates Jr. New York: Oxford University Press, 1988.

Johnson, Charles. *Oxherding Tale*. 1982. Edinburgh, UK: Payback, 1999.

———. *Middle Passage*. 1990. London: Picador, 1991.

Jones, Edward P. *The Known World*. 2003. New York: Amistad, 2004.

Jones, Gayl. *Corregidora*. 1975. London: Camden Press, 1988.

———. *Eva's Man*. 1976. Boston: Beacon, 1987.

———. *Xarque and Other Poems*. Detroit, MI: Lotus, 1985.

Joyce, James. *Ulysses*. 1922. London: Penguin, 1992.

———. *Portrait of the Artist*. 1916. London: Wordsworth Classics, 1992.

Marshall, Paule. *Praisesong for the Widow*. London: Plume, 1983.

Martin, Valerie. *Property*. London: Abacus, 2003.

Morrison, Toni. *The Bluest Eye*. 1970. London: Picador, 1994.

———. *The Bluest Eye*. 1970. London: Picador, 1990.

———. *Sula*. 1973. London: Picador, 1991.

———. *Beloved*. 1987. London: Picador, 1988.

———. *Song of Solomon*. 1977. London: Picador, 1989.

———. *A Mercy*. New York: Vintage, 2008.

Naylor, Gloria. *Linden Hills*. 1985. London: Minerva, 1992.

———. *Mama Day*. 1988. New York: Vintage Books, 1993.

Perry, Phyllis. *Stigmata*. 1998. London: Piatkus, 1999.

Prince, Mary. *The History of Mary Prince, A West Indian Slave: Related by Herself*. 1831. In *Six Women's Slave Narratives*, edited by Henry Louis Gates Jr. New York: Oxford University Press, 1988.

Reed, Ishmael. *Flight to Canada*. 1976. New York: Scribner Paperback Fiction, 1998.

Shange, Ntozake. *Sassafrass, Cypress and Indigo*. 1983. London: Minerva, 1996.

Tademy, Lalita. *Cane River*. London: Headline, 2001.

Trice, Dawn Turner. *Only Twice I've Wished for Heaven*. New York: Anchor Books, 1997.

Walker, Alice. *Meridian*. 1976. London: Women's Press, 1997.

———. "Everyday Use." In *The Complete Stories*. London: Women's Press, 1994.

Walker, Margaret. *For My People*. 1942. New Haven, CT: Yale University Press, 1969.

———. *Jubilee*. 1966. New York: Bantam Books, 1967.

———. *This Is My Century: New and Collected Poems*. Athens: University of Georgia Press, 1989.

Wheatley, Phillis. *Poems on Various Subjects, Religious and Moral*. 1773. Edited by John C. Shields. New York: Oxford University Press, 1988.

Williams, Sherley Anne. *Dessa Rose*. 1986. London: Virago, 1998.

———. *Peacock Poems*. Hanover, NH: Wesleyan University Press, 1975.

Wilson, Harriet E. *Our Nig; or, Sketches from the Life of a Free Black, In a Two Story House, North. Showing that Slavery's Shadows Fall Even There.* 1859. New York: Vintage Books, 1983.

Secondary Sources

Abel, Elizabeth. "Black Writing, White Reading: Race and the Politics of Feminist Interpretation." In *Female Subjects in Black and White: Race, Psychoanalysis, Feminism*, edited by Elizabeth Abel, Barbara Christian, and Helen Moglen. Berkeley: University of California Press, 1997.

Ammons, Elizabeth. "Stowe's Dream of the Mother-Saviour: *Uncle Tom's Cabin* and American Women Writers Before the 1920s." In *New Essays on Uncle Tom's Cabin*, edited by Eric Sunquist. New York: Cambridge University Press, 1986.

Andrews, William L. "The Representation of Slavery and the Rise of Afro-American Realism 1865–1920." In *Slavery and the Literary Imagination: Selected Papers from the English Institute, 1987*, edited by Deborah E. McDowell and Arnold Rampersad. Baltimore, MD: Johns Hopkins University Press, 1989.

Aptheker, Herbert, ed. *A Documentary History of the Negro People in the United States: From the Reconstruction Era to 1910.* New York: Citadel Press, 1951.

Armitt, Lucie. "Space, Time, and Female Genealogies: A Kristevan Reading of Feminist Science Fiction." In *Image and Power: Women in Fiction in the Twentieth Century*, edited by Sarah Sceats and Gail Cunningham. London: Longman, 1996.

Athey, Stephanie. "Reproductive Health, Race and Technology: Political Fictions and Black Feminist Critiques 1970s–1990s." *SAGE: A Scholarly Journal on Black Women* 22, no. 1 (February 1997): 3–27.

Baccolini, Raffaella. "Gender and Genre in the Feminist Critical Dystopias of Katharine Burdekin, Margaret Atwood, and Octavia Butler." In *Future Females, The Next Generation: New Voices and Velocities in Feminist Science Fiction Criticism*, edited by Marleen S. Barr. Lanham, MD: Rowman & Littlefield, 2000.

Baker, Houston A., Jr. "Balancing the Perspective, a Look at Early Black American Literary Artistry." *Negro American Literary Forum* 6, no. 3 (August 1972): 65–71.

———. *Long Black Song: Essays in Black American Literature and Culture.* Charlottesville: University Press of Virginia, 1972.

———. *The Journey Back: Issues in Black Literature and Criticism.* Chicago: University of Chicago Press, 1980.

———. "Generational Shifts and the Recent Criticism of Afro-American Literature." In *Within the Circle: An Anthology of African American Literary Criticism from the Harlem Renaissance to the Present*, edited by Angelyn Mitchell. London: Duke University Press, 1994.

———. *Blues, Ideology, and Afro-American Literature: A Vernacular Theory.* 1984. Chicago: University of Chicago Press, 1987.

———. *Workings of the Spirit: The Poetics of Afro-American Women's Writing.* Chicago: University of Chicago Press, 1991.

Bal, Mieke. *Narratology: Introduction to the Theory of Narrative.* Toronto: University of Toronto Press, 2002.

Baldwin, James. *Notes of a Native Son.* London: Michael Joseph, 1964.

Baraka, Amiri. "The Myth of a 'Negro Literature.'" In *Within the Circle: An Anthology of African American Literary Criticism from the Harlem Renaissance to the Present,* edited by Angelyn Mitchell. London: Duke University Press, 1994.

Barksdale, Richard K. "Margaret Walker: Folk Literature and Historical Prophecy." In *Praisesong of Survival: Lectures and Essays: 1957–1989.* Chicago: University of Illinois Press, 1992.

———. "Castration Symbolism in Recent Black American Fiction." *College Language Association Journal* 29, no. 4 (June 1986): 400–413.

Barrio-Vilar, Laura. "Racial Uplift Ideology and Black Womanhood in Frances Harper's Serialized Novels." In *Popular Nineteenth-Century American Women Writers and the Literary Marketplace,* edited by Earl Yarington and Mary De Jong. Newcastle upon Tyne, UK: Cambridge Scholars, 2007.

Barthes, Roland. *The Pleasure of the Text.* Translated by Richard Miller. Oxford: Blackwell, 1992.

Bassard, Katherine Clay. "Gender and Genre: Black Women's Autobiography and the Ideology of Literacy." *African American Review* 26, no. 1 (Spring 1992): 119–29.

Basu, Biman. "Public and Private Discourses and the Black Female Subject: Gayl Jones' *Eva's Man.*" *Callaloo: A Journal of African American and African Arts and Letters* 19, no. 1 (Winter 1996): 193–208.

Beal, Frances M. "Black Women and the Science Fiction Genre: Interview with Octavia Butler." *Black Scholar* 17, no. 2 (April 1986): 14–18.

Beaulieu, Elizabeth Ann. *Black Women Writers and the American Neo-Slave Narrative: Femininity Unfettered.* London: Greenwood Press, 1999.

Bell, Bernard W. *The Afro-American Novel and Its Tradition.* Amherst: University of Massachusetts Press, 1987.

———. "*Beloved*: A Womanist Neo-Slave Narrative; or Multivocal Remembrances of Things Past." *African American Review* 26, no. 1 (Spring 1992): 7–15.

———. *The Contemporary African American Novel: Its Folk Roots and Modern Literary Brances.* Amherst: University of Massachusetts Press, 2004.

Benberry, Cuesta. *Always There: The African-American Presence in American Quilts.* Louisville: Kentucky Quilt Project, 1992.

Benjamin, Walter. "Theses on the Philosophy of History." In *Illuminations,* edited by Hannah Arendt. Translated by Harry Zohn. New York: Harcourt, Brace & World, 1969.

Berlant, Lauren. "The Queen of America Goes to Washington City: Harriet Jacobs, Frances Harper, Anita Hill." *American Literature: A Journal of Literary History, Criticism, and Bibliography* 65, no. 3 (September 1993): 549–74.

Bigsby, Christopher, and William Edgar. *The Second Black Renaissance: Essays in Black Literature.* London: Greenwood Press, 1980.

Bjork, Patrick Bryce. *The Novels of Toni Morrison: The Search for Self and Place within the Community.* New York: Peter Lang, 1992.

Bonetti, Kay. "An Interview with Margaret Walker Alexander." *The Missouri Review* 15, no. 1 (1992): 112–31.

———. "Margaret Walker." In *Conversations with American Novelists: The Best Interviews from the Missouri Review and the American Audio Prose*, edited by Kay Bonetti, Greg Michalson, Speer Morgan, Jo Sapp, and Sam Stowers. Columbia: University of Missouri Press, 1997.

Bonner, Frances. "Difference and Desire, Slavery and Seduction: Octavia Butler's Xenogenesis." *Foundation: The Review of Science-Fiction* 48 (Spring 1990): 50–62.

Bonnet, Michele. "'To Take the Sin out of the Slicing Tress': The Law of the Tree in *Beloved*." *African American Review* 31, no. 1 (Spring 1997): 41–54.

Boudreau, Kristin. "Pain and the Unmaking of the Self in Toni Morrison's *Beloved*." *Contemporary Literature* 36, no. 3 (Fall 1995): 447–65.

Wisconsin: University of Wisconsin Press, Boyd, Melba Joyce. *Discarded Legacy: Politics and Poetics in the Life of E. W. Harper, 1825–1911*. Detroit, MI: Wayne State University Press, 1994.

Braxton, Joanne M. "Ancestral Presence: The Outraged Mother Figure in Contemporary Afra-American Writing." In *Wild Women in the Whirlwind: Afra-American Culture and the Contemporary Literary Renaissance*, edited by Joanne M. Braxton and Andrée Nicola McLaughlin. London: Serpent's Tail, 1990.

Broad, Robert L. "Giving Blood to the Scraps: Haints, History, and Hosea in *Beloved*." *African American Review* 28, no. 2 (Summer 1994): 189–96.

Brock, Sabine. "Transcending the 'Loophole of Retreat': Paule Marshall's Placing of Female Generations." *Callaloo: A Journal of African American and African Arts and Letters* 10, no. 1 (Winter 1987): 79–90.

Brondum, Lene. "'The Persistence of Tradition': The Retelling of Sea Islands Culture in Works by Julie Dash, Gloria Naylor, and Paule Marshall." In *Black Imagination and the Middle Passage*, edited by Maria Diedrich, Henry Louis Gates Jr., and Carl Pedersen. Oxford: Oxford University Press, 1999.

Boutry, Katherine. "Black and Blue: The Female Body of Blues Writing in Jean Toomer, Toni Morrison, and Gayl Jones." In *Black Orpheus: Music in African American Fiction from the Harlem Renaissance to Toni Morrison*, edited by A. Saadi Simawe. New York: Garland, 2000.

Brown, Sterling A. "The New Negro in Literature (1925–1955)." In *Remembering the Harlem Renaissance*, edited by Cary D. Wintz. New York: Garland, 1996.

Bryant, Jacqueline K. *The Foremother Figure in Early Black Women's Literature: Clothed in My Right Hand*. New York: Garland, 1999.

Buncombe, Marie H. "From Harlem to Brooklyn: The New York Scene in the Fiction of Meriwether, Petry, and Marshall." *MAWA-Review* 1, no. 1 (Spring 1982): 16–19.

Bush, Glen. "Creative Orality: Writing Orality into African American Literature." *Publications of the Mississippi Philological Association* 94 (1994): 8–14.

Busia, Abena P. B. "Words Whispered Over Voids: A Context for Black Women's Rebellious Voices in the Novel of the African Diaspora." In *Black Feminist*

Criticism and Critical Theory, edited by Joe Weixlmann and A. Houston Baker Jr. Penkevill, FL: Greenwood Press, 1988.

———. "What Is Your Nation?: Reconnecting Africa and Her Diaspora through Paule Marshall's *Praisesong for the Widow*." In *Changing Our Own Words: Essays on Criticism, Theory, and Writing by Black Women*, edited by Cheryl A. Wall. New Brunswick, NJ: Rutgers University Press, 1989.

Bussey, Susan Hays. "Whose Will Be Done?: Self-Determination in Pauline Hopkins's *Hagar's Daughter*." *African American Review* 39, no. 3 (Fall 2005): 299–313.

Callahan, John Francis. *In the African-American Grain: The Pursuit of Voice in Twentieth-Century Black Fiction*. Urbana: University of Illinois Press, 1988.

Carby, Hazel V. *Reconstructing Womanhood: The Emergence of the Afro-American Woman Novelist*. New York: Oxford University Press, 1987.

———. "'Ideologies of Black Folk': The Historical Novel of Slavery." In *Slavery and the Literary Imagination: Selected Papers from the English Institute, 1987*, edited by Deborah E. McDowell and Arnold Rampersad. Baltimore, MD: Johns Hopkins University Press, 1989.

Carmean, Karen. *Toni Morrison's World of Fiction*. New York: Whitston, 1993.

Carmichael, Jacqueline Miller. *Trumpeting a Fiery Sound: History and Folklore in Margaret Walker's Jubilee*. Athens: University of Georgia Press, 1998.

Carpenter, Alejo. "On the Marvelous Real in America." In *Magical Realism: Theory, History, Community*, edited by Lois Parkinson Zamora and Wendy B. Faris. Durham, NC: Duke University Press, 1995.

Cash, Floris Barnett. "Kinship and Quilting: An Examination of an African-American Tradition." *Journal of Negro History* 80, no. 1 (Winter 1995): 30–41.

Chauche, Catherine. "Beloved, A Principle of Order and Chaos in Toni Morrison's Novel *Beloved*." *Imaginaires: Revue du Centre de Recherche sur l'Imaginaire dans les Littératures de Langue Anglaise* 12 (2008): 345–58.

Childs, Dennis. "'You Ain't Seen Nothin' Yet': *Beloved*, the American Chain Gang, and the Middle Passage Remix." *American Quarterly* 61, no. 2 (June 2009): 271–97.

Christian, Barbara. "'Somebody Forgot to Tell Somebody Something': African-American Women's Historical Novels." In *Wild Women in the Whirlwind: Afra-American Culture and the Contemporary Literary Renaissance*, edited by Joanne M. Braxton and Andrée Nicola McLaughlin. London: Serpent's Tail, 1990.

———. *Black Feminist Criticism: Perspectives on Black Women Writers*. New York: Pergamon, 1985.

———. *Black Women Writers: The Development of a Tradition, 1892–1976*. Westport, CT: Greenwood Press, 1980.

———. "Ritualistic Process and the Structure of Paule Marshall's *Praisesong for the Widow*." *Callaloo: A Journal of African American and African Arts and Letters* 6, no. 18 (Spring–Summer 1983): 74–84.

Clabough, Casey. "Toward Feminine Mythopoetic Vision: The Poetry of Gayl Jones." *African American Review* 41, no. 1 (Spring 2007): 98–114.

———. "'Toward an All-Inclusive Structure': The Early Fiction of Gayl Jones." *Callaloo: A Journal of African Diaspora Arts and Letters* 29, no. 2 (Spring 2006): 634–57.

Clarke, Michael Tavel. "Reclaiming Literary Territory: Paule Marshall's Response to Joseph Conrad." *Conradiana: A Journal of Joseph Conrad Studies* 28, no. 2 (Summer 1996): 138–50.

Clark-Lewis, Elizabeth. *Living In, Living Out: African American Domestics and the Great Migration*. New York: Kodansha, 1995.

Cobham, Rhonda. "Revisioning Our Kumblas: Transforming Feminist and Nationalist Agendas in Three Caribbean Women's Texts." In *Postcolonial Theory and the United States: Race, Ethnicity, and Literature*, edited by Amritjit Singh and Peter Schmidt. Jackson: University Press of Mississippi, 2000.

Collier, Eugenia. "Fields Watered with Blood: Myth and Ritual in the Poetry of Margaret Walker." In *Black Women Writers (1950–1980): A Critical Evaluation*, edited by Mari Evans. Garden City, NY: Anchor-Doubleday, 1984.

Condé, Mary. "Some African-American Fictional Responses to *Gone with the Wind*." *Yearbook of English Studies* 26 (1996): 208–17.

Connor, Kimberly Rae. "*To Disembark*: The Slave Narrative Tradition." *African American Review* 30, no. 1 (Spring 1996): 35–57.

———. "Spirituals." In *The Oxford Companion to African American Literature*, edited by William L. Andrews, Frances Smith Foster, and Trudier Harris. New York: Oxford University Press, 1997.

Cooper, A. J. "Discussion of the Same Subject [The Intellectual Progress of the Colored Women of the United States Since the Emancipation Proclamation]." 1893. Address in *The World's Congress of Representative Women*, edited by May Wright Sewall, 711–15. Chicago: Rand McNally, 1894.

Cordell, Sigrid Anderson. "'The Case Was Very Black Against' Her: Pauline Hopkins and the Politics of Racial Ambiguity at the Colored American Magazine." *American Periodicals: A Journal of History, Criticism, and Bibliography* 16, no. 1 (2006): 52–73.

Cornis-Pope, Marcel. "Narrative Innovation and Cultural Rewriting: The Pynchon Morrison Sukenick Connection." In *Narrative and Culture*, edited by Janice Carlisle and Daniel R. Schwarz. London: University of Georgia Press, 1994.

Corti, Lillian. "*Medea* and *Beloved*: Self-Definition and Abortive Nurturing in Literary Treatments of the Infanticidal Mother." In *Disorderly Eaters: Texts in Self-Empowerment*, edited by Lillian R. Furst and Peter W. Graham. University Park: Pennsylvania State University, 1992.

Coser, Stelamaris. *Bridging the Americas: The Literature of Paule Marshall, Toni Morrison, and Gayl Jones*. Philadelphia: Temple University Press, 1995.

———. "Stepping-Stones between the Americas: The Narratives of Paule Marshall and Gayl Jones." *PALARA: Publication of the Afro-Latin American Research Association* 1 (Fall 1997): 80–88.

Couser, G. Thomas. "Oppression and Repression: Personal and Collective Memory in Paule Marshall's *Praisesong for the Widow* and Leslie Marmon Silko's *Ceremony*." In *Memory and Cultural Politics: New Approaches to American Ethnic

Literatures, edited by Amritjit Singh, Joseph T. Skerrett Jr., and Robert E. Hogan. Boston: Northeastern University Press, 1996.

Cutter, Martha J. "The Story Must Go On: The Fantastic, Narration, and Intertextuality in Toni Morrison's *Beloved*." *African American Review* 34, no. 1 (Spring 2000): 62–75.

Darling, Marsha. "In the Realm of Responsibility: A Conversation with Toni Morrison." In *Conversations with Toni Morrison*, edited by Danielle Taylor-Guthrie. Jackson: University Press Mississippi, 1994.

Davies, Carole Boyce. "Black Woman's Journey into Self: A Womanist Reading of Paule Marshall's *Praisesong for the Widow*." *Matatu: Journal for African Culture and Society* 1, no. 1 (1987): 19–34.

———. "Mother Right/Write Revisited: *Beloved* and *Dessa Rose* and the Construction of Motherhood in Black Women's Fiction." In *Narrating Mothers: Theorizing Maternal Subjectivities*, edited by Brenda O. Daly and Maureen T. Reddy. Knoxville: University of Tennessee Press, 1991.

Davis, Angela Y. *Women, Race and Class*. New York: Random House, 1981.

———. "Black Women and Music: A Historical Legacy of Struggle." In *Wild Women in the Whirlwind: Afra-American Culture and the Contemporary Literary Renaissance*, edited by Joanne M. Braxton and Andrée Nicola McLaughlin. London: Serpent's Tail, 1990.

Davis, Kimberly Chabot. "'Postmodern Blackness': Toni Morrison's *Beloved* and the End of History." In *Productive Postmodernism: Consuming Histories and Cultural Studies*, edited by John N. Duval. Albany: State University of New York Press, 2002.

Davis, Mary Kemp. "Everybody Knows Her Name: The Recovery of the Past in Sherley Anne Williams's *Dessa Rose*." *Callaloo: A Journal of African American and African Arts and Letters* 12, no. 3 (Summer 1989): 544–58.

Davis, Olga Idriss. "The Rhetoric of Quilts: Creating Identity in African-American Children's Literature." *African American Review* 32, no. 1 (Spring 1988): 67–76.

Davison, Carol Margaret. "'Love 'em and Lynch 'em': The Castration Motif in Gayl Jones's *Eva's Man*." *African American Review* 29, no. 3 (Fall 1995): 393–410.

Dawson, Emma Waters. "Psychic Rage and Response: The Enslaved and the Enslaver in Sherley Anne Williams's *Dessa Rose*." In *Arms Akimbo: Africana Women in Contemporary Literature*, edited by Janice Lee Liddell and Yakini Belinda Kemp. Gainesville: University Press of Florida, 1999.

Debo, Annette. "Margaret Walker" In *Contemporary African American Novelists: A Bio-Bibliographical Critical Sourcebook*, edited by Emmanuel S. Nelson. Westport, CT: Greenwood Press, 1999.

Denard, Carolyn. "The Convergence of Feminism and Ethnicity in the Fiction of Toni Morrison." In *Critical Essays on Toni Morrison*, edited by Nellie Y. McKay. Boston: Hall, 1988.

———. "The Long, High Gaze: The Mythical Consciousness of Toni Morrison and William Faulkner." In *Unflinching Gaze: Morrison and Faulkner Re-Envisioned*, edited by Carol A. Kolmerten, Stephen M. Ross, and Judith Bryant Wittenberg. Jackson: University Press of Mississippi, 1997.

———, ed. *Toni Morrison: What Moves at the Margin, Selected Non-Fiction*. Jackson: University Press of Mississippi, 2008.

———, ed. *Toni Morrison: Conversations*. Jackson: University Press of Mississippi, 2008.

D'Emilio, John, and Estelle B. Freedman. *Intimate Matters: A History of Sexuality in America*. New York: Harper & Row, 1988.

D'haen, Theo L. "Magical Realism and Postmodernism: Decentering Privileged Centers." In *Magical Realism: Theory, History, Community*, edited by Lois Parkinson Zamora and Wendy B. Faris. Durham, NC: Duke University Press, 1995.

DeLancey, Dayle B. "The Self's Own Kind: Literary Resistance in Sherley Anne Williams' *Dessa Rose*." *MAWA Review* 5, no. 2 (December 1990): 59–62.

Diana, Vanessa Holford. "Narrative Patternings of Resistance in Frances E. W. Harper's *Iola Leroy* and Pauline Hopkins' *Contending Forces*." In *Black Women's Intellectual Traditions: Speaking Their Minds*, edited by Kristin Waters and Carol B. Conaway. Burlington, VT: University Press of New England, 2007.

Dingledine, Donald. "Women Can Walk on Water: Island, Myth, and Community in Kate Chopin's *The Awakening* and Paule Marshall's *Praisesong for the Widow*." *Women's Studies: An Interdisciplinary Journal* 22, no. 2 (1993): 197–216.

Dobbs, Cynthia. "Toni Morrison's *Beloved*: Bodies Returned, Modernism Revisited." *African American Review* 32, no. 4 (Winter 1998): 563–78.

Dubey, Madhu. "Gayl Jones and the Matrilineal Metaphor of Tradition." *Signs: Journal of Women in Culture and Society* 20, no. 2 (Winter 1995): 245–67.

Durkin, Anita. "Object Written, Written Object: Slavery, Scarring, and Complications of Authorship in *Beloved*." *African American Review* 41, no. 3 (Fall 2007): 541–56.

Eckstein, Lars. "A Love Supreme: Jazzthetic Strategies in Toni Morrison's *Beloved*." *African American Review* 40, no. 2 (Summer 2006): 271–83.

Egejuru, Phanuel, and Robert Elliot Fox. "An Interview with Margaret Walker." *Callaloo: A Journal of African American and African Arts and Letters* 2, no. 2 (1979): 29–35.

Elder, Arlene. *The "Hindred Hand": Cultural Implications of Early Afro-American Fiction*. Westport, CT: Greenwood Press, 1978.

Elia, Nada. *Trances, Dances, and Vociferations: Agency and Resistance in Africana Women's Narratives*. New York: Garland, 2001.

Elkins, Marilyn. "Reading Beyond the Conventions: A Look at Frances E. W. Harper's *Iola Leroy, or, Shadows Uplifted*." *American Literary Realism* 22, no. 2 (Winter 1990): 44–53.

Ellison, Ralph. *Shadow and Act*. New York: Vintage Books, 1972.

Erickson, Daniel. *Ghosts, Metaphor, and History in Toni Morrison's Beloved and Gabriel García Márquez's One Hundred Years of Solitude* New York: Palgrave Macmillan, 2009.

Fabi, M. Giulia. "The 'Unguarded Expressions and Feelings of the Negroes': Gender, Slave Resistance, and William Wells Brown's *Clotel*." *African American Review* 27, no. 4: 639–54.

———. "Reconstructing Literary Genealogies: Frances E. W. Harper's and William Dean Howells's Race Novels." In *Soft Canons: American Women Writers and Masculine Tradition*, edited by Karen L. Kilcup. Iowa City: University of Iowa Press, 1999.

Fabre, Michel. "Margaret Walker's Richard Wright: A Wrong Righted or Wright Wronged?" *Mississippi Quarterly: The Journal of Southern Culture* 42, no. 4 (Fall 1989): 429–50.

Fahy, Thomas. "Unsilencing Lesbianism in the Early Fiction of Gayl Jones." In *After the Pain: Critical Essays on Gayl Jones*, edited by Fiona Mills and Keith Mitchell. New York: Peter Lang, 2006.

Faris, Wendy B. "Sheherazade's Children: Magical Realism and Postmodern Fiction." In *Magical Realism: Theory, History, Community*, edited by Lois Parkinson Zamora and Wendy B. Faris. Durham, NC: Duke University Press, 1995.

———. *Ordinary Enchantments: Magical Realism and the Remystification of Narrative*. Nashville, TN: Vanderbilt Press, 2004.

Ferguson, Rebecca. "History, Memory and Language in Toni Morrison's *Beloved*." In *Contemporary American Women Writers: Gender, Class, Ethnicity*, edited by Lois Parkinson Zamora. New York: Longman, 1998.

Finkenbine, Roy E. *Sources of the African-American Past: Primary Sources in American History*. New York: Longman, 1997.

Foreman, P. Gabrielle. "The Spoken and the Silenced in *Incidents in the Life of a Slave Girl* and *Our Nig*." *Callaloo: A Journal of African American and African Arts and Letters* 13, no. 2 (Spring 1990): 313–24.

———. "Past-On Stories: History and the Magically Real, Morrison and Allende on Call." In *Magical Realism: Theory, History, Community*, edited by Lois Parkinson Zamora and Wendy B. Faris. Durham, NC: Duke University Press, 1995.

Foster, Frances Smith. "Harper, Frances Ellen Watkins." In *The Oxford Companion to African American Literature*, edited by William L. Andrews, Frances Smith Foster, and Trudier Harris. New York: Oxford University Press, 1997.

———. *A Brighter Coming Day: A Frances Ellen Watkins Harper Reader*. New York: Feminist Press, 1990.

———. *Written by Herself: Literary Production by African American Women, 1746–1892*. Bloomington: Indiana University Press, 1993.

———. "'In Respect to Females . . .': Differences in the Portrayals of Women by Male and Female Narrators." *Black American Literary Forum* 15, no. 2 (Summer 1981): 66–70.

———. "Octavia Butler's Black Female Future Fiction." *Extrapolation: A Journal of Science Fiction and Fantasy* 23, no. 1 (Spring 1982): 37–49.

Fowler, Shelli B. "Marking the Body, Demarcating the Body Politic: Issues of Agency and Identity in *Louisa Picquet* and *Dessa Rose*." *College Language Association Journal* 40, no. 4 (June 1997): 467–78.

Fox-Genovese, Elizabeth. *Within the Plantation Household: Black and White Women of the Old South*. Chapel Hill: University of North Carolina Press, 1988.

Fox-Good, Jacquelyn A. "Singing the Unsayable: Theorizing Music in *Dessa Rose*." In *Black Orpheus: Music in African American Fiction from the Harlem Renaissance to Toni Morrison*, edited by Saadi A. Simawe. New York: Garland, 2000.

———. *Race and History: Selected Essays 1938–1988*. Baton Rouge: Louisiana State University Press, 1989.

Franklin, Jimmie Lewis. "Black Southerners, Shared Experience, and Place: A Reflection." *The Journal of Southern History* 60, no. 1 (February 1994): 3–18.

Franklin, John Hope. "The New Negro and the New Deal." In *Remembering the Harlem Renaissance*, edited by Cary D. Wintz. New York: Garland, 1996.

Franklin, John Hope, and Alfred A. Moss. *From Slavery to Freedom: A History of African Americans*. New York: McGraw-Hill, 1994.

Franklin, John Hope, and Loren Schweninger. *Runaway Slaves: Rebels on the Plantation*. New York: Oxford University Press, 2000.

Frazier, Franklin E. "The New Negro Middle Class." In *Remembering the Harlem Renaissance*, edited by Cary D. Wintz. New York: Garland, 1996.

Freibert, Lucy M. "Southern Song: An Interview with Margaret Walker." *Frontiers: A Journal of Women Studies* 9, no. 3 (1987): 50–56.

Friend, Beverley. "Time Travel as a Feminist Didactic in Works by Phyllis Eisenstein, Marlys Millhiser, and Octavia Butler." *Extrapolation: A Journal of Science Fiction and Fantasy* 23, no. 1 (Spring 1982): 50–55.

Fryar, Imani L. B. "Literary Aesthetics of the Black Woman Writer." *Journal of Black Studies* 20, no. 4 (June 1990): 443–66.

Fuller, Hoyt. "Towards a Black Aesthetic." In *The Norton Anthology of African American Literature*, edited by Henry Louis Gates Jr. and Nellie Y. McKay. New York: Norton, 1997.

Gabbin, Joanne V. "A Laying On of Hands: Black Women Writers Exploring the Roots of Their Folk and Cultural Tradition." In *Wild Women in the Whirlwind: Afra-American Culture and the Contemporary Literary Renaissance*, edited by Joanne M. Braxton and Andrée Nicola McLaughlin. London: Serpent's Tail, 1990.

———. "Conversation: Margaret Alexander Walker and Joanne V. Gabbin." In *The Furious Flowering of African American Poetry*, edited by Joanne V. Gabbin. Charlottesville: University of Virginia Press, 1999.

Gates, Henry Louis, Jr. "Frederick Douglass and the Language of the Self." *The Yale Review* 70 (July 1981): 592–611.

———. *The Signifying Monkey: A Theory of African-American Literary Criticism*. New York: Oxford University Press, 1988.

———. "Criticism in the Jungle." In *Black Literature and Literary Theory*, edited by Henry Louis Gates Jr. New York: Methuen, 1984.

Gayle, Addison, Jr. "The Black Aesthetic." In *The Norton Anthology of African American Literature*, edited by Henry Louis Gates Jr. and Nellie Y. McKay. New York: Norton, 1997.

Genovese, Eugene D. *Roll, Jordan, Roll: The World the Slaves Made*. New York: Vintage Books, 1976.

Gerzina, Gretchen Holbrook. "Frances E. W. Harper (1825–1911)." In *Nineteenth-Century American Women Writers: A Bio-Bibliographical Critical Sourcebook*, edited by Denise Knight and Emmanuel S. Nelson. Westport, CT: Greenwood Press, 1997.

Giddings, Paula. "'A Shoulder Hunched against a Sharp Concern': Some Themes in the Poetry of Margaret Walker." *Black World* 21, no. 2 (1971): 20–25.

Goldman, Anne E. "'I Made the Ink': (Literary) Production and Reproduction in *Dessa Rose* and *Beloved*." *Feminist Studies* 16, no. 2 (Summer 1990): 313–30.

Goodman, Charlotte. "From Uncle Tom's Cabin to Vyry's Kitchen: The Black Female Folk Tradition in Margaret Walker's *Jubilee*." In *Tradition and the Talents of Women*, edited by Florence Howe. Urbana: University of Illinois Press, 1991.

Goodman, Susan. "Competing Histories: William Styron's *The Confessions of Nat Turner* and Sherley Ann Williams's *Dessa Rose*." In *The World Is Our Culture: Society and Culture in Contemporary Southern Writing*, edited by Jeffrey J. Folks and Nancy Summers Folks. Lexington: University Press of Kentucky, 2000.

Gordon, Nickesia S. "On the Couch with Dr. Fraud: Insidious Trauma and Distorted Female Community in Gayl Jones' *Eva's Man*." *Obsidian III: Literature in the African Diaspora* 6, no. 1 (Spring–Summer 2005): 66–89.

Gottfried, Amy S. "Angry Arts: Silence, Speech, and Song in Gayl Jones's *Corregidora*." *African American Review* 28, no. 4 (Winter 1994): 559–70.

Govan, Sandra Y. "Homage to Tradition: Octavia Butler Renovates the Historical Novel." *MELUS: The Journal of the Society for the Study of the Multi-Ethnic Literature of the United States* 13, no. 1–2 (Spring–Summer 1986): 79–96.

———. "Connections, Links, and Extended Networks: Patterns in Octavia Butler's Science Fiction." *Black American Literature Forum* 18, no. 2 (Summer 1984): 82–87.

Graham, Maryemma, and Deborah Whaley. "Introduction: The Most Famous Person Nobody Knows." In *Fields Watered with Blood: Critical Essays on Margaret Walker*, edited by Maryemma Graham. Athens: University of Georgia Press, 2001.

———. "The Fusion of Ideas: An Interview with Margaret Walker Alexander." *African American Review* 27, no. 2 (Summer 1993): 279–86.

Griffin, Farah Jasmine. "Textual Healing: Claiming Black Women's Bodies, the Erotic and Resistance in Contemporary Novels of Slavery." *Callaloo: A Journal of African American and African Arts and Letters* 19, no. 2 (Spring 1996): 519–36.

Griffiths, Jennifer. "Uncanny Spaces: Trauma, Cultural Memory, and the Female Body in Gayl Jones's *Corregidora* and Maxine Hong Kingston's *The Woman Warrior*." *Studies in the Novel* 38, no. 3 (Fall 2006): 353–70.

Gwin, Minrose C. "Jubilee: The Black Woman's Celebration of Human Community." *Conjuring: Black Women, Fiction, and Literary Tradition*, edited by Marjorie Pryse and Hortense J. Spillers. Bloomington: Indiana University Press, 1985.

Gyant, La Verne. "Passing the Torch: African American Women in the Civil Rights Movement." *Journal of Black Studies* 26, no. 5 (May 1996): 629–47.

———. *Black and White Women of the Old South: The Peculiar Sisterhood in American Literature*. Knoxville: University of Tennessee Press, 1985.

Hajek, Friederike. "Margaret Walker's *Jubilee*: Oral History, the Fiction of Literacy and the Language of a Black Text." In *Rewriting the South: History and Fiction*, edited by Lothar Honnighausen and Valeria Gennaro Lerda. Tübingen, Germany: Francke, 1993.

Handley, William R. "The House a Ghost Built: *Nommo*, Allegory, and the Ethics of Reading in Toni Morrison's *Beloved*." *Contemporary Literature* 36, no. 4 (Winter 1995): 676–701.

Hardack, Richard. "Making Generations and Bearing Witness: Violence and Orality in Gayl Jones's *Corregidora*." *Prospects: An Annual Journal of American Cultural Studies* 24 (1999): 645–61.

Harper, Frances E. W. "Woman's Political Future." 1893. Address in *The World's Congress of Representative Women*, edited by May Wright Sewall, 433–37. Chicago: Rand McNally, 1894.

Harris, Janice. "Gayl Jones's *Corregidora*." *Frontiers: Journal of Women Studies* 5, no. 3 (Fall 1980): 1–5.

Harris, Trudier. "Escaping Slavery but Not Its Images." In *Toni Morrison: Critical Perspectives Past and Present*, edited by Henry Louis Gates Jr. and K. A. Appiah. New York: Amistad, 1993.

Harris, William J. "Black Aesthetic." In *The Oxford Companion to African American Literature*, edited by William L. Andrews, Frances Smith Foster, and Trudier Harris. New York: Oxford University Press, 1997.

Harrison, Suzan. "Mastering Narratives/Subverting Masters: Rhetorics of Race in *The Confessions of Nat Turner*, *Dessa Rose*, and *Celia, a Slave*." *Southern Quarterly: A Journal of the Arts in the South* 35, no. 3 (Spring 1997): 13–28.

Hartman, Saidiya V. *Scenes of Subjection: Terror, Slavery, and Self-Making in Nineteenth Century America*. New York: Oxford University Press, 1997.

Heinze, Denise. *The Dilemma of "Double-consciousness": Toni Morrison's Novels*. London: University of Georgia Press, 1993.

Helford, Elyce Rae. "'Would You Really Rather Die Than Bear My Young?': The Construction of Gender, Race, and Species in Octavia Butler's 'Bloodchild.'" *African American Review* 28, no. 2 (Summer 1994): 259–71.

Henderson, Mae G. "The Stories of O(Dessa): Stories of Complicity and Resistance." In *Female Subjects in Black and White: Race, Psychoanalysis, Feminism*, edited by Elizabeth Abel, Barbara Christian, and Helen Moglen. Berkeley: University of California Press, 1997.

———. "Toni Morrison's *Beloved*: Re-Membering the Body as Historical Text." In *Comparative American Identities: Race, Sex, and Nationality in the Modern Context. Essays from the English Institute*, edited by Hortense Spillers. New York: Routledge, 1991.

Heyman, Richard. "Universalization and Its Discontents: Morrison's *Song of Solomon*—A (W)hol(e)y Black Text." *African American Review* 29, no. 3 (Autumn 1995): 381–92.

Hill, Patricia Liggins. "'Let Me Make a Song for the People': A Study of Frances Watkins Harper's Poetry." *Black American Literature Forum* 15, no. 2 (Summer 1981): 60–65.

Hines, Maude. "Body Language: Corporeal Semiotics, Literary Resistance." In *Body Politics and the Fictional Double*, edited by Debra Walker King. Bloomington: Indiana University Press, 2000.

Hite, Molly. *The Other Side of the Story: Structures and Strategies of Contemporary Feminist Narratives*. Ithaca, NY: Cornell University Press, 1989.

Hoefel, Roseanne. "Praisesong for Paule Marshall: Music and Dance as Redemptive Metaphor in *Brown Girl, Brownstones* and *Praisesong for the Widow*." *MaComere: Journal of the Association of Caribbean Women Writers and Scholars* 1 (1998): 134–44.

Hoeller, Hildegard. "Self-Reliant Women in Frances Harper's Writings." *American Transcendental Quarterly* 19, no. 3 (September 2005): 205–20.

Holden-Kirwan, Jennifer L. "Looking into the Self That Is No Self: An Examination of Subjectivity in *Beloved*." *African American Review* 32, no. 3 (Autumn 1998): 415–26.

Holloway, Karla F. C. *Moorings & Metaphors: Figures of Culture and Gender in Black Women's Literature*. New Brunswick, NJ: Rutgers University Press, 1992.

Holmes, Kristine. "'This Is Flesh I'm Talking about Here': Embodiment in Toni Morrison's *Beloved* and Sherley Anne Williams' *Dessa Rose*." *Literature Interpretation Theory* 6, no. 1–2 (April 1995): 133–48.

Holt, Thomas C. *African-American History*. Washington, DC: American Historical Association. 1997.

Homans, Margaret. "'Her Very Own Howl': The Ambiguities of Representation in Recent Women's Fiction." *Signs: Journal of Women in Culture and Society* 9, no. 2 (Winter 1983): 186–205.

hooks, bell. "Representing Whiteness in the Black Imagination." In *Cultural Studies*, edited by Lawrence Grossberg et al. London: Routledge, 1992.

Horvitz, Deborah. "'Sadism Demands a Story': Oedipus, Feminism, and Sexuality in Gayl Jones's *Corregidora* and Dorothy Allison's *Bastard Out of Carolina*." *Contemporary Literature* 39, no. 2 (Summer 1998): 238–61.

Hyman, Rebecca. "Women as Figures of Exchange in Gayl Jones's *Corregidora*." *Xanadu: A Literary Journal* 14 (1991): 40–51.

Jacobe, Monica F. "Ursa Finds Her Voice: Sex, History, and Self in Gayl Jones's *Corregidora*." *Journal of Kentucky Studies*. 24 (September 2007): 117–24.

Johnson, E. Patrick. "Wild Women Don't Get the Blues: A Blues Analysis of Gayl Jones' *Eva's Man*." *Obsidian II: Black Literature in Review* 9, no. 1 (Spring–Summer 1994): 26–46.

Johnson, Maria V. "Shange and Her Three Sisters 'Sing a Liberation Song': Variations on the Orphic Theme." In *Black Orpheus: Music in African American Fiction from the Harlem Renaissance to Toni Morrison*, edited by Saadi A. Simawe. New York: Garland, 2000.

Johnson, Rebecca O. "African American Feminist Science Fiction." *Sojourner: The Women's Forum* 19, no. 6 (February 1994): 12–14.

Johnson, Sherita L. "'In the Sunny South': Reconstructing Frances Harper as Southern." *Southern Quarterly: A Journal of the Arts in the South* 45, no. 3 (Spring 2008): 70–85.

Jones, Gayl. *Liberating Voices: Oral Tradition in African American Literature*. London: Harvard University Press, 1991.

Kalfopoulou, Adrianne. "Gendered Silences and the Problem of Desire in Nathaniel Hawthorne's *The Scarlet Letter*, Gertrude Stein's 'Melanctha' and Gayl Jones's *Corregidora*." In *Nationalism and Sexuality: Crises of Identity*, edited by Yiorgos Kalogeras and Domna Pastourmatzi. Thessaloniki, Greece: Hellenic Association of American Studies, Aristotle University, 1996.

Karenga, Maulana. "Black Art: Mute Matter Given Force and Function." In *The Norton Anthology of African American Literature*, edited by Henry Louis Gates Jr. and Nellie Y. McKay. New York: Norton, 1997.

Kekeh, Andrée Anne. "Sherley Anne William's *Dessa Rose*: History and the Disruptive Power of Memory." In *History and Memory in African-American Culture*, edited by Genevieve Fabre and Robert O'Meally. New York: Oxford University Press, 1994.

Kenan, Randall. "An Interview with Octavia E. Butler." *Callaloo: A Journal of African American and African Arts and Letters* 14, no. 2 (Spring 1991): 495–504.

Kester, Gunilla T. "The Blues, Healing, and Cultural Representation in Contemporary African American Women's Literature." In *Women Healers and Physicians: Climbing a Long Hill*, edited by Lillian R. Furst. Lexington: University Press of Kentucky, 1997.

King, Lovalerie. "Resistance, Reappropriation, and Reconciliation: The Blues and Flying Africans in Gayl Jones's *Song for Anninho*." In *After the Pain: Critical Essays on Gayl Jones*, edited by Fiona Mills and Keith Mitchell. New York: Peter Lang, 2006.

King, Nicole R. "Meditations and Mediations: Issues of History and Fiction in *Dessa Rose*." *Soundings: An Interdisciplinary Journal* 76, no. 2–3 (Summer–Fall 1993): 351–68.

Kitch, Sally L. "Motherlands and Foremothers: African American Women's Texts and the Concept of Relationship." In *Analyzing the Different Voice: Feminist Psychological Theory and Literary Texts*, edited by Jerilyn Fisher and Ellen S. Silber. Lanham, MD: Rowman & Littlefield, 1998.

Klotman, Phyllis Rauch. "'Oh Freedom': Women and History in Margaret Walker's *Jubilee*." *Black American Literature Forum* 11 (1977): 139–45.

Koolish, Lynda. "Fictive Strategies and Cinematic Representations in Toni Morrison's *Beloved*: Postcolonial Theory/Postcolonial Text." *African American Review* 29, no. 3 (Autumn 1995): 421–38.

Kreiger, Georgia. "Playing Dead: Harriet Jacobs's Survival Strategy in *Incidents in the Life of a Slave Girl*." *African American Review* 42, no. 3–4 (Fall–Winter 2008): 607–21.

Krumholz, Linda. "The Ghost of Slavery: Historical Recovery in Toni Morrison's *Beloved*." *African American Review* 26, no. 3 (Autumn 1992): 395–408.

Larson, Jennifer. "Converting Passive Womanhood to Active Sisterhood: Agency, Power, and Subversion in Harriet Jacobs's *Incidents in the Life of a Slave Girl*." *Women's Studies: An Interdisciplinary Journal* 35, no. 8 (December 2006): 739–56.

Lee, Dorothy H. "The Quest for Self: Triumph and Failure in the Works of Toni Morrison." In *Black Women Writers (1950–1980): A Critical Evaluation*, edited by Mari Evans. Garden City, NY: Anchor-Doubleday, 1984.

Lee, Judith. "'We Are All Kin': Relatedness, Mortality, and the Paradox of Human Immortality." In *Immortal Engines: Life Extension and Immortality in Science Fiction and Fantasy*, edited by George Slusser, Gary Westfahl, and Eric S. Rabkin. Athens: University of Georgia Press, 1996.

LeSeur, Geta. "From Nice Colored Girl to Womanist: An Exploration of Development in Ntozake Shange's Writings." In *Language and Literature in the African American Imagination*, edited by Carol Aisha Blackshire-Belay. Westport, CT: Greenwood Press, 1992.

Levander, Caroline. "'Following the Condition of the Mother': Subversions of Domesticity in Harriet Jacobs's *Incidents in the Life of a Slave Girl*." In *Southern Mothers: Fact and Fiction in Southern Women Writing*, edited by Nagueyalti Warren and Sally Wolff. Baton Rouge: Louisiana State University Press, 1999.

Levecq, Christine. "Power and Repetition: Philosophies of (Literary) History in Octavia E. Butler's *Kindred*." *Contemporary Literature* 41, no. 1 (Spring 2000): 525–53.

Li, Stephanie. "Motherhood as Resistance in Harriet Jacobs's *Incidents in the Life of a Slave Girl*." *Legacy: A Journal of American Women Writers* 23, no. 1 (2006): 14–29.

Liddell, Janice Lee. "Voyages Beyond Lust and Lactation: The Climacteric as Seen in Novels by Sylvia Wynter, Beryl Gilroy, and Paule Marshall." In *Arms Akimbo: Africana Women in Contemporary Literature*, edited by Janice Lee Liddell and Yakini Belinda Kemp. Gainesville: University Press of Florida, 1999.

Lionnet, Françoise. "Geographies of Pain: Captive Bodies and Violent Acts in the Fictions of Myriam Warner-Vieyra, Gayl Jones, and Bessie Head." *Callaloo: A Journal of African American and African Arts and Letters* 16, no. 1 (Winter 1993): 132–52.

Litwack, Leon F. *Been in the Storm So Long: The Aftermath of Slavery*. New York: Vintage Books, 1979.

Lock, Helen. "'Building Up from Fragments': The Oral Memory Process in Some Recent African-American Written Narratives." *College Literature* 22, no. 3 (October 1995): 109–20.

Logan, Shirley Wilson. "'What's Rhetoric Got to Do with It?': Frances E. W. Harper in the Writing Class." *Composition Forum: A Journal of the Association of Teachers of Advanced Composition* 7, no. 2 (Fall 1996): 95–110.

Luckhurst, Roger. "'Horror and Beauty in Rare Combination': The Miscegenate Fictions of Octavia Butler." *Women: A Cultural Review* 7, no. 1 (Spring 1996): 28–38.

Lyotard, Jean-François. *The Postmodern Condition: A Report on Knowledge*. Minneapolis: University of Minnesota Press, 1984.

Macpherson, Heidi Slettedahl. "Perceptions of Place: Geopolitical and Cultural Positioning in Paule Marshall's Novels." In *Caribbean Women Writers: Fiction in*

English, edited by Mary Condé and Thorunn Lonsdale. New York: St. Martin's, 1999.

Maida, Patricia. "*Kindred* and *Dessa Rose*: Two Novels That Reinvent Slavery." *CEA Magazine: A Journal of the College English Association, Middle-Atlantic Group* 4, no. 1 (Fall 1991): 43–52.

Marsh-Lockett, Carol. "A Woman's Art; A Woman's Craft: The Self in Ntozake Shange's *Sassafras, Cypress, and Indigo*." In *Arms Akimbo: Africana Women in Contemporary Literature*, edited by Janice Lee Liddell and Yakini Belinda Kemp. Gainesville: University Press of Florida, 1999.

Martin, Valerie. "The Means of Evil." *The Guardian: Guardian Review*, July 31, 2004.

Mason, Mary G. "Travel as Metaphor and Reality in Afro-American Women's Autobiography, 1850–1972." *Black American Literature Forum. 20th Century Autobiography* 24, no. 2 (Summer 1990): 337–56.

Mathison-Fife, Jane. "*Dessa Rose*: A Critique of Received History of Slavery." *Kentucky Philological Review* 8 (1993): 29–33.

Mayer, Sylvia. "'You Like Huckleberries?' Toni Morrison's *Beloved* and Mark Twain's *Adventures of Huckleberry Finn*." In *The Black Columbiad: Defining Moments in African American Literature and Culture*, edited by Werner Sollors and Maria Diedrich. Cambridge, MA: Harvard University Press, 1994.

McDowell, Deborah E. "Negotiating between Tenses: Witnessing Slavery after Freedom—*Dessa Rose*." In *Slavery and the Literary Imagination: Selected Papers from the English Institute, 1987*, edited by Deborah E. McDowell and Arnold Rampersad. Baltimore, MD: Johns Hopkins University Press, 1989.

———. *"The Changing Same": Black Women's Literature, Criticism and Theory*. Bloomington: Indiana University Press, 1995.

———. "Conversation: Sherley Anne Williams and Deborah McDowell." In *The Furious Flowering of African American Poetry*, edited by Joanne V. Gabbin. Charlottesville: University Press of Virginia, 1999.

McDowell, Margaret B. "The Black Woman as Artist and Critic: Four Versions." *The Kentucky Review* 7, no. 1 (Spring 1987): 19–41.

McEntee, Grace. "The Ethics of Motherhood and Harriet Jacobs' Vision of Racial Equality in *Incidents in the Life of a Slave Girl*." In *The Literary Mother: Essays on Representations of Maternity and Child Care*, edited by Susan Staub. Jefferson, NC: McFarland, 2007.

McKible, Adam. "'These Are the Facts of the Darky's History': Thinking History and Reading Names in Four African American Texts." *African American Review* 28, no. 2 (Summer 1994): 223–35.

McKoy, Sheila Smith. "The Limbo Contest: Diaspora Temporality and Its Reflection in *Praisesong for the Widow* and *Daughters of the Dust*." *Callaloo: A Journal of African American and African Arts and Letters* 22, no. 1 (Winter 1999): 208–22.

Mehaffy, Marilyn, and Ana Louise Keating. "Radio Imagination: Octavia Butler on the Poetics of Narrative Embodiment." *MELUS: The Journal of the Society for the Study of the Multi Ethnic Literature of the United States* 26, no. 1 (Spring 2001): 45–76.

Metting, Fred. "The Possibilities of Flight: The Celebration of Our Wings in *Song of Solomon, Praisesong for the Widow*, and *Mama Day*." *Southern Folklore* 55, no. 2 (1998): 145–68.

Michaels, Walter Benn. "Political Science Fictions." *New Literary History: A Journal of Theory and Interpretation* 31, no. 4 (Autumn 2000): 649–64.

Miller, R. Baxter. "The 'Etched Flame' of Margaret Walker: Biblical and Literary Re-Creation in Southern History." *Tennessee Studies in Literature* 26 (1981): 157–72.

Mills, Fiona. "Telling the Untold Tale: Afro-Latino/a Identifications in the Work of Gayl Jones." In *After the Pain: Critical Essays on Gayl Jones*, edited by Fiona Mills and Keith Mitchell. New York: Peter Lang, 2006.

Miskolcze, Robin. "The Middle Passage of Nancy Prince and Harriet Jacobs." *Nineteenth-Century Contexts* 29, no. 2–3 (June–September 2007): 283–93.

Mitchell, Keith B. "'Trouble in Min': (Re)visioning Myth, Sexuality, and Race in Gayl Jones's *Corregidora*." In *After the Pain: Critical Essays on Gayl Jones*, edited by Fiona Mills and Keith Mitchell. New York: Peter Lang, 2006.

Mobley, Marilyn Sanders. *Folk Roots and Mythic Wings in Sarah Orne Jewett and Toni Morrison: the Cultural Function of Narrative*. Baton Rouge: Louisiana State University Press, 1991.

———. "A Different Remembering: Memory, History, and Meaning in *Beloved*." In *Toni Morrison: Critical Perspectives Past and Present*, edited Henry Louis Gates Jr. and K. A. Appiah. New York: Amistad, 1993.

Moglen, Helen. "Redeeming History: Toni Morrison's *Beloved*." In *Female Subjects in Black and White: Race, Psychoanalysis, Feminism*, edited by Elizabeth Abel, Barbara Christian, and Helen Moglen. Berkeley: University of California Press, 1997.

Moore, Geneva Cobb. "A Freudian Reading of Harriet Jacobs' *Incidents in the Life of a Slave Girl*." *Southern Literary Journal* 38, no. 1 (Fall 2005): 3–20.

Morgenstern, Naomi. "Mother's Milk and Sister's Blood: Trauma and the Neoslave Narrative." *Differences: A Journal of Feminist Cultural Studies* 8, no. 2 (Summer 1996): 101–26.

Morrison, Toni. *Playing in the Dark: Whiteness and Literary Imagination*. London: Harvard University Press, 1992.

———. "Rootedness: The Ancestor as Foundation." In *Black Women Writers (1950–1980): A Critical Evaluation*, edited by Mari Evans. Garden City, NY: Anchor-Doubleday, 1984.

———. "Unspeakable Things Unspoken: The Afro-American Presence in American Literature." In *Within the Circle: An Anthology of African American Literary Criticism from the Harlem Renaissance to the Present*, edited by Angelyn Mitchell. London: Duke University Press, 1994.

Mossell, Gertrude N. F., ed. *The Work of Afro-American Women*. 1894. Philadelphia: George S. Ferguson, 1908.

Muñoz-Cabrera, Patricia. "(Em)Bodying the Flesh: Mythmaking and the Female Body in Gayl Jones' *Song for Anninho* and *Corregidora*." *PALARA: Publication of the Afro-Latin American Research Association* 1 (Fall 1997): 106–16.

Neal, Larry. "The Black Arts Movement." In *Within the Circle: An Anthology of African American Literary Criticism from the Harlem Renaissance to the Present*, edited by Angelyn Mitchell. London: Duke University Press, 1994.

Nelson, Emmanuel S. "Black America and the Anglophone Afro-Caribbean Literary Consciousness." *Journal of American Culture* 12, no.4 (Winter 1989): 53–58.

Neubauer, Paul. "The Demons of Loss and Longing: The Function of the Ghost in Toni Morrison's *Beloved*." In *Demons: Mediators between This World and the Other. Essays on Demonic Beings from the Middle Ages to the Present*, edited by Ruth Petzolt and Paul Neubauer. Frankfurt, Germany: Peter Lang, 1998.

Novak, Terry D. "Frances Harper's Poverty Relief Mission in the African American Community." In *Our Sisters' Keepers: Nineteenth-Century Benevolence Literature by American Women*, edited by Jill Bergman and Debra Bernardi. Tuscaloosa: University of Alabama Press, 2005.

Olmstead, Jane. "The Pull to Memory and the Language of Place in Paule Marshall's *The Chosen Place, The Timeless People* and *Praisesong for the Widow*." *African American Review* 31, no. 2 (Summer 1997): 249–67.

Olney, James. "The Founding Fathers—Frederick Douglass and Booker T. Washington." In *Slavery and the Literary Imagination: Selected Papers from the English Institute, 1987*, edited by Deborah E. McDowell and Arnold Rampersad. Baltimore, MD: Johns Hopkins University Press, 1989.

Page, Philip. "Circularity in Toni Morrison's *Beloved*." *African American Review* 26, no. 1 (Spring 1992): 31–39.

Palmer-Mehta, Valerie. "'We Are All Bound Up Together': Frances Harper and Feminist Theory." In *Black Women's Intellectual Traditions: Speaking Their Minds*, edited by Kristin Waters and Carol B. Conaway. Burlington: University of Vermont/University Press of New England, 2007.

Pampling, Claire. "'Race' and Identity in Pauline Hopkins's *Hagar's Daughter*." In *Redefining the Political Novel: Women Writers, 1797–1901*, edited by Sharon M. Harris. Knoxville: University of Tennessee Press, 1995.

Parish, Peter J. *Slavery: History and Historians*. New York: Harper & Row, 1989.

Patton, Sharon F. *African-American Art*. New York: Oxford University Press, 1998.

Paulin, Diana R. "De-Essentializing Interracial Representations: Black and White Border-Crossings in Spike Lee's *Jungle Fever* and Octavia Butler's *Kindred*." *Cultural Critique* 36 (Spring 1997): 165–93.

Petrino, Elizabeth A. "'We Are Rising as a People': Frances Harper's Radical Views on Class and Racial Equality in the Sketches of Southern Life." *American Transcendental Quarterly* 19, no. 2 (June 2005): 133–53.

Petterson, Carla. "Unsettled Frontiers: Race, History, and Romance in Pauline Hopkins's *Contending Forces*." In *Famous Last Words: Changes in Gender and Narrative Closure*, edited by Alison Booth. London: University Press of Virginia, 1993.

Pettis, Joyce. "The Black Historical Novel as Best Seller." *Kentucky Folklore Record: A Regional Journal of Folklore and Folklife* 25 (1979): 51–59.

———. "Margaret Walker: Black Woman Writer of the South." In *Southern Women Writers: The New Generation*, edited by Tonette Bond Inge. Tuscaloosa: University of Alabama Press, 1990.

———. "Self Definition and Redefinition in Paule Marshall's *Praisesong for the Widow*." In *Perspectives of Black Popular Culture*, edited by Harry B. Shaw. Bowling Green, OH: Popular, 1990.

Pittman, Coretta. "Black Women Writers and the Trouble with Ethos: Harriet Jacobs, Billie Holiday and Sister Souljah." *Rhetoric Society Quarterly* 37, no. 1 (Winter 2007): 43–70.

Porter, Nancy. "Women's Interracial Friendships and Visions of Community in *Meridian, The Salt Eaters, Civil Wars*, and *Dessa Rose*." In *Tradition and the Talents of Women*, edited by Florence Howe. Chicago: University of Illinois Press, 1991.

Potts, Stephen W. "'We Keep Playing the Same Record': A Conversation with Octavia E. Butler." *Science-Fiction Studies* 23, no. 3(November 1996): 331–38.

Powell, Bertie J. "The Black Experience in Margaret Walker's *Jubilee* and Lorraine Hansberry's *The Drinking Gourd*." *College Language Association Journal* 21 (1977): 304–11.

Powell, Timothy. "Toni Morrison: The Struggle to Depict the Black Figure on the White Page." *Black American Literature Forum* 24, no. 4 (Winter 1990): 747–60.

Powers, Christopher. "The Third Eye: Love, Memory, and History in Toni Morrison's *Beloved, Jazz* and *Paradise*." In *Narrating the Past: (Re)Constructing Memory, (Re)Negotiating History*, edited by Nandita Batra and Vartan P. Messier. Newcastle upon Tyne, UK: Cambridge Scholars, 2007.

Raffel, Burton. "Genre to the Rear, Race and Gender to the Fore: The Novels of Octavia E. Butler." *Literary Review: An International Journal of Contemporary Writing* 38, no. 3 (Spring 1995): 454–61.

Ramos, Peter. "Beyond Silence and Realism: Trauma and the Function of Ghosts in *Absalom, Absalom!* and *Beloved*." *Faulkner Journal* 23, no. 2 (Spring 2008): 47–66.

Rampersad, Arnold. "Slavery and the Literary Imagination: Du Bois's *The Souls of Black Folk*." In *Slavery and the Literary Imagination: Selected Papers from the English Institute, 1987*, edited by Deborah E. McDowell and Arnold Rampersad. Baltimore, MD: Johns Hopkins University Press, 1989.

Randolph, Ruth Elizabeth, and Lorraine Elena Roses, eds. *Harlem Renaissance and Beyond: Literary Biographies of 100 Black Women Writers 1900–1945*. Cambridge, MA: Harvard University Press, 1990.

Ranson, Edward, and Andrew Hook. "The Old South." In *Introduction to American Studies*, edited by Malcom Bradbury and Howard Temperly. New York: Longman, 1998.

Raynaud, Claudine. "*Beloved* or the Shifting Shapes of Memory." In *The Cambridge Companion to Toni Morrison*, edited by Justine Tally. Cambridge, UK: Cambridge University Press, 2007.

Reyes, Angelita. "Politics and Metaphors of Materialism in Paule Marshall's *Praisesong for the Widow* and Toni Morrison's *Tar Baby*." In *Politics and the Muse: Studies in the Politics of Recent American Literature*, edited by Adam J. Sorkin. Bowling Green, OH: Popular, 1989.

———. "Reading Carnival as an Archaeological Site for Memory in Paule Marshall's *The Chosen Place, The Timeless People*, and *Praisesong for the Widow*." In *Memory, Narrative, and Identity: New Essays in Ethnic American Literatures*, edited by Amritjit Singh, Joseph T. Skerrett Jr., and Robert E. Hogan. Boston: Northeastern University Press, 1994.

Rice, Alan J. "'It Don't Mean a Thing If It Ain't Got That Swing': Jazz's Many Uses for Toni Morrison." In *Black Orpheus: Music in African American Fiction from the Harlem Renaissance to Toni Morrison*, edited by Saadi A. Simawe. New York: Garland, 2000.

Rigney, Barbara Hill. *The Voices of Toni Morrison*. Columbus: Ohio State University Press, 1991.

———. "'A Story to Pass On': Ghosts and the Significance of History in Toni Morrison's *Beloved*." In *Haunting the House of Fiction: Feminist Perspectives on Ghosts Stories by American Women*, edited by Lynette Carpenter and Wendy K. Kolmar. Knoxville: University of Tennessee Press, 1991.

Robinson, Sally. *Engendering the Subject: Gender and Self-Representation in Contemporary Women's Fiction*. Albany: State University of New York Press, 1991.

Rogers, Susan. "Embodying Cultural Memory in Paule Marshall's *Praisesong for the Widow*." *African American Review* 34, no. 1 (Spring 2000): 77–93.

Ronen, Ruth. *Possible Worlds in Literary Theory*. Cambridge: Cambridge University Press, 1994.

Rosenfelt, Deborah Silverton. "Feminism, 'Postfeminism,' and Contemporary Women's Fiction." In *Tradition and the Talents of Women*, edited by Florence Howe. Chicago: University of Illinois Press, 1991.

Rowell, Charles H. "An Interview with Margaret Walker." *Black World* 25, no. 2 (1975): 4–17.

———. "Poetry, History, and Humanism: An Interview with Margaret Walker." *Black World* 25, no. 2 (1975): 4–17.

———. "An Interview with Octavia E. Butler." *Callaloo: A Journal of African American and African Arts and Letters* 20, no. 1 (Winter 1997): 47–66.

———. "An Interview with Gayl Jones." *Callaloo: A Journal of African American Arts and Letters* 5:3, no. 16 (October 1982): 32–53.

Rushdy, Ashraf H. A. *Remembering Generations: Race and Family in Contemporary African American Fiction*. Chapel Hill: University of North Carolina Press, 2001.

———. "Relate Sexual to Historical': Race, Resistance, and Desire in Gayl Jones's *Corregidora*." *African American Review* 34, no. 2 (Summer 2000): 273–97.

———. "Reading Mammy: The Subject of Relation in Sherley Anne Williams' *Dessa Rose*." *African American Review* 27, no. 3 (Fall 1993): 365–89.

———. "Neo-Slave Narrative," in *The Oxford Companion to African American Literature*, ed. William L. Andrews et al. (New York: Oxford University Press, 1997).

Russell, Sandi. *Render Me My Song: African-American Women Writers from Slavery to the Present*. London: Pandora, 1990.

Saldivar, Jose David. "The Real and the Marvelous in Charleston, South Carolina: Ntozake Shange's *Sassafrass, Cypress & Indigo*." In *Genealogy and Literature*, edited by Lee Quinby. Minneapolis: University of Minnesota Press, 1995.

Sale, Maggie. "Critiques from Within: Antebellum Projects of Resistance." *American Literature: A Journal of Literary History, Criticism, and Bibliography* 64, no. 4 (December 1992): 695–718.

———. "Call and Response as Critical Method: African-American Oral Traditions and *Beloved*." *African American Review* 26, no. 1 (Spring 1992): 41–50.

Salvaggio, Ruth. "Octavia Butler and the Black Science-Fiction Heroine." *Black American Literature Forum* 18, no. 2 (Summer 1984): 78–81.

Sanchez, Marta E. "The Estrangement Effect in Sherley Anne Williams' *Dessa Rose*." *Genders* 15 (Winter 1992): 21–36.

Sandiford, Keith A. "Paule Marshall's *Praisesong for the Widow*: The Reluctant Heiress; or, Whose Life Is It Anyway?" *Black American Literature Forum* 20, no. 4 (Winter 1986): 371–92.

Savory, Elaine. "Ex/Isle: Separation, Memory and Desire in Caribbean Women's Writing." *MaComere: Journal of the Association of Caribbean Women Writers and Scholars* 1 (1998): 170–78.

Scarboro, Ann Armstrong. "The Healing Process: A Paradigm for Self-Renewal in Paule Marshall's *Praisesong for the Widow* and Camara Laye's *Le Regard du Roi*." *Modern Language Studies* 19, no. 1 (Winter 1989): 28–36.

Scarpa, Giulia. "'Couldn't They Have Done Differently?': Caught in the Web of Race. Gender. and Class: Paule Marshall's *Praisesong for the Widow*." *World Literature Written in English* 29, no. 2 (Autumn 1989): 94–104.

Sekora, John. "Black Message/White Envelope: Genre, Authenticity, and Authority in the Antebellum Slave Narratives." *Callaloo: A Journal of African American and African Arts and Letters* 32 (Summer 1987): 482–515.

Sensbach, Jon F. "Charting a Course in Early African-American History." *William and Mary Quarterly* 50, no. 2 (April 1993): 394–405.

Sharpe, Christina E. "The Costs of Re-Membering: What's at Stake in Gayl Jones's *Corregidora*." *African American Performance and Theatre History: A Critical Reader*, edited by J. Harry Elam Jr. and David Krasner. Oxford: Oxford University Press, 2001.

Shinn, Thelma J. "The Wise Witches: Black Women Mentors in the Fiction of Octavia E. Butler." In *Conjuring: Black Women, Fiction, and Literary Tradition*, edited by Marjorie Pryse and Hortense J. Spillers. Bloomington: Indiana University Press, 1985.

Sievers, Stefanie. "Escaping the Master('s) Narrative? Sherley Anne Williams's Rethinking of Historical Representation in 'Meditations on History.'" In *Re-Visioning the Past: Historical Self-Reflexivity in American Short Fiction*, edited by Bernd Engler and Oliver Scheiding. Trier, Germany: Wissenschaftlicher, 1998.

Simon, Bruce. "Traumatic Repetition: Gayl Jones's *Corregidora*." In *Race Consciousness: African-American Studies for the New Century*, edited by Judith Jackson Fossett and A. Jeffrey Tucker. New York: New York University Press, 1997.

Sitter, Deborah Ayer. "The Making of a Man: Dialogic Meaning in *Beloved*." *African American Review* 26, no. 1 (Spring 1992): 17–29.

Smith, Sidonie. "Resisting the Gaze of Embodiment: Women's Autobiography in the Nineteenth Century." In *American Women's Autobiography: Fea(s)ts of Memory*, edited by Mango Culley. Madison: University Press of Wisconsin, 1992.

Smith, Stephanie. "Harriet Jacobs: A Case History of Authentication." In *The Cambridge Companion to the African American Slave Narrative*, edited by Audrey A. Fisch. Cambridge, UK: Cambridge University Press, 2007.

Smith, Valerie. "'Circling the Subject': History and Narrative in *Beloved*." In *Toni Morrison: Critical Perspectives Past and Present*, edited by Henry Louis Gates Jr. and K. A. Appiah. New York: Amistad, 1993.

Smith-Wright, Geraldine. "In Spite of the Klan: Ghosts in the Fiction of Black Women Writers." In *Haunting the House of Fiction: Feminist Perspectives on Ghosts Stories by American Women*, edited by Lynette Carpenter and Wendy K. Kolmar. Knoxville: University of Tennessee Press, 1991.

———. "A Response to Williams." *Soundings: An Interdisciplinary Journal* 76, no. 2–3 (Summer–Fall 1993): 245–59.

Spears, James E. "Black Folk Elements in Margaret Walker's *Jubilee*." *Mississippi Folklore Register* 14, no. 1 (Spring 1980): 13–19.

Steinberg, Marc. "*Dessa Rose*: Putting the 'Story' Back into History." In *Reclaiming Home, Remembering Motherhood, Rewriting History: African American and Afro-Caribbean Women's Literature in the Twentieth Century*, edited by Verena Theile and Marie Drews. Newcastle upon Tyne, UK: Cambridge Scholars, 2009.

Steinitz, Hilary J. "Shaping Interior Spaces: Ntozake Shange's Construction of the 'Room' for Art." *West Virginia University Philological Papers* 38 (1992): 280–87.

Stepto, Robert. *From Behind the Veil: A Study of Afro-American Narrative*. Urbana: University of Illinois Press, 1979.

Stone, Albert E. *The Return of Nat Turner: History, Literature, and Cultural Politics in Sixties America*. Athens: University of Georgia Press, 1992.

Story, Ralph. "An Execution into the Black World: The 'Seven Days' in Toni Morrison's *Song of Solomon*." *Black American Literature Forum* 23, no. 1 (Spring 1989): 149–58.

Strandness, Jean. "Reclaiming Women's Language, Imagery, and Experience: Ntozake Shange's *Sassafrass, Cypress & Indigo*." *Journal of American Culture* 10, no. 3 (Fall 1987): 11–17.

Tate, Claudia, ed. *Black Women Writers at Work*. New York: Continuum, 1983.

———. "Allegories of Black Female Desire; or, Rereading Nineteen-Century Sentimental Narratives of Black Female Authority." In *Changing Our Own Words: Essays on Criticism, Theory and Writing by Black Women*, edited by Cheryl A. Wall. New Brunswick, NJ: Rutgers University Press, 1989.

Thomas, H. Nigel. *From Folklore to Fiction: A Study of Folk Heroes and Rituals in the Black American Novel*. Westport, CT: Greenwood Press, 1988.

Thompson-Cager, Chezia. "Superstition, Magic and the Occult in Two Versions of Ntozake Shange's Choreopoem *for colored girls* and Novel *Sassafrass, Cypress and Indigo*." *MAWA Review* 4, no. 2 (December 1989): 37–41.

Taylor-Thompson, Betty, and Gladys Washington. "Mothers, Grandmothers, and Great Grandmothers: The Maternal Tradition in Margaret Walker's *Jubilee*."

In *Southern Mothers: Fact and Fictions in Southern Women's Writing*, edited by Nagueyalti Warren and Sally Wolff. Baton Rouge: Louisiana State University Press, 1999.

Todorov, Tzvetan. *The Fantastic: A Structural Approach to a Literary Genre*. Translated by Richard Howard. New York: Cornell University Press, 1975.

Trapasso, Ann E. "Returning to the Site of Violence: The Restructuring of Slavery's Legacy in Sherley Anne Williams's *Dessa Rose*." In *Violence, Silence, and Anger: Women's Writing as Transgression*, edited by Deirdre Lashgari. Charlottesville: University Press of Virginia, 1995.

Traylor, Eleanor W. "Music as Theme: The Blues Mode in the Works of Margaret Walker." In *Black Women Writers (1950–1980): A Critical Evaluation*, edited by Mari Evans. Garden City, NY: Anchor-Doubleday, 1984.

———. "'Bolder Measures Crashing Through': Margaret Walker's Poem of the Century." *Callaloo: A Journal of African American and African Arts and Letters* 10, no. 4 (Fall 1987): 570–95.

Tricomi, Albert H. "Harriet Jacobs's Autobiography and the Voice of Lydia Maria Child." *ESQ: A Journal of the American Renaissance* 53, no. 3 (2007): 216–52.

———. "Dialect and Identity in Harriet Jacobs's *Autobiography and Other Slave Narratives*." *Callaloo: A Journal of African Diaspora Arts and Letters* 29, no. 2 (Spring 2006): 619–33.

Turner, Darwin T. "Theme, Characterization, and Style in the Works of Toni Morrison." In *Black Women Writers (1950–1980): A Critical Evaluation*, edited by Mari Evans. Garden City, NY: Anchor-Doubleday, 1984.

Walker, Daniel E. "Suicidal Tendencies: African Transmigration in the History and Folklore of the Americas." *Griot: Official Journal of the Southern Conference on Afro-American Studies, Inc.* 18, no. 2 (Fall 1999): 10–18.

Walker, Margaret. *Richard Wright, Daemonic Genius: A Portrait of the Man, A Critical Look at His Work*. New York: Warner Books, 1988.

———. "Natchez and Richard Wright in Southern Literature." *The Southern Quarterly Review: A Journal of the Arts in the South* 24, no. 4 (Summer 1991): 171–75.

———. *How I Wrote Jubilee and Other Essays on Life and Literature*. Edited by Maryemma Graham. New York: Feminist Press, 1990.

———. "New Poets." In *Within the Circle: An Anthology of African American Literary Criticism from the Harlem Renaissance to the Present*, edited by Angelyn Mitchell. London: Duke University Press, 1994.

———. *On Being Female, Black, and Free: Essays by Margaret Walker, 1932–1992*. Edited by Maryemma Graham. Knoxville: University of Tennessee Press, 1997.

———. "'I Want to Write the Songs of My People': The Emergence of Margaret Walker." In *Fields Watered by Blood: Critical Essays on Margaret Walker*, edited by Maryemma Graham. London: University of Georgia Press, 2001.

Walker, Melissa. *Down from the Mountain Top: Black Women's Novels in the Wake of the Civil Rights Movement, 1966–1989*. New Haven, CT: Yale University Press, 1991.

Ward, Jerry W., Jr. "A Writer for Her People: An Interview with Dr. Margaret Walker Alexander." *Mississippi Quarterly: The Journal of Southern Culture* 41, no. 4 (Fall 1988): 515–27.

———. "Black South Literature: Before Day Annotations (For Blyden Jackson)." *African American Review* 27, no. 2 (Summer 1993): 315–26.

Warner, Anne Bradford. "Harriet Jacobs at Home in *Incidents in the Life of a Slave Girl*." *Southern Quarterly: A Journal of the Arts in the South* 45, no. 3 (Spring 2008): 30–47.

Warren, Robert Penn. "The Uses of History in Fiction." *Southern Literary Journal* 1, no. 2 (Spring 1969): 57–90.

Washington, Mary Helen. *Invented Lives: Narratives of Black Women, 1860–1960.* London: Virago 1989.

———. "Walker, Margaret." In *The Oxford Companion to African American Literature*, edited by William L. Andrews, Frances Smith Foster, and Trudier Harris. New York: Oxford University Press, 1997.

———. "Teaching Black Eyed Susans: An Approach to the Study of Black Women Writers." *Black American Literary Forum* 11, no. 1 (Spring 1977): 20–24.

Waxman, Barbara Frey. "The Widow's Journey to Self and Roots: Aging and Society in Paule Marshall's *Praisesong for the Widow*." *Frontiers: A Journal of Women Studies* 9, no. 3 (1987): 94–99.

———. "Dancing Out of Form, Dancing into Self: Genre and Metaphor in Marshall, Shange, and Walker." *MELUS: The Journal of the Society for the Study of the Multi-Ethnic Literature of the United States* 19, no. 3 (Fall 1994): 91–106.

Weinstein, Philip M. *What Else But Love?: The Ordeal of Race in Faulkner and Morrison.* New York: Columbia University Press, 1996.

Weixlmann, Joe. "An Octavia E. Butler Bibliography." *Black American Literature Forum* 18, no. 2 (Summer 1984): 88–89.

Wells, Kimberly A. "'The Dream of My Life Is Not Yet Realized': Harriet Jacobs and the Failure of the Ideal." *Griot: Official Journal of the Southern Conference on Afro-American Studies, Inc.* 26, no. 1 (Spring 2007): 65–75.

White, Deborah Gray. *Ar'n't I a Woman? Female Slaves in the Plantations of the South.* New York: Norton, 1985.

Wilcox, Janelle. "Resistant Silence, Resistant Subject: (Re)Reading Gayl Jones's *Eva's Man*." In *Bodies of Writing, Bodies in Performance*, edited by Thomas Foster, Carol Siegel, and E. Ellen Berry. New York: New York University Press, 1996.

Wilentz, Gay. "Towards a Spiritual Middle Passage Back: Paule Marshall's Diasporic Vision in *Praisesong for the Widow*." *Obsidian II: Black Literature in Review* 5, no. 3 (Winter 1990): 1–21.

———. "Civilizations Underneath: African American Heritage as Cultural Discourse in Toni Morrison's *Song of Solomon*." *African American Review* 26, no. 1 (Spring 1992): 61–76.

Williams, Fannie Barrier. "The Intellectual Progress of the Colored Women of the United States Since the Emancipation Proclamation." 1893. Address in *The World's Congress of Representative Women*, edited by May Wright Sewall, 696–711. Chicago: Rand McNally, 1894.

Williams, Sherley Anne. "Some Implications of Feminist Theory." *Griot: Official Journal of the Southern Conference on Afro-American Studies, Inc.* 6, no. 2 (1987): 40–45.

———. "The Lion's History: The Ghetto Writes Back." *Soundings: An Interdisciplinary Journal* 76, no. 2–3 (Summer–Fall 1993): 245–59.

———. "Telling the Teller: Memoir and Story." In *The Seductions of Biography*, edited by Mary Rhiel and David Suchoff. New York: Routledge, 1996.

———. "The Blues Roots of Contemporary Afro-American Poetry." In *Chant of Saints: A Gathering of Afro-American Literature, Art, and Scholarship*, edited by Michael Harper and Robert Stepto. London: University of Illinois Press, 1979.

Willis, Susan. *Specifying: Black Women Writing the American Experience.* London: Routledge, 1990.

Wilson, Lucy. "Aging and Ageism in Paule Marshall's *Praisesong for the Widow* and Beryl Gilroy's *Frangipani House.*" *Journal of Caribbean Studies* 7, no. 2–3 (Winter 1989–Spring 1990): 189–99.

Winchell, Donna Haisty. "Cries of Outrage: Three Novelists' Use of History." *Mississippi Quarterly: The Journal of Southern Cultures* 49, no. 4 (Fall 1996): 727–42.

Woodard, Vincent. "Deciphering the Race-Sex Diaspora in Pauline Hopkins's *Contending Forces.*" *Interdisciplinary Literary Studies: A Journal of Criticism and Theory* 8, no. 1 (Fall 2006): 72–93.

Wright, Lee Alfred. *Identity, Family, and Folklore in African American Literature.* New York: Garland, 1995.

Wright, Richard. "Blue Print for Negro Writing." In *The Norton Anthology of African American Literature*, edited by Henry Louis Gates Jr. and Nellie Y. McKay. New York: Norton, 1997.

Yellin, Jean Fagan. "*Incidents* in the Life of Harriet Jacobs." In *The Seductions of Biography*, edited by Mary Rhiel and David Suchoff. New York: Routledge, 1996.

Young, Elizabeth. "Warring Fictions: Iola Leroy and the Color of Gender." *American Literature Forum: A Journal of Literary History, Criticism, and Bibliography* 64, no. 2 (June 1992): 273–97.

Zaki, Hoda M. "Utopia, Dystopia, and Ideology in the Science Fiction of Octavia Butler." *Science Fiction Studies* 17, no. 2 (July 1990): 239–51.

Zamora, Lois Parkinson. "Magical Romance/Magical Realism: Ghosts in U.S. and Latin American Fiction." In *Magical Realism: Theory, History, Community*, edited by Lois Parkinson Zamora and Wendy B. Faris. Durham, NC: Duke University Press, 1995.

Index